PERSONAL LETTERS *OF A* PUBLIC MAN

PERSONAL LETTERS *OF A* ∾∾∾ PUBLIC MAN

The Family Letters of
JOHN G. DIEFENBAKER

Edited by
THAD McILROY

With an Introduction by
J.L. GRANATSTEIN

AN ARCADIA HOUSE BOOK

DOUBLEDAY CANADA LIMITED, TORONTO, CANADA
DOUBLEDAY AND COMPANY, INC., GARDEN CITY, NEW YORK
1985

AN ARCADIA HOUSE BOOK
Jack Jensen
Thad McIlroy
David Montle

The Personal Letters of a Public Man
The Family Letters of John G. Diefenbaker
Copyright © 1985 by Arcadia House Inc.

The family papers of John G. Diefenbaker are held by the University of Saskatchewan
at the Right Honourable John G. Diefenbaker Centre. They are printed here by permission.
The photographs that appear in this book are also held at the Diefenbaker Centre.
While every effort has been made to trace the copyright holders of these photographs,
Arcadia House would appreciate receiving notification of any errors or omissions.

Canadian Cataloguing in Publication Data

Diefenbaker, John G., 1895-1979.
  The personal letters of a public man

Includes index.
ISBN 0-385-25005-3

1. Diefenbaker, John G., 1895-1979.
2. Prime ministers - Canada - Correspondence.
I. McIlroy, Thad, 1956-   . II. Granatstein,
J.L., 1939-   . III. Title.

FC616.D5A4 1985   971.064'2   C85-099273-7
F1034.3.D5A4 1985

Library of Congress Cataloging-in-Publication Data

Diefenbaker, John G., 1895-1979.
  The personal letters of a public man.

   1. Diefenbaker, John G., 1895-1979 -- Correspondence.
2. Diefenbaker, John G., 1895-1979 -- Family.
3. Diefenbaker, John G., 1895-1979 -- Friends and
associates. 4. Prime ministers -- Canada -- Correspondence.
I. McIlroy, Thad, 1956-   . II. Title.
E1034.3.D5A4 1985   971.064'2'0924   85-15928
ISBN 0-385-25005-3 (Doubleday)

Design Direction by David Montle

Typeset on a Macintosh 512K ® and LaserWriter ® at Elm Street
Computer Terminal

Printed and Bound in Canada by John Deyell Co.

Published by Doubleday Canada Limited
105 Bond Street
Toronto, Ontario M5B 1Y3

CONTENTS

FOREWORD

I HAD THOUGHT TO WRITE A PASSIONATE NOTE about my reasons for editing the Diefenbaker family letters. But I imagine that my reasons for editing these letters are roughly the same as yours for getting hold of a copy of this book – I thought John Diefenbaker was an extraordinary Canadian whose personal life was much overshadowed by his public life, and I thought his family papers might be important and revealing. I wasn't disappointed, and I don't think you will be either, but let me throw in a few words of caution.

John Diefenbaker was very much aware that he would occupy a prominent position in Canadian history. Consequently he knew that all his written documents, be they Cabinet memoranda or letters home to his mother, might one day be subject to public scrutiny. This realization was bound to make Diefenbaker slightly circumspect in what he committed to paper. At the same time, in writing a letter home, he wanted to communicate some news, some feelings and a few ideas, otherwise the exercise would have been pointless. This precarious balance is much in evidence in the Diefenbaker family letters. At times, evaluating their importance is as much a question of what is not said at a significant moment as what is.

There are some 65,000 documents in the Family Series of the Diefenbaker Papers held in the Diefenbaker Centre at the University of Saskatchewan. There are about 250 letters in this book. Daunted by the need to offer a volume of reasonable length, I've endeavored to make the best representative selection possible.

A great many of the letters concern themselves with the everyday minutiae that is of little interest to the general reader and were easily omitted. Long portions of many of the letters chosen would fall into the same classification, and so were edited in order that more letters could be included. Spelling for the most part was corrected, as was punctuation, although the unique grammar was left intact.

I think that the reader will find that J.L. Granatstein's introductory material – at the beginning of the book, and before each chapter – serves well to locate the time in which these letters were written. In some cases notes have been added where I thought it helpful to explain references, though my general policy has been to keep these to a minimum, to let the letters flow and to permit the reader to make his or her own evaluation. Names are clarified where they first occur, or if they haven't been encountered in a while, except where the name was a personal friend of no political standing. A few of the surnames of these friends have been deleted where the nature of the communication seemed to make such an identification undesirable. The dating of the letters has been made uniform (again with a few exceptions), and the name of the place of writing has been added where not originally specified.

A few thanks are in order. My partners in Arcadia House have backed this project from its inception, and have provided much support in ensuring its completion. Sharon Mitchell and all of the staff of the Diefenbaker Centre were co-operative and generous to a fault. Without their help this book could not have been attempted. The staff of the Elm Street Computer Terminal in Toronto saw to it that these words got off the ubiquitous diskettes and onto pieces of paper. J.L. Granatstein was brought into the project to write an introduction, and ended up unbidden as the virtual co-editor of this book – his knowledge of the Diefenbaker era has been invaluable. And last, but by no means least, I would like to thank my editors at Doubleday, Denise Schon and Gwyneth Runnings. They were enthusiastic at the beginning, quietly supportive for the duration, and gently prodding when I found myself behind schedule – one can ask for nothing more.

– Thad McIlroy
Toronto, 1985

INTRODUCTION

THE PRIVATE LETTERS OF PUBLIC MEN can always tell us much. Nowadays, we see the public faces of our leaders on television every night, always smiling, always polite, almost always in full control of the carefully arranged events their public relations experts decide are right for their images. But what, if anything, goes on behind those well-composed facades? What do our leaders really say and feel and think when they talk to their parents or wives or children?

We know something of our past leaders. Most of the political papers of Canada's prime ministers have been preserved and are housed in the Public Archives of Canada in Ottawa. Here we can find Sir John A. Macdonald planning for Confederation and worrying over the details of patronage. Here is Sir Wilfrid Laurier mulling over the details involved in sending a Canadian contingent to the Boer War or Sir Robert Borden agonizing over the difficulties of imposing conscription in 1917. Here too are Arthur Meighen and Louis St. Laurent, Alexander Mackenzie and Sir Charles Tupper, Lester Pearson and Pierre Trudeau. Their records are essential for historians trying to reconstruct the past, struggling to fit motive onto the bare bones of historical fact.

But what were the prime ministers really like as individuals? Most Canadians know that Macdonald drank, but how many today remember that his daughter, Mary, was hydrocephalic? Did that familial tragedy affect Macdonald? To ask the question, of course, is to answer it. We all know that it must have affected the Prime Minister, day in and day out, in a thousand different ways. How unfortunate for historians then that Macdonald's papers do not contain hundreds of letters to his wife talking over the details of the daughter's illness and expressing the Old Man's fears and concerns. Sir John Thompson, one of John A's successors as Prime Minister in the 1890s, did write regularly to his wife, in part because she remained in Nova Scotia throughout most of his Ottawa career. That correspondence, tender and personal and political, forms the very heart of Peter Waite's fine new biography of Thompson, *The Man from Halifax*, and it serves to remind us what we are missing from the others.

Then there is Mackenzie King, Canada's longest-serving Prime Minister, a man who dominated Canadian politics from 1921 until his retirement in 1948. King's papers are a national treasure, a record of all events of importance and a storehouse of trivia, including Christmas cards and engraved invitations to long-ago dinner parties. But the King record also includes an extraordinary diary, an almost life-long recounting of events from Mackenzie King's own perspective. That source is important for all aspects of twentieth century Canadian politics, of course, but it is just as important for what it tells us about the fussy and complex bachelor who ruled us for so long. As we now know, King was a spiritualist who revelled in seances; he was a man who was attracted to women but who never married, in substantial part because he could never overcome the baleful influence exercised by his mother on his psyche – both while she was alive and after her death. And some historians and novelists also argue, unconvincingly in this author's view, that King repeatedly used the services of prostitutes. The point is not whether or not King was crazy or wicked; the point is that Mackenzie King's diaries, for better or worse, allow Canadians to grapple with the full complexity of an extraordinary man. Worth considering too is that King's will left instructions for his diaries to be destroyed, a decision that his literary executors later overrode (resulting in substantial damage to King's reputation).

And now we have John Diefenbaker's papers. The Diefenbaker Papers are housed in the Diefenbaker Centre in Saskatoon (with a microfilm copy at the Public Archives of Canada) and, although all the Diefenbaker correspondence and memoranda are not yet open for public scrutiny, it is already clear that the collection as a whole is of first-rank importance. The Papers comprise legal papers, material on the years prior to 1940, on the years from 1940 to 1956, and on Diefenbaker's first period as Leader of the Opposition in 1956-57, all of which are now open. The bulk of the most important political material, still closed to scrutiny, undoubtedly will be found in the Prime Minister's Office papers and in the Leader of the Opposition files from 1963 to 1967.

Happily, Diefenbaker left a substantial body of private family correspondence, the raw material of this book, organized by the Centre's archivists into the Diefenbaker Family Series. Because he outlived all the members of his family, because he was a lawyer and the executor of his family's estates, and because he wished to preserve the story of his forebears, the family correspondence in the Diefenbaker collection is probably the most extensive of that of any Canadian prime minister. Here we can see the formative influences that shaped John Diefenbaker. We can read what his parents wrote to their son, we can watch his brother, Elmer, getting into scrapes all through his life, and we can come to know his old Uncle Ed. Most important, perhaps, here we can trace John Diefenbaker's relationship with his first wife, Edna, and follow the courtship of his second wife, Olive. In other words, the family letters of John Diefenbaker allow us that rarest and most privileged access of all – an insight into the private life of a most public man.

John Diefenbaker's parents had moved West from Ontario in 1903. William Diefenbaker was a school teacher – a bookish, dreamy man with an interest in politics – who had decided that the Prairies were to be the land of opportunity for his family. He purchased a homestead near Borden, Northwest Territories (which became Borden, Saskatchewan in 1905) soon after his arrival and, while waiting for the chance to build and to farm, he supported the family by teaching. With his brother Ed, William Diefenbaker broke ground in 1905 and built the shacks in which the family could live. Life was hard. By 1909, the Diefenbakers had cleared barely thirty acres and ran an operation that at its greatest extent comprised three cows and a single horse and had a cash value, including the wood used to build the house, of $400. The next year, failing at Prairie farming as so many did in those years, the Diefenbakers moved to Saskatoon where William took a job in the provincial civil service. William Diefenbaker retired in 1937 and died in 1945.

His wife, Mary Bannerman Diefenbaker, was the tough one in the family, the one who kept it together in the bad years and who clearly dominated her slightly feckless husband. Mary Diefenbaker was a largely unlettered woman, as her correspondence in this book makes clear, but she had far more determination and drive than her husband. If John Diefenbaker had a burning ambition to succeed in politics, it was because his mother force-fed this to him with his daily bread; if he wanted to do good, it was because his mother would not tolerate anything else and continued to remind him so in her letters; and if he married relatively late, it was almost surely because he could not find a woman who was either the same as, or markedly different from, Mary

Diefenbaker. Her influence on her son was enormous and powerful, lasting until her death in 1961 when her boy was Prime Minister of Canada.

Mary Diefenbaker had less success in transmitting her drive and grit to her younger son, Elmer. Born in 1899, four years after John, Elmer was his father's boy. He too was a dreamer, an almost carefree young man who went to university, served in both world wars, and worked at a variety of selling jobs, often drumming through rural Saskatchewan. Elmer's real talent was as a local political organizer, a gatherer of political information that could be, and often was, of great use to his brother; even so, Elmer, who remained unmarried and who lived for a long stretch near the end of his life in a YMCA, was always a trial to his older and vastly more successful brother. To his credit John almost never allowed his exasperation to show through more than fifty years of correspondence that ended only with Elmer's death in 1971.

Edna Brower, John's first wife, was in her own way another trial for John Diefenbaker. Pretty, slender and vivacious, Edna was a few years younger than the 34-year-old lawyer she married in 1929. She was much livelier and more personable than her politically-minded husband, and it was Edna who put whatever verve there was in Diefenbaker's early political campaigns and who, some observers claimed, had really won the election in Lake Centre, Saskatchewan for her husband in 1940. The Diefenbaker marriage had its difficulties, particularly after the move to Ottawa, and Edna, depressed and frightened, was institutionalized for a time in 1945-46. The letters she wrote to John from the sanitarium are surely among the most poignant ever addressed to a public figure from his spouse. Edna's last years were a torment for her and her husband. She died of leukemia in 1951.

But for John Diefenbaker it all worked out well in the end when he met Olive Freeman Palmer, an acquaintance from Saskatoon in the days of the Great War. Olive, a widow with one child, Carolyn, worked for the Ontario Department of Education in Toronto as a specialist in guidance counselling. The two fell in love very shortly after Edna's death, and the courtship, despite a few minor squalls that show in the letters they exchanged, progressed smoothly to marriage in December, 1953. Olive Diefenbaker became the rock upon which John now built his political career, his unfailing supporter in every crisis of his years as Conservative leader, and she quickly drove the memories of Edna from his mind (and until recently from the history books). As the chatelaine of the Prime Minister's residence, she set a model of hospitality and warmth that endeared her to the country. Her death in 1976, following a long and painful struggle with arthritis and a stroke, left her husband bereft and deprived him of the last of the three remarkable women on whom he had depended for so much and for so long. Mary, Edna and Olive Diefenbaker had had much to do with the successful political figure that he became.

And what of John Diefenbaker? What do these family letters tell us about this man from Prince Albert? The first point that emerges clearly is that Diefenbaker lived politics to an extraordinary (and perhaps unhealthy) extent. Almost all his letters, no matter the family member to whom they were written, talk about politics and those involved in them. Moreover, they demonstrate how remarkably single-minded Diefenbaker was in his determination to get into politics and to succeed once there. This shows best in the remarkable first letter he wrote home to Saskatoon from Ottawa after his election in 1940. The Conservative leader, Dr. R.J. Manion, had been defeated in the general election and the caucus unceremoniously dumped him. That meant that the Tories needed a House leader for the parliamentary session, and John Diefenbaker, still a novice politician with nothing but a long record of defeats behind him, actually contemplated running for the post. Not only that, but he seemed to feel it necessary to explain to his family, and especially to his mother, why he had not. Clearly, John was the bearer of his determined mother's hopes, and that burden was the spur that drove him on.

Something else stands out clearly from the first Ottawa letters. As it had in the Great War, Diefenbaker's Germanic-sounding surname was a definite liability in wartime Ottawa and in the proudly British Conservative party. Again and again, Diefenbaker referred to this problem, his sensitivity never easing over the years. Indeed, as late as the mid-1960s, the Chief almost sued *Maclean's* for running a cartoon that showed him dressed as a Prussian officer. That sensitivity unquestionably was at the root of Diefenbaker's long crusade for "One Canada," a nation where people were not French-Canadians or English-Canadians or German-Canadians, but just Canadians, pure and simple. He had suffered for his name and, to his credit, he did not want others to suffer for theirs. As these letters demonstrate, those attitudes required him to rise above the casual prejudice and ethnic slurs that he had grown up with. One Canada was a noble goal, but it flew in the face of Québecois sensitivities and the desires of many other Canadians to preserve their heritage against the forces of assimilation.

The discrimination that Diefenbaker suffered for his name probably led also to his concern for civil liberties, the single issue that first drew him to public attention during the war and kept him there in peace. The Liberal governments of Mackenzie King and Louis St. Laurent had grown used to power between 1935 and 1957 and were unafraid to exercise it; in the process, peoples' rights sometimes got trampled, and Diefenbaker was always on the watch for abuses. He opposed rule by order-in-council, he stood for the rights of Parliament and the rights of the little man against big government, and in power he passed the Canadian Bill of Rights, a milestone in our history. The one blot on this honorable record is that, despite the claims in his memoirs, Diefenbaker did *not* speak out against the removal of Canadians of Japanese ethnicity from the Pacific Coast in the months after Pearl Harbor brought North America to war with Japan.

If Diefenbaker's sensitivity and concern for civil liberties stand out in the family letters, one trait that is almost always absent is the bitterness that, in the judgment of many observers, poisoned his political life. The string of five political defeats he suffered in federal, provincial and municipal politics before 1940 clearly had helped to convince Diefenbaker that people were out to get him. "They" did not want him and, over his career, "they" expanded to include the Grits and the socialists, elements in his own party, Toronto and Montreal corporations and businessmen, the armed forces, the public service, the press, the Americans, and even, on occasion, the British. As much as anything else, the bitterness and suspicion Diefenbaker fostered and generated in his party led to the fall of his government in 1963 and, almost certainly, to the tenacious way he hung on to the leadership of his party so as not to give "them" the satisfaction of driving him out. But that trait, while not wholly absent from the family letters, does not dominate. Probably some things were so well understood that they did not have to be said to those at home; some things were best left unsaid.

Who then was John Diefenbaker? As the letters in this book show, he was a man who loved those who had borne him and shaped his personality and career. He depended on them all, and they did not ever really let him down. He was a Westerner, a man whose ideas and attitudes had been formed on the Prairies. He was a *progressive* Conservative, a man who knew that the state had to help alleviate people's suffering. He was a civil libertarian who understood that the state could not have untrammelled authority and could be allowed to go only so far. He was a great orator who struck a responsive chord in millions of Canadians with his vision of what Canada might be. John Diefenbaker was a great Canadian, a leader who will be remembered as the man who toppled the entrenched, impregnable and smug Grits. But he was neither a great administrator nor a great prime minister, not one who could marshall his colleagues and the bureaucracy to implement his vision for his country. He found decisions very difficult to make, for their consequences affected hundreds of thousands of people and even the security of the state. As a private Member of Parliament, Diefenbaker had agonized over such questions as where he might run for election; as Prime Minister, the scale and the complexity of the problems increased in quantum leaps, and he found genuine agony in making the hard choices that every leader must. The Diefenbaker promise, then, was probably greater than the performance, but that judgement is one over which historians will argue for generations.

Few will disagree that John Diefenbaker was one of Canada's most "human" leaders, a man of the people with few pretensions. Now and for the first time, thanks to these family letters, we can see the Chief complete – as son and brother, as lover and husband and, of course, always as politician and public figure.

– J.L. Granatstein
Toronto, 1985

1

PREPARING FOR PARLIAMENT

JOHN DIEFENBAKER WAS AN UNUSUAL CHILD who knew precisely what he wanted to do with his life: he wanted to be a lawyer, a Member of Parliament, and then the Prime Minister of Canada, and his course of action was fixed on those goals from the time he began school. As every Canadian knows, he turned his dream into reality, but inevitably there was a long road between the genesis of those goals and their accomplishment.

Certainly, his family was supportive. His father, William Diefenbaker, was variously a school teacher, struggling farmer and provincial civil servant; most important for his son, William had loved the war of words in the House of Commons sessions at Ottawa in the early 1890s. John Diefenbaker's mother, Mary Bannerman, was a woman of great determination who held the family together through the hard times – and there were plenty of those. Then there was the younger brother, Elmer, always trying to be helpful, but always a potential source of difficulty for his ambitious older sibling.

Unfortunately, John Diefenbaker did not write many revealing letters in the years before he went to the House of Commons and acquired secretaries and filing cabinets. For his youth and university years, there are only scraps or fragments. For his whole Great War service, only two postcards survive. For the years in which he built his law practice in Wakaw and Prince Albert, almost nothing. The Diefenbaker family was always close by in Saskatoon, too near at hand to necessitate letter writing.

And when he began to court Edna Brower in 1927 and then married her in 1929, there was also little need for an exchange of letters, and certainly none have survived in the Diefenbaker papers. The young lawyer, trying hard to build a practice and make a political name for himself in Prince Albert, did his wooing in person in the little time he could spare between the law and politics.

The young Diefenbaker was absorbed by politics – despite his total lack of success at it. A man who had become politically aware during the great 1911 reciprocity election and who first worked in an election in the 1917 conscription campaign, he was obsessed with winning office. He ran federally in Prince Albert in 1925 and 1926 and lost, the second time to Prime Minister Mackenzie King; he ran in the Saskatchewan provincial election of 1929 and lost; he lost a race for mayor of Prince Albert in 1933; then despite this record, he was selected as leader of the virtually defunct Saskatchewan Conservative party and led it to a crushing defeat in the 1938 provincial election, a victim of the formidable Liberal machine. Not until 1940 did he finally secure election. Characteristically, Diefenbaker did it the hard way, winning a seat in Lake Centre, Saskatchewan, in a wartime election swept by the Liberals. John Diefenbaker was one of only 40 Tory M.P.s, but at last he had made it to Ottawa. The first part of the lifelong dream had been fulfilled.

From Elmer to John   *Humboldt, Sask.*
[Postcard]   *July 13, 1915*

Dear John,

I am out here at Humboldt. Arrived here 1:30 today. Going to sell books just as you are doing now. I went to Rev. Coldwell and received a fine recommend [sic] and am going to sell tomorrow. Write me. Address mail to Humboldt. I will write in a few days.

> With Love,
> Yr. Bro.,
> Elmer

From Elmer to John   Humboldt
[Postcard]   *July 19, 1915*

Dear John,

Everything is full around here. If I don't get some decent place to
work I'm going home. Mostly foreigners and Catholics around here and
you know how easy it is to sell to those darn fools. The Catholic priest is
much in favor of work [?], but if he recommends it to people he is afraid
of being fired. He says they are sore at him now. If you are not going to
Yorkton we would like that burg. It's a little piece of Canora. Write me
as soon as you can and tell me if we can have it.

                              Elmer

                         ↶

From John to Elmer   *[Pas de Calais, France]*
[Postcard]   *July 27, 1936*

Leaving today for Ypres battlefields and then to Antwerp tonight and
to England in the morning. King passed down my rank. Boyish as ever
and apparently bashful.

                              John

                         ↶

From Mother to John   *[Saskatoon]*
                                     [September 18, 1938]

Dear John,

Another year has passed and you are one year older.

I hope you will have a Happy Birthday and many of them.

I don't mind getting old myself but I hate to see you kids getting to be
old men.

Your dad went shopping today. Hope you like what we got for you.
Also hope they fit.

We are both pretty well.

Lots of love to you and Elmer.

                              From Mother.

In early 1940 John's aging parents moved to Victoria to escape the Saskatoon winter. They stayed only until spring.

From Father to John   *118 Howe St.*
                                         Victoria, B.C.
                                         February 19, 1940

Dear John,

    Now for a letter from me and a note from your mother. And I trust the note, though the shorter of the two, will also be very acceptable to you.

    To begin with Mary can smile and chuckle, and outside of some rheumatism the last day or two, seems to be gradually benefiting in health from the change.

    In certain ways I like it very much here and from my present feeling of body and inclination, I am in no wise in a hurry to leave. We are getting used to the change in water and eating etc. which certainly means much....

    You know too well that we shall follow your election battle with great interest....

    I was highly pleased to hear of your gain in weight....

    May this letter also interest Edna. Such is my wish.

                              With love from
                              Father...

From John to Mother   *Canadian Pacific Telegraphs*
                                         Prince Albert, Sask.
                                         March 27, 1940

MRS W T DIEFENBAKER
118 HOWE ST VICTORIA

MY ELECTION IS ALMOST CONCEDED AS I AM LEADING BY ABOUT TWO HUNDRED WITH FIVE SMALL POLLS UNREPORTED AND THE SOLDIERS VOTE TO BE HEARD FROM STOP HOPE THAT FATHER ELMER AND YOU ARE ALRIGHT STOP I SHALL WRITE FULLY TODAY STOP LOVE TO YOU

                        JOHN

From Elmer to John   *118 Howe Street*
                                              Victoria, B.C.
                                              March 27, 1940

Dear John,

I think congratulations are in order as I gather your election is practically conceded. I went downtown last night for awhile but could get no
information. I went to bed about midnight and right after that the
messenger arrived with your wire. Mother received your other wire
this morning.

Well, you can consider that a great personal victory because I venture
to say that nobody else could have done that. You might as well run in a
Hitler election as an opposition candidate. I consider you are as well as
elected now provided there are no auxiliary ballots – in that case the results of the ballots of Jack Rabbit, Peter Rabbit, Bunny Cottontail, Harry
Crow, Sammy Muskrat – have not yet been counted. Well boy, that is a
grand victory considering the big shots that were left. You fought hard
and surmounted all obstacles and I can say that I received a great surprise when I got your telegram. I had forgotten all about the business
when I was awakened and came to the conclusion that you had just
dropped by the wayside along with the rest....

Well I must get along. Carry the good work on and best of luck.

                                              Brother
                                              Elmer

P.S. At 6 A.M. when the first results came (after the polls closed here)
and the first statement was to the effect that the election of the Liberal
party was assured, Mother was quite disinterested in the whole matter
from then on and went to sleep....

From Father to John   *118 Howe St.*
                                         Victoria, B.C.
                                         April 1, 1940

Dear John,

    ...As to leadership etc., that is of course, so to say, another thing. I am exceedingly well pleased that you have got onto a foundation – in a position – where you can no longer be prevented to *show* what you can do. Go ahead and try to do what is right in the matter of serving the people who are trusting you with their political and state affairs. In my own humble way I thank God for it all as the Foster's seemed, as we seem to feel, to think – we have in a way been separated from the people generally, in that we must from now on be careful in our political or national utterances, lest we say something that might (possibly disadvantageously) be construed as coming from you....

    John, I have met some fine people here and have in a way become very much attached to this beautiful and climatically magnificent Victoria....

    I am constrained to think that Edna's natural ability to be bright and polite should add materially in the advancement of your future political success. And Mrs. Brower [Edna's mother], dear lady, I can imagine her not necessarily feeling proud, but modestly glad at the outcome of your strenuous campaign....

                                         With love to you both
                                         from Father....

From Mother to John   *[Victoria]*
                                         April 1st [1940]

Dear John,

    The Battle is over and the victory won and I bet you feel pretty proud of yourself. Well, I feel that way myself, so do we all. You put up a good fight and you must be very tired. I can see by your letter that the aim of your ambition is to fill [Prime Minister Mackenzie] King's chair. Well, I think you will get there someday if you work hard enough. There is a lot of hard work ahead for there has to be some changes in this old world of ours. The rich have to live on less and the poor have more than they have today and I hope you will be one of them that will work for those changes whatever they may be, and I want you to be honest and upright in all you do and don't try and get rich on other people's money. You will find that it pays in the end to be honourable and just at all times.

I don't want to preach to you but I mean all I say and I think you will do just what I want you to do....

Lots of love from us all,
M. & D.

2

MAKING A NAME

THE OTTAWA TO WHICH JOHN DIEFENBAKER came in 1940 was the
political cockpit of a nation at war. Just as the new Parliament opened,
the Allies suffered a catastrophic defeat in the Low Countries and
France, and the British army, if very little of its equipment, was saved
only by the miracle of Dunkirk. From being a war of limited liability
for Canada, the Second World War was suddenly a struggle for
survival.

Diefenbaker played his part, quickly establishing himself as a scourge
of government policies despite the difficulties his Germanic surname
caused him in wartime. Like almost all his party, Diefenbaker wanted
conscription for overseas service and a greater war effort; he wanted
Canada to stay close in foreign policy to Britain; and, as a shrewd
politician, he wanted a fair share of war spending for his province of
Saskatchewan. That was normal. But Diefenbaker, unlike many of his
colleagues, had another concern – civil liberties. As a lawyer who had
defended ordinary men and women, as a devoted Canadian who had
suffered slurs because of his difficult surname, Diefenbaker's interest in
individual rights was perhaps understandable and natural. Certainly the
Second World War increased his concerns. The conflict had to be prose-
cuted to the fullest, but because it was a struggle for democracy, the state
had to ensure that it did not trample on the liberties of its citizens. If
anything made Diefenbaker's name in the war years and after, it was his
constantly pressing the government to respect the rights of the people. In
addition, he was forming his own views on social questions, and characteristically he was unafraid to express them. Diefenbaker, for example,

stood almost alone in the Tory caucus in 1944 in supporting family allowances, a measure to help poor families that many in his party saw only as a Liberal "bribe" to Quebeckers who had resisted conscription.

At the same time, Diefenbaker was trying to advance his fortunes in the party. His very first letter from Ottawa in May, 1940, noted that he had refused to let his name stand for the House leadership of the party, but that this parliamentary novice had even considered the idea was astonishing. So too was his decision to contest the leadership at the Conservative party's great convention in Winnipeg in December, 1942, a contest won by Premier John Bracken of Manitoba. Diefenbaker placed third on the first ballot after a "stiff and starched" speech, and third and last on the second and final vote. Undoubtedly, Diefenbaker had realized that his chances were slim in that contest, but he was shattered when the caucus passed him by early in 1943 and selected the lacklustre Gordon Graydon as House leader until Bracken entered Parliament. He was hurt, but Diefenbaker soldiered on, addressing every party gathering anywhere in the country that would have him, attending day in and day out to his constituents' needs, and even attracting letters from those with problems across the country. He was a fighter and people liked that, even if his caucus colleagues sometimes found him difficult and testy. Nonetheless, when he tried once more for the crown in 1948 after Bracken retired from the political wars, again it was not to be: the party machine threw its full weight behind Premier George Drew of Ontario. Diefenbaker won the overwhelming support of the Saskatchewan delegates, but he lost on the first ballot to the Ontarian by 827 to 311 votes. The Prairie politician was still too progressive for his conservative party.

From John to Mother   *House of Commons*
                                          [Ottawa]
                                          May 15, 1940

My dear Mother,

Well, I have my seat – third row on the right in the same column as [Conservative House Leader, Richard Burpee] Hanson and the whip [A.C. Casselman] – I have been sworn in and am now a full-fledged member.

I refused to let my name stand for the leadership as I couldn't hope to get anywhere as everything was pretty well cut and dried.

[Conservative M.P.] Joe Harris had Edna and I to dinner last evening and we had a good time.

I will write you tomorrow after the House opening and will tell you *all* the news.

George Tustin is my seatmate, so with Joe Harris & [Robert] McGregor on the front bench the "four horsemen" are all set to go.

Between ourselves there is more log-rolling and backbiting here in one day than there is elsewhere in a year.

I have no private office yet – there are two of us together but I am hopeful that I may get by myself tomorrow.

The war situation makes us all very fearful and there will be no functions after the opening. I hope you are feeling well again and that father too is all right. I had a letter from Elmer today – newsy, as usual. He knows how to write letters that are interesting.

I am writing this letter in haste so as to get it on the airmail.

Affectionately,
John

From Mother to John   *[Saskatoon]*
                                         May 24th [1940]

Dear John,

How does it feel to be sitting in the seats of the mighty? Hope you are enjoying yourself and that you like it at Ottawa. You know John, ambition is a funny thing. It drives one on to greater things and when you get it it means nothing. At least you are never satisfied.

Well I hope you will do good work down there. The war comes first of all. The British need all Canada can give her in everything. I am afraid we are going to have a bad time fighting those devils. The loss of life has been terrible. One wonders why it should be. One thing I know [is that] that cruel, bloodthirsty nation will get what is coming to her in the end. It looks as if the Government [is] at last trying to get busy. If they had done the right thing a year ago, things would be a lot better today....

How does Edna like it there? She must get fed up sometimes. She has a lot of time to put in.

When are you going to make your [maiden] speech? I am looking forward to hear it or at least read it. See you make a real good one. I am betting on you.

I have been very well the last while and have gone out more than usual, but it is hot and dry here, no rain at all, lots of dust. Have not seen or heard of Mrs. Brower. Don't know where she is.

Your Dad is well. He waters the garden. Nothing much up yet.

Love to you both from us both. Write very soon.

> Lots of love and
> a wee kiss.
> [no signature]

From Father to John   *117 Albert Ave.*
                                  Saskatoon, Sask.
                                  June 10, 1940

Dear John,

It's not your mother's fault that I am not producing my quota of letters to you. That says enough.

Well, your mother received a letter from you today (A.M.) but apparently you neglected to enclose the end portion of the same. However, as you well know, we readily snatch up anything that comes from you – including Hansard and such matter as papers, etc. dealing with Ottawa as a city.

Your address about subversive elements in Saskatchewan was put up in very nice form. But we are today told of the tragic death of the very man in the Ministry who answered you in most kindly and considerate terms.* Very sad indeed! According to my ideas of procedure on your part in Parliament, you are showing great judgement and doubtless someday you will reap your reward for your restraint (I mean in regard to rushing in to speak, etc.)....

A person almost becomes sick of the terrible war situation. The poor French people! How they are fighting so valiantly. I pray and trust that they may still break the back of that demon Hitler's hordes before Paris....

I am glad that our Edna is standing with you as she is. Give her a kiss on top of her head. Ha! Ha!

* The Honourable Norman McLeod Rogers, then Minister of National Defence, died in a plane crash on June 10, 1940.

Now John, I shall draw my letter to a close and trust at least in some degree to satisfy your desire to hear from us fairly regularly periodically.

With love from us both to you both.

> Your affectionate
> Father...

ॐ

From Mother to John

[Saskatoon]
Sunday
[July, 1940?]

Dear John,

We were in church today and heard Arch Ivord [?] preach and I have come to the conclusion that he is the most remarkable man I ever knew. He preaches a marvellous sermon. He spoke about the changes that are to come and what a wonderful day it will be for the poor people. He also told us about the blind and what wonderful things are being done by them and for them. Speaking of his own case he said it was so hard he used to pray the Lord would let him die. Now he is doing a great work and seems so happy and looks so well. I was not the only one in the church with wet eyes either.

How I would like to live to see that change that I know will come and how nice it would be if you did your small bit to bring it about. You people down there have a wonderful opportunity to do good if you would only forget politics and try to do some real service for our country.

So you would like to be home for a change. I don't blame you. You two have been away for a long time. I would kind of like to see you myself. Edna must be fed up sitting in the gallery so much. She will get a real education in politics. She should be able to get ahead of Duncan [?] in an argument and that would be going some for he knows his stuff. Have not heard from him yet....

I think on the whole they have been very nice to you in the House. They have given you a good hearing. I think you are right not to have too much to say in the first session. Friend [Minister of Agriculture, Jimmy] Gardiner got a little het up. You should keep after that boy.

How I would like to see you sitting in the house. Maybe I will some day. I don't know. It will be a long time before the next session....
Write soon. Lots of love to you and Edna.

> From us both
> [unsigned]

✎

From Mother to John   *Saskatoon*
                                          March 6 [1941?]

Dear John,

How is the little crabbie boy that thinks he don't get enough news from home. Just how long do you think you have been away? Well we will try and do better in the future. We were glad to hear Edna is all right again. I have not heard from Sheila [Brower] for some time. Hope she is all right. It's a week today since I heard from Elmer. He is very busy.

Well John, you sure can stir those fellows up when you start in. Give them lots of it. It makes good reading. It also sounds good over the radio. Last week you were on twice....

How is our polite little leader getting along [Hanson]? He doesn't cause much of a stir, does he? You just keep right after it and someday you will have old King's place, and that is the truth....

> Lots of love from us to you
> [unsigned]

✎

From Father to John   *117 Albert Ave.*
                                          Saskatoon, Sask.
                                          March 20, 1941

Dear John,

I don't know what particular letter I am answering, but shall proceed with this one just the same. Now nearly 3:30 P.M., somewhat dark outside and the temperature about 31° above 0.

Your mother has prepared a postal parcel – shirt and handkerchief – for Elmer. You know tomorrow will be the 21st of March.

As to our health, I am pretty well – much better than I was even not long ago. Your mother got downtown the other day, weighed 166 lbs. And came home in pretty good shape. She was at the Dr.'s office – to pay his bill.

Her face looks better and if you saw her now, I think you would feel glad. As to our going East? Well, that still depends to a great extent on your mother's condition. I imagine I wrote almost in a similar tone before. Up here (at our place) the snow still covers the ground....

In a letter from you received by your mother today, you speak of your name. Now, as you likely know, the broadcaster last evening spoke it out nicely and as I think, in an attractive manner. Throughout Canada, it went. Another – to my notion – good boost for you, by way of valuable publicity. In fact, *now* the people of Canada will no doubt find it an easier matter to say your name, and may forget its pronunciation and devote more time to considering the ability of the person onto whom it is tagged and of the worthiness of such person of the confidence which they someday may have the opportunity to place in him. Go ahead John. Reading such editorial matter as appeared in the Hamilton paper, we certainly feel rather overcome. And it's not only one of the larger city dailies that is eulogizing you. Do what is right. Your fellow citizens cannot help but appreciate the sincere services which you may render them and which will redound to their present and future benefit.

Trusting that you and Edna may be well. I shall close now with love to you both.

Your affectionate Father

Additional –
I am still glad when I think how nicely he pronounced your name. Further, if I remember correctly, he said *the* Saskatchewan Conservative member (?), John Diefenbaker. I have written at some length of this particular matter, but feel that I had to do so to make myself clear.

Your mother has just told me that she will write to you on Saturday. She too, sends her love to both of you.

From Mother to John   *[Saskatoon]*
                                          Sat. [March] 22nd [1941]

Dear John,

    I received your letter the other day and was glad to hear that everything was looking so favourable for you – do try and forget that name of yours. Surely you have lived that down. It is not your friends but enemies that talk that way. You have made a great name for yourself in a very short time. It is amazing how quickly you have come to the front. I don't think I need tell you how proud I am of you. You should know that. You know I am not the kind to hand out a lot of soft soap, but I assure you there is a lot inside that I don't talk about. I suppose one reason for that is I hear so much at home about it all. I don't think he ever thinks of anything else....

    John, you will have to be very careful and watch your step and don't do anything foolish. Don't let your temper get the better of you, for I am afraid they will all be after you so watch out. Someday you will get where you want to be, if not now, later. You are still young, at least the papers seem to think so. When I look at the picture you had taken in Hamilton, you do look young beside those big fat boys....

    Love and the best of good wishes for you both from us all.

    I want to get a new coat and will you ask Edna if they are close-fitted or loose-back?

Love XX

Oh, I must tell you my winter birds are still there. Just now the tree is full of them.

✍

From Father to John   *117 Albert Ave.*
                                          Saskatoon, Sask.
                                          2:45 P.M.
                                          March 27, 1941

Dear John,

    ...There are a few things I wish to speak about, bearing in a way on the present all-important matter of your not alone political but national well being.

    Publicity is certainly making you known from coast to coast.

Adjectives have a strong part to play in the use of language, and do not as a rule need much of additional modifying words to make their meaning stronger. "Studied, whirlwind." Then nouns like "brains, ability, drive, logic, delivery." Then the words "debating" etc.

Now I am not boasting hereby. It only goes to show what others who are not by any means given to showering eulogistic epithets upon others who they think do not deserve them – I mean "others" who write for or are editors of the metropolitan papers – in this case of Canada.

And what you lead us to expect soon further to see, the movement is continuing. I wish I could at this moment speak to you personally. Your name? Well, I imagine in the end in regard thereto, any opposition will disappear from the very fact that they are making so much of *your* being *able* to qualify as leader. Already I should judge the people are beginning to get used to it. And they certainly gave you a nice and prominently situated write-up in the Financial Post. And the Montreal Financial Times by no means made anything of a point against you....

Then too *possibly* the best thing for you to do in the matter of jealousy is to strive unnoticed to hide any feelings of dislike for any such apparent attitude on the part of any of your party or other fellow members.

Now, I have spoken out my heart on these things and I do not think you can take amiss what I have said.

You are to proceed with this object before you that you will do what is right and what is best for your country, which I trust you are trying to serve as best you can.

The Easter Vacation should benefit you. We shall be looking forward to seeing you both at that time.

With love from both of us to both of you.

> From your affectionate
> Father

ᴄᴏ

From Mother to John   *Saskatoon*
                                         May 8th [1942]

Dear John,

I received your Mothers' Day letter. Thank you for all the nice things you said to me. I don't think I deserved that much praise. However, I tried to do the best I could under very trying conditions. If I had to do it over again and knew as much about it as I do now I think I could have made a much better job of it....

Love to you both.
[unsigned]

&

From Father to John   *117 Albert Ave.*
                                         Saskatoon, Sask.
                                         Afternoon
                                         February 24, [1943?]

Dear John,
      Another letter from me. I received another letter from you this forenoon.

   Well I am not feeling very jubilant at the apparently disconcerting information you give us as to the prospective appointment of a House Leader. From all we know, in plain words, *you* are the one, the logical one, that should get the appointment. That talk about "awkward name" or whatever else it may be, appears to be a miserable resort of propagandists to defeat you in the matter of your being granted fair play – British fair play – at this rather momentous time of your career as a public servant. *Those* opposing you *thus* know very well that a man in public life who gets the opportunity to act and then shows himself capable is esteemed, and then it has become a pretty difficult matter to throw you down – and that irrespective of the name that one happens to have you cannot make people easily change their mind, when once they have involuntarily got to love a lover or in their hearts have begun to consider a man able according to their standard. Is it not so? Edna, am I not reasonably right in this?

   Mr. Hanson must know that too.

   Had I written this letter earlier in the day, I might have used some pretty strong language about him but had better forbear.... You are not looking for the leadership of the party in Canada – at this time – but in the House only.

   With love from both of us to you and Edna and her mother.

Your affectionate Father

From Mother to John   *Saskatoon*
                                         May 2nd [1944]

Dear John,

I was sorry I did not do better over the phone. I took aspirin all morning trying to keep cool so as I could talk to you but just before you called the roses arrived and it knocked me out. Fifty roses when all I wanted was sons. I never was so disappointed in all my life, even after getting Edna's letter saying she wished you folks could be here but that politics seemed to have upset everything. I never thought that politics would keep you from coming home to our golden wedding. As you told me it was the one reason why you did not take (or want to take) the trip to Australia. I told you then to forget about it. But when you didn't go I did think you would be here today. But politics comes first. I did not know you loved them that much.

Well John, I have shed a lot of tears today, and I heard your Dad crying too, but he is not like me, he don't say anything and I just rave....

Well, the *Big* day will soon be over and I am thankful for that. I have not eaten a thing since morning. I got some dinner for Will but could not choke anything down myself. There are very few live to see their fiftieth anniversary. I am not saying this to make you feel bad but I just can't understand it....

Now John, write and tell me why.

                                         Love.
                                         [unsigned]

Father to John   *[Saskatoon]*
                                         P.M., May 2, 1944

Dear John,

It was fifty years ago today that your mother and I were married. The time has passed and that is all there is about it. From what I know, there were few if any of those, according with my acquaintanceship, in my own close relations, that actually reached the fifty years mark of married life.

And when one considers the measure of health both of us enjoy at this time, I can but say Thank God for it all.

All seems a little strange....

All in all, that was quite a write-up about you in the Saturday Night. The manager of the Bank spoke to me about it. The picture is fine. Seems to me it shows a strong character or whatever you may call it....

Well John, I cannot say anything definitely just at the moment about our going to Ontario. Shall try to let you know soon.

With love to both of you.

From your affectionate
Father.

From John to Elmer   *House of Commons*
                                  Ottawa
                                  May 5, 1944

Dear Elmer,

I have your letter of the 4th instant, and I am equally disturbed at not having been present at the anniversary. I had the same experience as you did, and I think the only thing that can be done is to hold some reunion at a later date.

I will try and forward you some material on a flag address, if what it is is an address in honor of the flag. I had one delivered at one time, and I think you could use most of it. I will dig it up on Monday and will send it on. I do not think that you will have to read the address. You can have it before you, and having gone over it sufficiently you will be able to follow it through just as is generally done, by having the manuscript there and turning over page by page, which gives you a sense of security that is otherwise absent....

I wrote home today explaining the situation as much as I could, but apparently there is nothing that can be done now.

Best wishes,
John

From Mother to John   *Saskatoon*
                                   July 30th [1944]

Dear John,

This is going to be a short note for I think we will be seeing you next week. John, I don't know how you do it. That speech was really a masterpiece. You were for the bill but you say it is unconstitutional.* I don't know what to think of it. You didn't commit yourself, did you? How I wish we had been there to hear you. You know how proud we are of you. John, the Lord has given you wonderful talents and a great mind and I hope you will use them in the right way and I am sure you will. I want you to do all you can for your country and help the poor that work so hard and get nothing. I know some day you will be in King's place. I just know you will. I think it was nice of the old boy to send you a note of congratulations. Now I want you to tell me what you really think of little Willie's diaper dole [baby bonus]? I had my family thirty years too soon.

I had a letter from Elmer. He seems happy doing nothing, wearing shorts and getting a good tan. That will do him good.

I got a kick out of Edna and her Chinese. You will have a nice lunch. I suppose there will be a Dominion election by Oct. That will be a big worry for us all....

Your Dad went to the fair Friday. Left here at three and got back at eleven. Had a wonderful time, not tired at all. Nothing hurts him but work. The very thought of it kills him. We have been living on the garden. If you don't come home soon it will all be gone....

> Lots of love from
> us both.
> [unsigned]

∽

From John to Elmer   *House of Commons*
                                        Ottawa
                                        May 24, 1946

Dear Elmer,

Edna says that I write the same kind of letter to her as I do to mother and you. It is without any information. However, if I only write when I can think of something to write about, there would never be a letter.

The debate is still going on, as you know, in connection with Agriculture, and I may speak again today, to answer Mr. Coldwell

---

* A bill had been introduced to stabilize farm prices as Canada moved away from the restrictions of the War Measures Act. Diefenbaker pointed out that while he supported the concept of farmers receiving a fair price for their grain, fixed prices might cause problems several years down the road, and that there were constitutional problems in the bill.

[M.J. Coldwell, CCF M.P. for Rosetown-Biggar], who spoke last night. There is very little progress being made. For some reason the government is not rushing, and seem to be taking all the time in the world, apparently having no legislation available.

The Redistribution Act will be brought in one of these days, and Saskatchewan will lose one seat instead of four as originally anticipated. I have no idea at all what the redistribution will be, but Gordon Graydon's [P.C. M.P., Peel] view is (and I have talked to two or three Liberal members) that they would not dare pick my seat out for the one to wipe out completely because it would look too obvious, and there would be very strong reaction against it everywhere across the country. It would look as though the government was intending to build up the CCF at the expense of one who has been consistent in his opposition to Socialism and believes in private enterprise.

I was going to go to Toronto today to attend the International Affairs convention, but I felt that this weekend I should rest. I am rather tired, although feeling exceptionally well, so I think that it will be rest instead of travel.

I have not got any further word in regard to the trip to Bermuda, excepting that it will be ten days altogether. The CCF representative will be Mr. Castleden [George Castleden, Yorkton], but who the Liberals will be, I don't know.

Edna looks exceptionally well, and is having a really warm homecoming. Next Wednesday the Cabinet Ministers' wives are going to entertain in honor of the Governor General [Lord Alexander] and Lady Alexander, and Edna's worry now is whether she has the proper clothes. That apparently is a matter of major consideration.

I hope that your garden was not completely frozen down. You worked so hard on it, and it deserves a better fate. How is the insurance business going? Do let me know – and also whether you have found a purchaser for your lots. Real estate down here is going ahead very fast. In one case Bill Brunt* had a piece of land that he was willing to sell for $6,000.00, he listed it at $9,000.00, and when approached by a Toronto millionaire one morning, this man just driving into the yard, stated that his price was $13,000.00 – and got cash for it. Inflation is certainly here with a vengeance!

Love to Mother,
John

---

* William Brunt, a lawyer, was a lifelong friend and political associate of Diefenbaker's, who rewarded him by an appointment to the Senate in 1957.

William Diefenbaker died in February, 1945. No letters were available from this time.

From John to Mother   *[Ottawa?]*
                                          Feb. 12th [1947]

My Dearest Mother,
    My heart goes out to you today.
    Two years has gone by and father's memory is with me every passing day and I know what it must be to you.
    Elmer and I have been blessed in having you with us during these years and while sometimes we may not act that way, we do appreciate it and our hope and prayer is that you may long be with us.
    You mean more to us, can we would like to say [sic] – and you should know it.
    My feeling is that I should have told father that more than I did.

                                          Love,
                                          John

                              ✍

From his early days in Parliament, Diefenbaker lobbied for legislation ensuring fundamental human rights. Finally on May 16, 1947, Ian MacKenzie, Minister of Veterans Affairs, moved that a committee be established to "consider the question of human rights and fundamental freedoms," and proposed that John be made a member of this committee.

From Elmer to John   *117 Albert Ave.*
                                          Saskatoon, Sask.
                                          May 24, 1947

Dear John,
    You have won a great victory and you certainly deserve congratulations. I have just read your speech on civil liberties in Hansard and it is outstanding and you show an exceptional knowledge of history and biography.
    I have also read the newspaper accounts, which are more than laudatory. They give you an immense build up in the London Free Press and it is more than amazing to find two large leading editorials in the Toronto Star. Tories are mentioned there very seldom, but they have really played you up.

You have carved yourself a niche in history. It stands out as a milestone in Canadian history and is the Magna Carta of Canada. King John's men forced the writing of a Bill of Rights in England. In Canada, John, humble subject of the King, forced another King in Canada to recapitulate and sign a Bill of Rights for the people of Canada. This seems to be a converse theorem – but you have really scored and you have something to your credit that comes very seldom in a lifetime. You will always be quoted as the authority on civil liberties and you come up regularly on that subject over the radio, including forums.

Ian Mackenzie delivered a masterly address. He said he had given the subject a great deal of study in the past few months and that is very evident....

You will be pleased to learn that I am getting down to business at last. I have something definite now. I have the provincial agency for a brand new sensational Bowers Pipe and a line of outstanding lighters. Did you see the pipe when you were here? It is the only pipe with a lighter and once it catches on it will move. There are none in Saskatchewan yet. The lighters are heaters. I went out with it yesterday but had trouble making appointments, but those who saw it really talked. I saw Rolly Howes at Birney's Hardware and he gave me a fine order for lighters without hesitation and that is just his first order. I told him about the wagons and kiddy cars and he wants to see them. The samples have not arrived yet. I expect to do a big business with the wholesales on that. Ashdown's are just waiting for the samples....

But I gather from Ashdown's buyer, they will take about 100 kiddy cars here immediately and what I gathered from his conversation he may pave the sale of at least 450 or 500 in Winnipeg. He told me if they buy in Winnipeg they will take at least 450 or 500. I hope those samples arrive this week.

So with the wagons for Western Canada and the pipe and lighters for Sask. I am pretty well set up now. It's just a matter of push now. The Bowers Pipe and lighters are fine to deal with and they are distributing now from St. Thomas. They sent me a fine bunch of samples and good advertising.

If you see Bill Brunt, tell him I really appreciate that wagon agency he got me as it has great possibilities.

I'm showing the stuff at the Retail Merchants' Convention. Incidentally, they are tickled to death you are speaking there.

Well that is all. Keep up the good work.

Elmer

In September, 1948, Diefenbaker made his second run at the leadership of the Conservative Party.

From John to Mother   *Chateau Laurier*
                               Ottawa
                               September 17, 1948

My dear Mother,

I cannot hope to win but it's a good fight. I had a press conference today and told them I would defeat Drew!! That's cheek in his view.

Tomorrow I go to Montreal for my birthday party.

So glad to hear your voice today. Strong it was – I am glad you are keeping up your great spirit.

Lots of publicity – and work too, but I am enjoying it.

Wish I didn't have to go back to N.B. for Monday. A long trip and a tiring one without much hope there.

Glad to hear from Elmer today. He's a cheerful spreader of hope.

Love,
John

3

EDNA

THE SERIOUS DIFFICULTIES John Diefenbaker was experiencing in his political career were more than equalled by the problems he was having at home. His father had died in 1945, leaving his mother increasingly dependent on him for advice, counsel and support. More difficult still was his relationship with, and the condition of, his wife, Edna.

Edna May Brower had been four years younger than John Diefenbaker when they married in 1929. Vivacious, slender and attractive (and more than a little vain about her good looks), Edna was the livelier half of the Diefenbaker partnership, a tireless worker in her husband's losing campaigns and someone who could talk to canvassers and party workers in a way that the still-stiff candidate could not. In fact, many thought that Edna's charm and personality had been the decisive factor in the 1940 election win. Their marriage, like most, had its difficulties, and it remained childless, but it was working well enough when Diefenbaker went to Ottawa as the Member of Parliament from Prince Albert.

Ottawa put new strains on the relationship. The city was still not far removed from the lumber town it had been only a few years before, but it was far livelier than Prince Albert. There were attractive men and women in and out of uniform, powerful politicians and their ambitious aides, civil servants and journalists – a scene that Edna fitted into more easily than her husband. His personality would never allow him to play the social butterfly, and he was always too much of a maverick, too often at war with the government side of the House and with the members of his own caucus, to enjoy all the social benefits of Ottawa. And the buffeting Diefenbaker's career suffered in 1942 and 1943 must have tested the couple sorely.

There were to be other tests. Not long after Diefenbaker's triumphant re-election in 1945, Edna sought medical help for her growing depression and entered a sanitarium. The course of treatment was slow and, as her pathetic and poignant letters amply demonstrate, frightening and painful for Edna. In early 1946 she agreed to undergo electroconvulsive therapy (shock treatments) – a dangerous course of treatment then much in use. Edna eventually left the sanitarium and resumed her married life. For much of 1947 she stayed in Prince Albert, embarrassed at the way she now looked, but she did emerge to labor at John's side during the leadership convention of 1948 and in his successful general election campaign of 1949. But her health was breaking down once more. This time it was leukemia, a cancer that she died of in February, 1951. Unfortunately John Diefenbaker's letters to Edna during this period have almost all been destroyed, but Edna's fragmentary correspondence suggests strongly that she never lost her love for her husband.

All of Edna's letters to John are undated, but appear to have been written between 1945 and 1947. None of John's letters to Edna still exist except the last one in this chapter.

From Edna to John   *[Prince Albert]*
                                       Monday Night

Dearest John,

You have been so wonderful about mail lately & it's a great help when there is so little to do with myself except work.

It's nearly 1:30 A.M. Jack [Brower, Edna's brother] has left to curl on the 2:15 draw.

Quite warm today. I'm busy cleaning house as I might entertain a few of the women one of these days to tea & maybe a supper bridge.

Mabel [Connell] was in yest. & again today. I'd die without her. Really she is a wonderful friend.

Don't send me Globe & Mail as I get it through the mail. I like Ottawa papers & anything for my scrap book. You would be surprised if you could see the amt. I have in two weeks.

I suppose there's lots of entertaining but until I feel and look well I can't go to Ottawa & how I loved those first years & people were so nice to me.

The papers are full of spring clothes. I want a light Navy suit & hat &

shoes & bag this year. It's young looking & doesn't make me look as big as in light color. I weigh 125 which seems a lot to me.

I ordered a new suit for you, dark grey with a light stripe. You will get it in April.

I wish your phone call had come through. When they reached me you couldn't be found.

Must go to bed. Will post this on plane tomorrow.

Be good & lots of Love,
Edna

Hope the cold is better. Take your sero Calcin [?] & keep warm. Perhaps your new undies are too light.

Love,
Edna

From Edna to John   *[Prince Albert]*
                             Sunday Night

Dearest John,

I should have written a day or so ago but didn't feel so well. Hope you are alright. The papers & your letters have been grand. It's all there is to break a very monotonous life, but that is not your fault. My throat has been very bad the last few days & I get very discouraged. I wonder if I am right in my conclusion. I'm being patient & hoping the poison is the cause & that it will eventually leave me.

We have had one week of lovely weather. The forecast is for more cold. I'm pretty sick of that damn furnace. Never again.

I'm lonesome for you & don't let myself think of how happy I was in Ottawa with you when I was well – if only this pain in my throat and head leaves I'll never ask for another thing.

I see how busy they are in Ottawa with gay parties & all & I don't envy them. All I want is my health.

How was the dance at Government House? Beautiful women & dresses I suppose. Oh well. Such is life.

There hasn't been much in the papers & you haven't said much. Of course you haven't had a chance to speak on the throne speech... seeing it was put off for two weeks & you coming West....

My Hansards are not coming. Please check. The last one sent Feb. 7th & I should have more later ones. Don't send Globe & Mail. I get it.

Mabel & Lorne [Connell] were here today. They send their love. She is some better.

Who is your stenographer? You never said if you can have Mr. Gratrix or not. Well I better close as I'm a bit low tonight. Tomorrow is another day and I'll be like Scarlet & go on.

Good Night Dear. Be as good as you can to me. It may not be for long.

> All my Love,
> Edna

ᴄ₰

From Edna to John　　　　　　　　*[Prince Albert]*
　　　　　　　　　　　　　　　　　Sunday

Dearest John,

My it was nice to hear your voice yest. I guess you phoned to show me you were in Ottawa so I wouldn't worry. Well I was happy when you phoned. Today my throat has been terrible & I get very discouraged when it is like this as I'm desperately afraid it is something serious because if it was poison it should be gone now.

I felt pretty good all week but this day has surely taken the pep out of me. Just pray for me Dear. I want to get well & be with you. This is no life for either of us.

I'm sorry about redistribution.* It looks as if you will have to go elsewhere. What makes me sore is to think the Liberals would sooner have another CCF. They are pretty rotten. It's Tucker, of course.

Everyone liked your speech on Douglas. I'm waiting to see if he answers you on radio or press. I got your March 7th speech yest. Very good, I think.

I hope I feel better tomorrow & I'll write you a better letter but I'm sick tonight.

I love you, John & want to be with you always. Write often.

> All my Love,
> Edna

---

* Portions of John's Lake Centre riding were redistributed before an election was called on April 16, 1945. In his memoirs Diefenbaker claimed that the area removed included 1,000 of his supporters.

From Dr. Goldwin W. Howland   *Medical Arts Building*
to John   *Toronto*
                                   July 10, 1945

Dear Mr. Diefenbaker,

I think we are becoming regular correspondents. However, your wife has asked me to write again. After a certain relapse last month, she is again improved and has been quite like herself. I think we may expect, from time to time, relapses, but she will finally get well. She says you are always asking what sort of treatment she has. On the first hand she had the late night superintendent from Homewood in full charge of her night and day. I always feel that a competent nurse much more valuable than anything else. Secondly I have handled the case with very careful attention, studying her every mental condition, studying all the underground condition of her mind, using every modern method of psychotherapeutic measures, using much the same methods you would use in your legal practice. I have had to judge her reactions to people and to those not living about her and I might say it is one of the hardest cases I have had, causing me great anxiety as to whether this was going to be a permanent case or not.

I am not anxious about her recovery now, but am anxious how you will manage the case when you take over and it will depend on you more than anyone else whether she remains well or not. She is a very fine woman, indeed, and her ideals are the best and she is completely wrapped up in your interests but it would be better if she had more interests of her own. She dislikes housekeeping which is, unfortunately part of her life's work.

I have a feeling that between now and the time the House opens in Ottawa that perhaps it would be possible for you and your wife to take a holiday together for two or three weeks. I do not feel certain whether starting her directly at work at home is quite the wisest thing after such a serious illness. Perhaps you and she might decide to have a holiday and I almost think she would sooner go to Ottawa than back at home. She was tremendously interested in your saying you might start practice in partnership in Vancouver. She said "it is the wish of my life and perhaps my husband is becoming tired of sitting on the Opposition of the House."

During her whole time here I do not think she has said a single thing against you, which is very unusual for a wife. But she is terribly afraid you will be disappointed when you see her, so, for Heaven's sake, when you do come be delighted with her condition. She does not think you realize how ill she has been. She certainly was in a poor condition when she arrived in Toronto.

                                        Yours sincerely,
                                        Goldwin Howland

                          ✍

From Edna to John   *[Guelph, Ontario]*
                                       Sunday
                                       [February, 1946 ?]

Dear John,

Really John, you must come to see the situation. Dr. MacKinnon has no interest in me whatever, he won't see me. Now John, this is just a place for people who can afford to keep their relatives out of mental hospitals.

They are practically all mental here, Dear, or have no home. They give shock [treatment] for those who can afford it & can take it but apparently they don't want you cured here –

There is no routine at all. Oh God, if I only could explain it to you Dear.

John, you couldn't get well here seeing what I see. I thought it would only be nervous patients – but it's everything. On my floor they are on their own & will be here for years – there isn't a hostess to arrange our day or walk with us. Nobody sleeps & everybody is on pills.

You must come. I'll never improve here. Talk about throwing your money away for no purpose. You must get up at 7:30 & then stay alone as the living room is filled with people who seem to look normal but in reality they are not.

There is a sweet girl here who had too many drugs & spent 13 months in a rest [home] in Toronto & is cured. She has a glandular upset & came to see if she could have shock but can't so is going home today. She is the only person I can talk to normally. I can see why Dr. MacKinnon doesn't want you here for a month. He is a liar and [has] no heart. Thinks he is quite the big shot. What all did you tell him? He told me you had explained my case & won't let me give him my history. Told me frankly he didn't believe me. Now John, you know I want my feelings back & I liked my life.

My hair has practically gone dead & is coming out completely. Apparently they have never had a case like this before.

If you don't come I'm going to leave. I'll try home, Ottawa, or any place but there is nothing conducive to health here. They are really tough John. How I wish I knew if it was drugs or breakdown. No one here has had the head or vacancy I have had so I wonder if it's too many drugs for years.

[Doctor] Howland knew his stuff when he said don't come here.

I could battle the hair, get a wig if necessary.

Well John, do something. I'm not committed and you know I'm sane.

Please, please come, otherwise I'll write Mother & she will come I know. There must be someone who can tell why this stony feeling is here. My skin is dead, also my head & they must have run into like cases somewhere – I'm not hysterical nor panicky. I'm reasoning it out & if you were here you would understand it just means years if you leave me dear. It's just a money-making place John – you must investigate.

Your speech was fine dear. I'm hungry for news. No one here talks my language Dear – I think an apt. with a nurse would be better & not much more.

Miss Cooper told me drugs took her feelings & taste away altho she never lost her sense of touch in her skin & body. She said her head was stony, not as bad as mine, but she only had them 3 months. It was sodium amythal, she took every 2 hours for 2 months. A Dr. gave them to her to get settled enough to work.

Now you must do something John as I definitely realize this state will never change here. Even you will see there is a definite change for the worse here.

If Mabel [Connell] were only in Toronto & could come up she would see how this environment is so injurious to one – it's fine for people who are definitely mental, they rave on & enjoy the place, but my place is in Ottawa with you. My brain is so clear. It's just something has gone wrong with my nervous system. It's either drugs or the breakdown. I'd like so much to see another psychiatrist, as he would know which is wrong with me if my feelings come back.

You would not waste your money. As for drugs, they are giving me new ones that make me sleep longer & I know they are stronger. Well, that isn't a cure, is it? They gave me pheno Barb after meals & I throw it down the toilet as I have turned to stone so I don't need them at all.

Dr. MacKinnon isn't the man you think he is. Dr. Baugh is human & believes me when I say my head has such queer sensations at times & then stony & tells me he thinks it's drugs plus a depression due to my age & he did say they were considering shock.

Please tell me you will come soon, otherwise I'll go clean crazy &

disgrace you Dear & so far I've been normal through it all. I've been alone in my room now for hours & you never expected that & if you are upstairs you are confined to barred rooms & John you wouldn't let them do that when my mind is clear. It's all emotions & nerves & fear from my hair which is wrong & you know it.

Come, come soon & try & find out if I can have shock & get well.

All my Love,
Edna

ᴄᴏ

From Goldwin W. Howland to John   *Medical Arts Building*
Toronto
February 27, 1946

Dear Mr. Diefenbaker,

I have had reports regarding your wife from time to time and I note she is now going to take electric shock treatments, so that she is getting her own way.

I, personally, am pleased she is going to take them, but thought she was going to take them when she first went there.

I still feel that she is an extreme case of an obsession and it is a big obsession including her home and your family and I think, yourself. The obsessions in these three quarters are greater than her judgment and these cases are always very difficult.

I, personally, feel that the main hope is in shock treatment and if this fails, the proposition only becomes a bigger one.

Yours sincerely,
Goldwin Howland

This invoice was sent to John from the Homewood Sanitarium where Edna had been treated.

Homewood Sanitarium
Guelph, Ontario
March 31, 1946

Wellington A. Cameron, Pres.
David E. Kennedy, V.P.
F.H.C. Baugh, Medical Superintendent
A.L. MacKinnon, Asst. Med. Sup.

Admitted: September 24, 1945
Discharged: March 26, 1946

Re: Mrs. Edna M. Diefenbaker

March	1	to balance	$358.65
	23	by cheque	(450.00)
	31	26 days care & treatment @ 8.50/day	221.00
		sundries	102.98
		5 electroshock treatments @ 7.50 each	37.50
		Balance	$270.13

From Edna to John   *[Prince Albert]*
                                    Friday Night [1947?]

Dearest John,
    No letter today so I'm a bit low. I seem to live for mail.
    Had a bad day with my throat yesterday and was very discouraged as I can't go to Ottawa feeling ill. You know that is one place a person needs to be well. I get almost panicky at times wondering what is wrong. This arrangement in my mouth is anything but a decent fit yet.
    I've just heard the eight o'clock news. You got a long report on your speech today on controls. I imagine it must have been a good speech....

Tomorrow night is the Press Club dinner. You will have fun. Tell me about it please. I'm so darn lonesome I feel I can't go on....

Oh, I wish the session was over and you were home.

I'm enclosing this note asking for a dollar. Do as you please. I've not been entertained very much so you can pay if you wish.

Send me anything you have for my scrapbook.

How is Mr. Graytrix liking the work? I hope you are both satisfied.

Be good dear & keep me from worrying as you know the things I fear.

> All my Love,
> Edna

From Edna to John   *[Prince Albert]*
                                 Wed. Night
                                 [February 5, 1947]

Dear John,

Your special delivery letter came late this afternoon. Where it was I'll never know.

I wrote a blue letter this afternoon & I'm sorry but I guess you will never realize how badly I was hurt last August. It just won't heal no matter what I do. I wake up out of a sound sleep with it on my mind and a pain in my heart. I hope you never suffer like this.

If I were well enough to go some place and get away from worry & too much responsibility, but Ottawa isn't the place. I have such an inferiority complex over myself & with everyone down there looking their best, I just can't face it.

It's pretty awful here. I never go anywhere and naturally you get introspective with no outside interest. You hated P.A. [Prince Albert] & longed to get east so you can't wonder. I've not been on a train for over 6 months.

Colin Baker [?] died. I sent flowers as I knew you liked him. He was found dead.

P.A. has been a place of tragedy this last while. No wonder, with weather 50 below, winds & snow....

All for now. Forgive me if I'm blue. I'm ill & nothing in my life but loneliness & see nothing much ahead.

> Love,
> Edna

From Edna to John   *[Prince Albert]*
                                       Sunday Night
                                       11 O'clock
                                       [March 9, 1947]

Dearest John,

Well Dear, only one letter from you this week. Try & do better this week. Dear – I'm so lonesome for you & my life is pretty dull after taking part in everything....

If I come east before or after Easter I'll need a smart new outfit. I'd like a fur-trimmed suit. It helps a person who has a horrid feeling about how they look.

You got great broadcasting on Friday, 8 o'clock, 10 o'clock Saskatoon. On 11 o'clock CBC the only one mentioned in detail. You should leave the CBC alone.

Write me about the Press dinner.

Be good Dear.

I love you so much & want to be well & with you if you want me.

                              All my Love,
                              Edna

                    ✑

From Edna to John   *[Prince Albert]*
                                       Friday Night
                                       [March, 1947]

Well, you haven't been a good boy this week. Only two small typewritten letters. Try & do better. I'm trying not to worry you & you know I'm ill & can't help but imagining things.

Your speech on Douglas last night was very good. Everyone says it has Douglas behind the eight ball....

I phoned your Mother. She is fine and was going to listen to your speech last night.

Had bottom impression taken, should get that appliance soon. How I'll ever get used to it I'll never know.

Your speech of March 8th in Hansard hasn't arrived yet. I'm anxious to get it.

I just spent one and a half hours on your scrapbook.

It was 23 below last night. I'll have to get more coal. No wonder my shoulders are all muscles, all the shovelling I've done this year.

Write soon Dear.

I'll write you again Sunday.

Wish I was down there if only I thought I was well enough & looked presentable.

All my Love,
Edna

ॐ

From John to Edna   *House of Commons*
                                              Ottawa
                                              April 28, 1947

My Dear Edna,

I received the enclosed letter today from Mrs. Charlton [not found] and I only wish that you could have been present for this visit. They are nice people and have a wonderful home near Brantford.

Last evening I had dinner with the Fultons. Mrs. Fulton is a very good cook and Davie [P.C. M.P., Kamloops] makes a good waiter. I needn't tell you that I did all the talking so a good time was had by all.

The Joe Harris party was a great success on Saturday night. By the time I left to get my train at 11 o'clock, Joe had spoken about every subject under the sun. He had been in successive paragraphs of his speech, leader and follower; he was servant of the people and messenger boy for his constituency; he was head of the East General Hospital and also the humble worker in the ranks of the supporters of that hospital. It was a great evening but Bob McGregor was not there.

Today I am going to see Mr. [Walter] Tucker in regard to the redistribution plan but do not believe there will be any change.

I am sending you herewith a clipping from the Ottawa Citizen which you can hand to Mabel dealing as it does with Queen's Alumni.

I received a letter from C. Morrison and I am sending it herewith [not found]. He invited me to speak to the Alumnae Association in Toronto.

Love,
John

Hope you are feeling better — and your mother too.

4

OLIVE

DESPITE HIS DEEP AND GENUINE GRIEF, John Diefenbaker did not remain alone for very long after Edna's death. When he had returned home from overseas in 1917 he had met a young teenager, Olive Freeman – "too young for me," he said. Their paths diverged. Olive went to Brandon College for her B.A., married Harry Palmer, a lawyer, in 1933, and was soon left a widow with a young daughter, Carolyn. Then at some impossible-to-determine date, John and Olive met again. The empathy between them was instant and, by early 1952, it seems they were on the closest of terms. Olive Palmer worked for the provincial Department of Education in Toronto as the Assistant Director of Vocational Guidance, and she was exactly what John Diefenbaker, now in his middle fifties, needed.

Her interest in politics was enormous, as her letters to John suggest, and her faith in her fiancé's star was as great as his own. Indeed, at the time of their courtship, her faith was probably greater than his, for Diefenbaker had become convinced that he could never overcome the entrenched power of central Canadian Conservatives and take over the leadership of his party. Moreover, Diefenbaker was certain that the government of Louis St. Laurent was bent on gerrymandering his Lake Centre seat out from under him, and much of the 1952-53 correspondence to Olive revolved around his agonizing and agonized efforts to decide what to do. Should he take a seat in the East? Should he go elsewhere in Saskatchewan? Or should he risk all by choosing to run in the difficult seat of Prince Albert? He knew that his political career hinged on making the correct choice. In the end Diefenbaker gambled and chose Prince Albert, where supporters – some of whom were long-time Liberals and CCFers – had already created Diefenbaker Clubs. He won the seat handily in the August, 1953 election (and held it as long as he lived). Not long afterwards, their engagement having remained a closely-guarded secret, he and Olive were married in Toronto on December 8. For the next 23 years until Olive Diefenbaker's death, they formed one of the most potent political partnerships in Canadian history, for Olive Diefenbaker provided the rock of stability at home that gave her husband the strength to run, to govern, and to fight.

The date of this letter is uncertain. It's unclear if the "P.C. Convention" referred to the 1948 leadership convention.

From John to Olive   *House of Commons*
                                        Ottawa
                                        Sunday

My dearest,

    Working in the office – wasting time – dictating to an inanimate machine which is more accurate in taking down what I dictate to it than the modern steno.

    Preparing a speech or drafting it – what a life!

    Nothing to write about so I am just writing you.

    I received a thrilling letter from Rev. Dr. McDonald [?] – he calls me "Mr. Conservative" and expresses his regrets at the P.C. Convention outcome. It was a kind and warmhearted message.

    Well, my dear, back to work.

                            Affectionately,
                            John

                        ✍

From John to Olive   *Royal York Hotel*
                                        Toronto
                                        4 P.M., Monday [1952]

My darling,

    This is unusual for me to write you so soon after seeing you but there's a reason. I don't like to see *you* saddened or disturbed – and this is to take you in my arms (figuratively) and to wipe away the tears. All of us have the days of everything being all wrong – all we need then is just a little bit of consideration. I should have been doing so this morning – and by the time you receive this you will be removed from the need of a word. Anyway, you were just Ollie of 35 years ago for a few minutes this morning.

I went to the Women's Meeting – 275 were out. I was told everything was excellent – speech, and even I was – by those who nailed me down 3 years ago [?]! Yes, I said in reply, without that degree of warmth that such eulogy should command....

I hope you have a good week – and the weekend with you will soon be here.

Lovingly,
John

꘎

From John to Olive

1 P.M.
Approaching Winnipeg.
May 6, 1952

My dear,

Well, it has been an ideal trip so far except that I am in a rear seat that doesn't tilt. The result is that when I fall asleep my head falls and I awaken! That is a novelty for me – to be kept awake – no matter what the consequences may be or *could have been.*

I should not have awakened you this morning before leaving the [Royal York] Hotel. Your dream of Scarborough was a strange one – it indicates that you are driving too much or what?

It was a wonderful interlude yesterday between flights – but now two weeks must elapse before seeing you again. I shall try to write occasionally – and will be looking for a letter when you feel like writing – and have the time. Yes it will be proper, fitting, etc. to address your letters to my S'toon address. Mother and Elmer know that I know your address – even if Hal [?] hasn't furnished it yet!

Well, I have my speech material for the B'nai B'rith for Tuseday night reviewed.

Historically, politically, scientifically, musically, and in every way, they arc the leaders! etc. etc.

Well, we approach our first stop so must bring these few unconnected words to a termination.

You were wonderful – as always, last evening. I shall remember the hours – and re-live them, during the next two weeks.

As Ever,
John

In July, 1952, John's Lake Centre riding was split into three parts and added onto neighbouring ridings, effective with the next election due the following year.

From John to Olive   *House of Commons*
                                        [Ottawa]
                                        July 3, 1952

[No salutation]

Well, I am "out" – the vote has taken place and L.C. [Lake Centre] is no more. St. Laurent hypocritically pretended that votes would be free – but he and every Liberal stood firm – and put Moose Jaw and 6000 people of Regina City into the new area. Drew has been wonderful as have all my colleagues – they fought on and on. It was most kind and is deeply appreciated.

Tomorrow afternoon I shall fly to Toronto – then will leave Sat. P.M. by car for Chicago. Davie Fulton will be with me. Tomorrow I will be met by a person who has never met me before – David Walker (Trustee and Goldring lawyer) at whose place I will spend the evening with them (enclosed his letter) [not found].

So you are having a good time – and you lifted the curtain a bit to explain your absence in Ottawa. I was very glad to get your letter today. It came at a time when I was very lonely – even a bit discouraged after the vote – and your words lifted me up. I wish I could call on you tomorrow, but no –

I shall be in Chicago from Sunday evening through Thursday – and then away for Saskatoon – I will be looking for a letter there if you have time to write.

I phoned Mother tonight – she was fine and asked about you. She saw Sadie B. [?], who is in very bad physical condition.

Elmer may come to Chicago too.

After that trip to Chicago I must take a vacation. I am tired – very tired.

Well, I must close for now.
Have a good time – and spend your full vacation, for you are tired too.
I will write you from Chicago in a few days.

> Affectionately,
> John

ᴄ

From John to Olive   *[Prince Albert]*
                                        Tuesday
                                        [July/August, 1952]

My dearest,

Well, I am in my office cleaning up old files and Ottawa papers and correspondence – and I am *not* working. It was quite an event yesterday to talk to you – it took me two minutes from "Call" to "Answering number." That was almost a record.

The weather is cool – there hasn't been a warm day since my return home – cool and raining and when I hear of your weather I use the Taft slogan on the lapel badges worn by his followers, "No like."

Law business is quiet – always at this season – everybody but Jack C. [Cuelenaere, one of John's law partners] and I are on vacation – with two stenos. No one wants to interview the "Phantom lawyer" so I am free from unnecessary interruptions....

I am counting the days – I have TCA [Trans-Canada Air Lines, Air Canada's predecessor] passage (it's only tentative yet) for August 10th, Sunday, in Saskatoon 2:45 P.M., and August 11th, 1 A.M.

P.S. The situation in M.J.-L.C. [Moose Jaw/Lake Centre] is very dangerous to my political survival – Prince Albert would like me to run here – today's mail brought an invitation to Calgary's rural seat – wouldn't that cause a surprise? Of course I am staying in Sask – and no doubt will be a wiser but sadder person on the morning after. One never knows what to do – However I have stopped worrying – now I am planning.

I may go up to Lac La Ronge tomorrow – it's a long trip but would be interesting – and I might add to my piscatorial knowledge.[*]

---

[*] Lac La Ronge, about 100 miles north of Prince Albert, is part of that federal riding, and was also one of John's favorite fishing spots.

Well, I must close now – Looking forward to hearing from you soon –
your letters are as wonderful as their writer – Yours of Saturday last arrived this afternoon.

> As Always
> and Ever,
> John...

From John to Olive   *Trans-Canada Air Lines*
                                  In flight
                                  7 P.M. Sunday
                                  August 17, 1952

My darling Ollie,

   Well, we are about to arrive in Saskatoon after a quiet – but for me, a
thoughtful trip. I arrived at the airport late – the bus ran out of oil and
came to a stop about a 1/4 mile from the airport – so finished on foot. By
the time I got on board I had an unreclinable seat – so my sleep was
restricted.

   Snyder [?] stayed for an hour – and as usual wanted me to come East.
Then I phoned you and went to sleep for 45 minutes.

   The result of the hectic week is that I am tired – and full of wonderful
memories.

   Ollie, you're a darling – you couldn't have been sweeter and more considerate than you were yesterday – and last evening as we parted – the
smile of the angelic after the momentary tears.

   And then the phone call – and the happy spirit, but when I asked you a
question – how quickly came the self-control to the rescue – "*we won't
speak about that*" – and that was final.

   I am sure the days will drag on – as they always do after a parting – but
I shall be counting them. What a happy time we had yesterday – and it's
only six hours since we parted, yet how long!

   This afternoon I shall be in P.A. [Prince Albert]. I hope that it will be
possible for you to go to Queenston today – seeing Carolyn will mean so
much.

   Well this letter would appear to be endless now. I shall be awaiting
your first letter promised for Sept. 7th – and when you get the first away
– do let me hear from you as often as you feel like writing....

   I shall have to return to Saskatoon the next morning [after a speaking
engagement] to be present at Mother's birthday (orchids and all).

What I am writing is my way of telling you how much our hours together mean to me – St. George and all. It was too bad we couldn't have sat around yesterday where we sat at St. George twenty-eight years ago.

Well, Saskatoon approaches – and it's now only 7:30 – 2000 miles from you.

As Ever and Always,
John

ᶞ

From John to Olive   [*Prince Albert*]
                                        Saturday
                                        [*August, 1952*]

My dear,

It was wonderful to hear your voice last evening – but you did seem so tired. You will be glad that the gathering will be history after next Friday, won't you? Knowing your capacity for taking infinite care, I am certain that the arrangements will be the best the "Brains" will ever have experienced.

I will write you tomorrow to tell you the news so this letter will be short.

The Brunts and I had a good time. Bill went with me to Lake Centre – but now I know I should have gone to Moose Jaw, as I had promised the President there that I would. He phoned this morning to advise that 30 members of the Executive in Moose Jaw City turned up to meet me. My failure to attend as promised will not be conducive to that unity which is so necessary.

Bill says P.A. is the last place I should consider as a constituency. I wonder. Frankly, I am bewildered by the prospects.

Today's mail offered me nomination in East York (a new riding) – and Essex South has done the same. I wonder sometimes why I don't go East. It would do away with those long intervals between visits to you, too.

I was out shooting and got five mallards. I tried to ship a couple to you but Foot & Mouth regulations prevent me doing so. However, when I come East for McMaster I will try to bring you a *goose*.

Saskatoon is celebrating its 70th anniversary. I lead off tomorrow night with a speech – poorly conceived and rather pointless it will be.

Now, don't overwork my darling – I hope to have your letter which was on the way last night before I leave here this afternoon.

I hope that your tremendous preparations will proceed without a hitch next week.

As Ever,
John

∽

From John to Olive   *[Prince Albert]*
                                       August 27, 1952

My dear,
   You sounded enthusiastic about your chat with Helen and Bill [Brunt] when I talked with you last evening. I am waiting to hear what took place. As I told you, Moose Jaw is terrible – every Tory is frightened. There is no organization and I am disgusted with their attitude!
   This afternoon I am going to Spiritwood – 80 miles west of P.A. – to speak to a Board of Trade dinner. Dr. Lorne Connell is going with me. Why do I? The answer is I don't know.
   Everything is in full harvest swing – 30-50 bushels to the acre – the finest crop in 50 years in Saskatchewan.
   P.A. is still an attraction politically. I wonder! Your letters were here when I arrived – and Carolyn's French is excellent.

Affectionately,
John

∽

From John to Olive   *Saskatoon*
                                       Sunday
                                       [September, 1952]

My dearest,
   Well, the air mail didn't arrive yesterday so the letter is still "in futuro" (that should establish a classical basis for believing that sometime or other I did indulge myself in the Classics).
   This evening's speech on the Pioneers of Saskatoon will give no such evidence!
   This afternoon a memorial cairn will be unveiled and dedicated and from what is said there my text for this evening will be suggested (I hope).

Tomorrow I have a case in P.A. This morning I was asked to take a retainer in a murder case at Whitehorse. The accused is in a dreadful position and his people came here from Geraldton, Ont. to see me. I don't know whether I will take it. During the week I turned down a fabulous fee to defend a wealthy dog fancier who during his stay here training his dogs violated a decent woman. I do not want that type of case under any circumstances – although my partners are displeased with me for refusing a fee which would have been shared by them. After all, I have to live with myself.

This will be your trying week. Shouldn't you have a week's rest? If you should, how about coming out to Winnipeg for a weekend?

The Autumn is here. Leaves have fallen – I am always a melancholy person at this season of the year!

Tomorrow morning I will be back in P.A. and looking for a letter. Letters do fill in – and bring us closer together.

All of the Best to you during this week of responsibility – and always.

Affectionately,
John

From John to Olive

Hotel Georgia
Vancouver, B.C.
September 3 [1952]

My dearest,

Well, there is a little break between functions – 6:30 P.M. now – and dinner at 7:30 P.M., so here is a few lines.

Your note was very welcome. The Brunts were on the plane and time went fast from Saskatoon to Vancouver. They expressed most warm sentiments about you (all of which were unanimously agreed to). More of that discussion later!

The weather is superb. The entertainment is fine, but the best of all is the number of friendships one makes or renews.

You will be working hard on your Educators' Convention. I told your A.G. Pater [?] that he made a great speech last year at Saskatoon. I wish the convention was to be in S'toon this year.

In haste,
Affectionately,
John

From Olive to John   *Office of the Director of*
                                        Guidance
                                        Ontario Department of
                                        Education [Toronto]
                                        Friday night
                                        [September 5, 1952]

Darling,

Your note from Vancouver today when I got home. I'm *glad* you are having a good time, seeing people, enjoying the Brunts. ("Bless them" is getting to follow that name automatically.) This should reach you in Saskatoon Monday.

I see that Mr. St. Laurent is making his comment on the U. of T. – Osgoode quarrel,* that your friend Mr. Garson's [Hon. Stuart Garson, Minister of Justice] stand re appointment of judges is not being supported,** that Dave Walker's Neilson case is starting: these in tonight's Star.

I'm enclosing the second in the Grandfather St. Laurent series. Last night's – passive resistance. Tonight – out-and-out rebellion. Tomorrow? – the voter's pride and joy kicks L.St.L. in the shins. I think the photographer must be a P.C. It looks to me like sabotage.

John, do you remember Pericles' Funeral Oration over the Albemores who died in the Peloponnesian War? I came across it today in something I was reading. Does it have an idea that might be used at ----- [?]. Those who died for their country have left everywhere "imperishable records of our valour" – those of us who are left must become enamored of [or] remember constantly her greatness, must serve as willingly, & as valiantly with all their gifts (this is the emphasis I think) – something to that effect. I remember it as a very powerful and moving speech, even in translation. I believe we read it in Greek under Mr. Ramsay at U. of Sask.

You know, I heard Anthony Eden when he received his degree at U. of T. [University of Toronto] in 1946. I had forgotten that. He spoke very briefly – very modestly and simply – and beautifully. I remember saying...that I considered him one of the greatest statesmen of the world, and remember that even then I was making comparisons with someone nearer and dearer.

---

* At the time the Law Society of Upper Canada felt they should handle all aspects of the training of lawyers, while others, supported by St. Laurent, suggested that the universities had a role to play.

** Garson argued that the Federal Cabinet as a whole should decide on the appointment of judges, while others argued it should be solely the responsibility of the Minister of Justice and the Prime Minister.

You and Bill [Brunt] will be away to Moose Jaw-Lake Centre. Will Helen [Brunt] go with you? I hope you like what you find better than the last time – hope it looks rosier through Bill's glasses.

> Good night now dear,
> Ollie

> Love to your mother.

From Olive to John

[Toronto]
Saturday night
[September 6, 1952]

Darling,
   Poor old Garfield Case [P.C. M.P., Grey North]: He doesn't have an inkling, does he, that he was elected last time because he happened to be useful?
   Did you read right through Blair Fraser's Sept. 1 Maclean's article*?
   And Mr. St. Laurent is hard at work on Young Canada.
   And Moose Jaw doesn't look very good to you.
   An election is in the making, isn't it? Only one thing of the slightest importance: What will it mean to you?
   I spent a long & very dull day at the Exhibition, home to the Brodie's for dinner at 7. Now it's 11 and I have ham on the stove and gingerbread in the oven against Carolyn's** homecoming tomorrow. She's bringing with her – to stay for a few days, I gather – a Japanese girl.
   This is the day of Jill's [?] wedding.
   A year ago I was looking forward to the trip West with a call in Winnipeg on the way, a longer one in Calgary, and a return to Saskatoon – all three very fresh and vivid in my mind, and very happily. The whole year – how full of you. The old iceberg metaphor is worn threadbare – but how much of what has been most poignant, below the surface.
   Goodnight my darling. You're with your mother tonight, I hope.

> Yours,
> Ollie

---

* Fraser made the point that in the 1942 P.C. leadership convention, Diefenbaker's nominator made veiled criticisms of John Bracken, who won the leadership. Fraser said that the Canadian style of politics, unlike the American, could not tolerate personal attacks on opponents.
** Olive's daughter by her first marriage.

From John to Olive   *Hotel Saskatchewan*
                                            Regina
                                            October 4, 1952

My dear,

Yesterday was the first meeting in Moose Jaw and it was not very well attended – only seventy-five women turned out. Tonight the public meeting will take place in a large hall – which will make the smallness of the attendance appear the worse.

I came into Regina at 6 P.M. for the Gov. General's [Vincent Massey] dinner – a quiet, poorly arranged and drab affair. I didn't get into the reception (being on feminine votes bent) and when the G.G. and his party were leaving the dinner, he left his party and came over to me and shook hands. Being the only Conservative at the dinner may be the reason for a rather unusual gesture.

All was informal – Tommy Douglas insists on that – not even the informality of one tuxedo – the brass of Church and State wore everything but overalls! This is like gossip. Anyway, I had a nice evening – had a long chat with Tommy Douglas – and the Judges called me over to give me the news that Chief Justice [of Saskatchewan, James Thomas] Brown (82 years of age) is about to be married to a 38-year-old secretary. They said he was heir-conditioned and having the authority of judicial pronouncement would seem to be meaningful!

After the dinner I retired and was happy to receive your two letters. The enclosures were interesting too. The synopsis of the Lawyer is an excellent one [?]. After all, all freedom is the direct result of fearless lawyer's advocacy – but that does not include the sinister activities of some who prostitute their profession by the advantage they take of its privileges. (I shall use the excerpt when I speak to the law students at the University.)

Well, tomorrow night I am to speak at the Ministerial meeting. I haven't one line – and but a few ideas. I must prepare it now – before returning to Moose Jaw for another shallow imitation of what could be.

The radio reported last evening that Saskatoon P.C.s had offered me nomination. What a hope that is – 13,000 CCF majority last June.

Mother is better – now I wonder whether she didn't have a virulent flu. She disclaims polio – and that's final.

Have a good time on your rounds – and don't overwork.

                                        Affectionately,
                                        John

The quotations that follow are from the introduction by J. L. Granatstein unless otherwise specified.

William Diefenbaker
in 1894

"(He) was variously a school teacher, struggling farmer and provincial civil servant..."

–Edwards, Waterloo

Wedding photo of William and Mary Diefenbaker, 1894.

Politics prevented John from being with them on their fiftieth wedding anniversary. His father wrote of the marriage, "the time has passed and that is all there is about it."

– J. B. Ferguson

*John after graduating
with a degree in law from
the University of
Saskatoon, 1919.*

*"During the week I
turned down a fabulous
fee to defend a wealthly
dog fancier who . . .
violated a decent woman.
I do not want that type
of case under any
circumstances . . . "*
　　　　*–John to Olive,
　　　　　September 1952*

John with unidentified group, no date.

*"John Diefenbaker was an unusual child who knew precisely what he wanted to
do with his life . . . "*

John and Elmer Diefenbaker about 1919.

". . . you deserve the first things in everything as far as I am concerned."
– John to Elmer, January 10, 1957

John in court, probably in Prince Albert.

"As a lawyer who had defended ordinary men and women . . . Diefenbaker's interest in individual rights was perhaps understandable and natural."

John with unidentified woman, no date.

"Unfortunately, John Diefenbaker did not write many revealing letters in the years before he went to the House of Commons and acquired secretaries and filing cabinets."

Edna, no date.

"... many thought Edna's charm and personality had been the decisive factor in the 1940 election win."

Edna, no date.

"Edna May Brower had been four years younger than John Diefenbaker when they married in 1929. (She was) vivacious, slender and attractive [and more than a little vain about her good looks]..."

John and Edna Diefenbaker outside 411 9th St. E., Saskatoon.

"During her whole time (at the hospital) I do not think she has said a single thing against you, which is very unusual for a wife."
    – Dr. G.W. Howland to John Diefenbaker, July 1945

Mary and Edna Diefenbaker outside 411 9th St. E., Saskatoon.

"Mary, Edna, and Olive Diefenbaker had had much to do with the successful political figure that he became."

William Diefenbaker

"You are to proceed with this object before you, that you will do what is right and what is best for your country which I trust you are trying to serve as best you can."
– William Diefenbaker to John, March 1941

Uncle Ed

"There was Diefenbaker's Uncle Ed, his father's brother, who seemed to believe that the Prime Minister of Canada was just the man to sort out his land-tax problems."

Elmer in uniform in 1939.

"Born in 1899, four years after John, Elmer was his father's boy."

Olive Diefenbaker

"Anyway, you were just Ollie of 35 years ago for a few minutes this morning."
    – John to Olive, 1952

Olive with koala bear, 1958 World Tour

"They formed one of the most potent political partnerships in Canadian history..."

John & Olive in Kildonan, Scotland, 1958.

"My great-grandfather, George Bannerman, came from the Kildonan strath in Sutherland in the Highlands."

– *John Diefenbaker,* Memoirs, *Vol. I*

*John and Mother
about 1958*

*"He had called her
'Canada's No. 1
Mother,' and for him it
was always true."*

John and Olive at Harrington Lake

*"This home consists of 10 rooms or more . . . located on the side of a lake which is
4 miles long . . . some 9,000 acres, all hills and dales and heavily treed . . . in
short, it is a wonderful place."*

– John to Elmer, 1958

John fishing.

"I may go to Lac La Ronge tomorrow . . . I might add to my piscatorial knowledge."
                                                    – John to Olive, 1952

– Bill Cadzow, Capital Press

The Chief with some chiefs, 1965 election campaign

"All reports indicate the Indian vote will be pretty solid..."

– Elmer to John, October 1965

Pearson and Diefenbaker:
Shades of World War I

Cartoon from Maclean's magazine February 15, 1965

"If you look at the February issue of Maclean's you will find a cartoon about which I am going to sue them for libel."

– John to Elmer, 1965

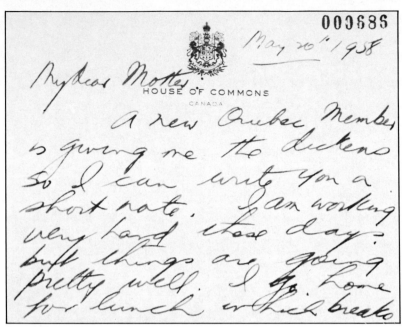

Letter from John to Mother
"If John Diefenbaker had a burning ambition to succeed in politics, it was because his mother force-fed this to him with his daily bread."
(See page 87 for full letter.)

Letter from Edna to John

"Not long after Diefenbaker's triumphant re-election in 1945, Edna sought medical help for her growing depression and entered a sanitarium."

(See page 46 for full letter.)

Letter from Olive to John

"Her interest in politics was enormous, as her letters to John suggest, and her faith in her fiancé's star was as great as his own."

(See page 55 for full letter.)

Letter from Mother to John

"Mary Diefenbaker was a largely unlettered woman, . . . the tough one in the family, the one who kept it together in the bad years and who clearly dominated her slightly feckless husband."

(See page 29 for full letter.)

John as "The Chief,"
June 4, 1969.

"The Chief had become a living icon, a treasured national relic . . . his outrageous quips and comments were repeated up and down the land."

John with crowd in Prince Albert, 1968 election campaign.

"Bill (Brunt) says P.A. is the last place I should consider as a constituency. I wonder. Frankly, I am bewildered by the prospects."

– John to Olive in 1952

From John to Olive   *[Prince Albert]*
                                              Tuesday
                                              October 7, 1952

My dear,
    Your letter written yesterday, prior to your departure on your
Exploration trip, came to me this afternoon.
    Yes, I am over my worry. I now know M.J.-L.C. is a "washout" politi-
cally and will do no more wondering about its potentialities....

                                              Affectionately,
                                              John

Re: *M.J.-L. Centre*
    I am still undecided. Very trying for me to decide against my friends
wishes from Lake Centre.
    I have usually been called decisive – sometimes abrupt. Yet this time I
postpone decision.

                              ✎

From John to Olive   *[Saskatoon ?]*
                                              Thursday Evg.
                                              [December, 1952]

My dear,
    The storm has broken now that the Diefenbaker Club of P.A. is
launched (see tonight's [Prince Albert] Herald).
    Tell Bill [Brunt?] of it – what should I do?
    Woe is me!
                                              Affectionately,
                                              John

                              ✎

From John to Olive   *[Saskatoon]*
                                              Christmas Day [1952]

My darling,
    Well, here I am having opened up the parcels from Ollie and
Carolyn. Beautiful and thoughtful yours and suggestive but most helpful

from Carolyn. I feel a bit of regret and even shame that I failed to get you the watch that I should have – but the plans I had fell through because of the overcast sky in Toronto. However, the postponement or delay will not be for long. The books – well I have read "The Old Man and the Sea" – finished the climactic last twenty pages this morning. A very thrilling story, well-told – and conveying quite a lesson.

Mother is fine and was so glad to talk with you yesterday (if only for a minute). Elmer gave me a Shnorkel pen – something to be lost without delay – and what a Christmas tree he had decorated up – the finest I have seen. It's his day for the year when he decorates the house and tree – in his own way!

1952 has been a happy year for me – thanks in abundant measure because of you. 1953 may be happier – even with all the uncertainties....

Well, I must get this away. For you my best of good wishes for the days ahead – I wish I could have you with me today – but have the memory of three days in Toronto, unforgettable.

Give Carolyn my thanks – I will be writing her later – and my best wishes – and for you,

As always and Ever,
John...

How did you know I needed white gloves? You're a rascal.

‿

From John to Olive   *[Prince Albert]*
Sunday, 6 P.M.
[December 28, 1952]

My darling,

What a day of aimless uncertainty! I arose at 8 and intended to work for awhile at the office – thence to Church – and after noon a meeting of the John G.D. Club. It all fell through in as far as the forenoon was concerned. I went to [Roy] Hall's for a key to my office – got them out of bed – spent two hours with them gossiping – then lunch – then three with the D. Club – the city of P.A. is plastered with my picture – almost every business place – but a moment ago I phoned Moose Jaw and Tupper McConnell, the President, says, "You're a shoo-in in M.J.-L.C.!" Oh, what a mess I am in! The Club in P.A. has raised $1900 in $1 subscriptions – oh woe, O Mores!

Last evening I spoke to the Masonic Lodges – made a fair speech – too long, but they couldn't leave before I finished (that's my explanation of the fact that none left).

I told them my gossip story – I think you know it. Four Ministers at a Ministerial meeting decided to reveal their secret sins – without the necessary detail, the outline is:

The Presbyterian   Smoking in stealth

The Anglican   The odd drink for his health (when
                      away from home).

The U.N.   Liked women, whether in or out of
                      the congregation.

The Baptist said nothing until specially asked whether his silence meant he had none. "No," he said, "Mine is gossip – and I am just dying to get this meeting over and get out of here."

I had dinner at the Connell's last evening too.

Incidentally, five copies of Sir John A's life and works have been added to my library for the Christmas season.

I hope you had a nice Christmas – sorry I failed to get you your present – but will make up for it in the New Year.

May you have a good New Year's Day – and 1953 bring you everything you desire in happiness and sweet content.

> Affectionately,
> John...

From John to Olive   *Prince Albert, Sask.*
                                        Wednesday
                                        April 1, 1953

My dearest,

...Mother is in bed – in good spirits but is very, very thin – and her face is very wrinkled for the first time.

How thankful that she is about at all.

This afternoon there will be a meeting of the D. Club – I have advised them that I have almost decided, "almost persuaded," would be more *appropriate* and would show my training.

Mother told Beulah I had met you again – so that is that!...

The political situation is in a state of flux here. Most of my friends are hopeful – some are optimistic. I am neither. However, a heavy load will pass from my shoulders when I decide finally and irrevocably....

> Affectionately,
> John

This is All Fools Day. Is there any significance for me in agreeing to run in P.A. today? I wonder too.

❧

From John to Olive   *[Prince Albert]*
                                        Wednesday, 8 A.M.
                                        [May, 1953]

My dear,

...A big movement is on to get me to run in P.A. – many claim that I could win – but if I ran and was defeated I would [be] *out*. If I run in M.J.-L.C. and go down people will believe that the constituency was fixed. What course to follow is a question which must be decided soon....

> As Ever,
> John

❧

From John to Olive   *Saskatoon*
                                        Sunday
                                        May 31, 1953

My dearest,

I am down here today trying to get my Radio work ready – and laying plans for the Campaign. I am a long-faced, dour, melancholy person every time I think of getting into the P.A. fight, but being in I must get out and work. There is quite a lot of encouraging support, but it couldn't bring a win at this time. I have to take 3000 votes from each of the other parties – what a menacing picture! However, faint heart never won an election either!

Mother is in good spirits, but very weak. She asked me today when you would be coming. I told her I hadn't heard – and anyway I had failed to ask you when I was talking with you. Have you decided whether you may or will not come? Let me know after you decide.

So the letter was under the steps! What a woman she is who failed to tell you for an hour! Mother has another here who keeps her B/P [blood pressure] up. She came up with a prize question today (in my absence). "When is John getting married?" She heard me talking to you on L.D. [long distance] telephone. And came to an early and emphatic conclusion.

I miss you so much my darling – and the campaign won't be over for at least 2 1/2 months. When I come East, even if you are on holiday, I must see you if only for a short hour. I will be writing Bill tomorrow. Elmer is going up with me tomorrow.

> Lovingly,
> John

∾

From John to Olive   *John Diefenbaker*
                                   Campaign Headquarters
                                   Prince Albert Riding
                                   Thursday, 9 A.M.
                                   [July, 1953]

My darling,

...Things are improving here but it is an awful battle – everything but swords and shotguns. Both Liberal and CCF opponents are after me, but not each other. I am the target for everything. Tell Bill how glad I am that the Social Credit didn't come in. The Provincial organizer tried so hard to get a nomination put in but without success. Then too the Communists – Mrs. Clarke is in. She will not be taking too many votes from me!...

So, on and on but I must go to work. Don't get the idea I have won (I am a way down yet to CCF) – far from it, but it is getting better and better.

Dave Walker has been pretty unreasonable – but I will have to speak for him even if all other Toronto members object to him being singled out by me. He refused a joint meeting with other P.C. candidates which isn't altogether fair.

Well I must get to work, Madame *Directress*.

> Lovingly,
> John

〜

From John to Olive　　　　　　　[Prince Albert]
　　　　　　　　　　　　　　　　　Saturday
　　　　　　　　　　　　　　　　　August 8, 1953

My dearest,

Well, this is the last campaign day – and I must now depart for the last "roundup" at Nipawin.

It has been a terrifically gruelling siege – never have I undergone more abuse without replying in kind. Possibly I made a mistake in following that course, but that was the strategy I mapped out to begin with.

I cannot even hope a prophecy. Most people concede that it is a fight between [CCF candidate David] Corney and me. What will be the outcome? I am neither hopeful nor hopeless. It is tough. I don't think we have lost ground during the last week – but haven't gained too much either.

I am frankly unable to say what I think. Will this be the last letter anyone will receive on H. of C. stationery? (I intend to write no more until after the election results are in.)

Drew can't win (that is certain). I doubt our total will exceed 82[*] – I am low as compared to other estimates.

Bill Brunt's work was completely successful and effective. Everybody liked him – and his speech of instruction to the scrutineers on Wednesday night was a remarkable one – (I wasn't present, but everyone who was is loud in his praise). What he has done for me is beyond words of thanks.

Now to summarize – since May 23 I have spoken at 65 meetings. Is it all to be ineffective? Monday will tell. If I win I shall be rewarded. If not, I shall not reveal any depression.

By the way, my letter to the constituency is enclosed herewith. It was most effective, even if you may consider it a bit "corney."

---

[*] In fact the P.C.s ended up with 50 seats.

Well my darling – your letters have been a source of deep strength to me. Next week I will go fishing – and (if elected) I will be down to see you soon.

Lovingly,
John

ᔎ

From John to Olive   *[Prince Albert]*
                                        Aug. 10 [1953] – 11 A.M.

My dearest,

This is the fateful day! I am not doing any work – just standing around in the Committee Room.

The Liberals have a large car force at the polls. So have the CCF. We have 75 cars.

I had only 6 hours sleep last night – got up at seven o'clock – why? I don't know.

Well, eight hours from now the polls will close*???* I am still hopeful.

Lovingly,
John

ᔎ

From John to Olive   *[Prince Albert]*
                                        August 11th [1953]

My dearest,

I *am* using H. of C. stationery again! *And* very happy at the unbelievable result here.*

Myriads of messages came to me today. Well, that's over – I mean the campaign. I will have to go to Saskatoon for a day or so before going fishing.

Dave Walker is perky – I am sorry he lost out. He wants you and me to visit them at the Lake, but it is going to be hard for me to get away just now. I have to speak to several organizations – to Saskatchewan Medical Society, and to open P.A. Horticultural Society *and* be made the Chief of

---

* The final results were: John Diefenbaker - 10,038 votes; David Corney (CCF) - 7,037; Floyd Glass (Liberal) - 5,409; and Phyllis Clarke (Labor Progressive) - 295.

the Cree Indians (16 tribes) on Aug. 22. Can't you see me smoking the pipe of peace after it has been sucked by about 25 other chiefs and headmen before I start (Carolyn will understand my predicament even if you cannot envision me sticking that pipe into my mouth). They tell me I dare not wipe it off before using....

∽

From John to Elmer   *Sunday*
                                        En route
                                        November 29, 1953

Dear Elmer:

Here's the plan in detail:

1. To be married on Tues. 8th, 7 P.M. at Park Road Baptist Church with a small reception at Royal York after the ceremony to which total number invited will be 20 people.

2. Leave Toronto CNR at 11 P.M. for Vancouver, passing through Saskatoon on Toronto section on 10th at 10 P.M. Shall Ollie and I try to run up to see Mother if only for a minute?

3. Leave Vancouver on 12th for Mexico – returning on 22nd Dec. and then on to Saskatoon for Christmas – we can have Xmas dinner at the Bessborough [Hotel] so there won't be a lot of excitement for Mother.

We will have to see a bull fight in Mexico – I've seen everything else.

Olive has one very strong determination and that is that everything must be done for the happiness of Elmer. Where did you get all the "stand-in"?

The Press has been most considerate to us in not making a lot of fool announcements.

Yesterday's Rugby game was worth seeing. Ollie couldn't go as she has a terrific cold which is on her chest – I hope she gets over it at an early date.

I hope that we shall be happy – we should know each other pretty well after these long years even with all the shortcomings revealed in the "Maclean's" article (most people are greatly taken with it even if it is full of critical remarks).*

---

* In an article entitled "Will Diefenbaker Lead the Tories?" in the December 1, 1953 issue of *Maclean's*, Blair Fraser pointed out that John was the "odds-on favorite" to succeed George Drew but, with remarkable insight, noted also that he was "morbidly sensitive to criticism" and that he "doesn't work well with other people," probably the two most decisive factors in John's later downfall.

I met some old friends of yours at the game – Bill MacDonald and Grant (a 33° Mason, both from Winnipeg). You have lots of friends.

I bought the rings down here but will buy something to make up from Stacey's [?] later.

John

The dress suit arrived in lots of time. Thanks for all your trouble. I hope Mother is feeling all right too. Carolyn will be lonesome for Christmas alone in Toronto....

These notes were inserted in the Diefenbaker papers in the John/Olive correspondence. All are undated, for obvious reasons.

From Olive to John

Wear white shirt marked X with new suit for opening – and new black & white tie. You will look really sharp!!!

Blue shirt with grey suit & blue striped tie.

Blue checked shirt with grey suit.

Have fun.

Love,
Ollie

From John to Olive

My darling,

I went up to say "good bye" – you were sleeping.

You looked so serene and beautiful.

To my Love,
John

From John to Olive

My *musings*:

[the page is blank]

5

INTO POWER

IN 1956 SERIOUS ILLNESS CAUSED GEORGE DREW to retire suddenly from the leadership of the Conservative party. John Diefenbaker's marriage to Olive was a great success, and no doubt gave him the heart to take another run at becoming Leader of the Opposition. He was a vigorous 61 years old, a striking man with a penetrating gaze, a head of curly hair now going grey, and a tall, spare frame. What is more, this time Diefenbaker believed he could win. Drew had failed to crack the Liberal stronghold of Quebec and his success in the West had been strictly limited. Perhaps now the Tory party would realize that is was time for a progressive Westerner?

Certainly many people thought so. While Gordon Churchill, the Winnipeg M.P., organized the bulk of the Conservative caucus behind Diefenbaker's candidacy, the candidate himself called in all those IOUs collected during the years of speaking and campaigning across the country. Diefenbaker was extraordinarily well known throughout the party and, if he was less than popular with the business communities of Toronto and Montreal, he had friends by the score in St. John's, Red Deer, Moosonee, Brandon, and Castlegar. Bolstered by favorable opinion polls and facing only weakly organized opposition from Davie Fulton of British Columbia and Donald Fleming of Toronto, Diefenbaker's campaign roared to a smashing first ballot victory at the beginning of December at the party's leadership convention in Ottawa.

John Diefenbaker was now the Leader of Her Majesty's Loyal Opposition, but that was not a post he would hold for very long. By the spring the country was in the midst of a general election campaign and, to everyone's surprise, the entrenched Liberals were running into trouble. There was a popular feeling that the St. Laurent government had grown arrogant and uncaring, that it had let down Britain and France by supporting American policies during the Suez crisis of October and November 1956, and that the government generally had grown too close to Washington. What was needed, Canadians had come to believe, was a new vision, and John Diefenbaker gave them that.

In a brilliant campaign Diefenbaker stumped the country, telling the people that while "sometimes I may be wrong...I'll never be on the side of wrong...." The Conservative chief roused the people with his promises of a new deal for the elderly, for the regions, for the provinces. "A New National Policy: Unity Requires It... Freedom Demands It... Vision Will Ensure It!..." the Conservative posters proclaimed. The people believed and when Canadians awoke on June 11, 1957, they discovered to their astonishment that the Diefenbaker Party had more seats than the Liberals (although too few to form a majority government). Ten days later Diefenbaker was Prime Minister: his childhood dream had been realized.

His task now, as he wrote his aged mother, was "to do well." And for the first months everything went very well indeed. There was a blizzard of good legislation, increased pensions for the aged and for veterans, and great vigor everywhere. Then the Liberals chose Lester Pearson as their leader and on his first post-convention appearance in Parliament, Diefenbaker savaged him in debate. Soon after, the Prime Minister sought and received a dissolution from the Governor General and in the election of 1958, the Canadian people rewarded him with the most seats in history to that point. John Diefenbaker was in the catbird seat, and the media pundits talked endlessly about the Conservative century and the man who had brought it about.

From John to Mother and Elmer   *Chateau Laurier*
                                     Ottawa
                                     Sunday, 25th Nov. [1956]

My dearest Mother, and Elmer,
    I am here today resting.
    Gee, isn't the enclosed Gallup Poll wonderful? Of course it doesn't mean votes at the Convention, but it shows what the Canadian people think.

It might be well to have Alvin Hamilton make copies and have same deliver to:

CFOC TV
CKOM

and send one to the "Herald" in P.A.

Subtract from 100 those who expressed no choice and it means I have 40 out of 63 of all voters.

55 out of 80 P.C.s
34 out of 60 Liberals
42 out of 56 CCF & Social Credit

It's quite amazing to me.

We went to Church today so our daily good deed is done....

Two weeks from tomorrow the Convention will be on. Who will win? I have a fair chance but the *Machine* is certainly working overtime against me.

> Love to Mother,
> The Best to Elmer,
> John

This presumably was a form letter inadvertently sent to Elmer.

From John to Elmer   *[Ottawa]*
                                  December 6, 1956

Dear Elmer,

I am writing you this note on the eve of the Convention in Ottawa which is so important to the future of our Party. I will be registered in the Chateau and will hope to see you there or at the Convention.

Yours will be an important role in the proceedings because you will be influencing decisions which will have great significance for our cause for many years to come.

It is encouraging to know that we have in our Party people like yourself who are willing to devote their time and talents to public affairs. It is my sincere hope that the contribution which you and the other delegates will make at the Convention will lay a solid foundation for a Progresive Conservative victory in the next election.

I shall be honored if you see fit to support me for the Leadership of our Party, and if chosen, I pledge myself to join with you and our fellow Conservatives in all ten provinces in an immediate Crusade for Victory.

Sincerely,
J. Diefenbaker

From John to Elmer

House of Commons
Leader of the Opposition
[Ottawa]
January 10, 1957

Dear Elmer,

Well, this is my first letter in longhand on my official stationery and it should be that way, for you deserve the first things in everything as far as I am concerned.

Your letter came today – 3 days late – but most welcome. It was good to hear your voice last evening on the phone.

I have been busy and will continue to be although since my speech yesterday I have been resting.

Tomorrow afternoon I shall fly to Toronto at 4 P.M. and will have several interviews on organization on Saturday and will come back here.

Just at the beginning of this letter Philpott [Elmore Philpott, Liberal, Vancouver South] started to speak and said a few bombastic words regarding me which I laughed at.* I'll get lots of this in the days ahead.

I am glad that Mother enjoys the TV junior set, but be sure to have the larger one installed for a test and choose the better one. Then have the company send me the bill and I'll send a cheque. (Also, one will come to you in a few days for automobile account as promised.)

The Drews are leaving the residence [Stornoway] soon but not to my pleasure as it means that we will have to furnish it at a fabulous cost.

Well, I must get along – Best wishes and good luck.

Affectionately,
John

* Among Philpott's remarks: "He [Diefenbaker] was waiting to see if the government was going to do something, in which case he would have said they should have done nothing; or he was waiting to see whether the government was going to do nothing, in which case he would have said they should have done something."

In the election held on June 10, 1957, the results were P.C.s, 112; Liberals, 105; CCF, 25; and Social Credit, 19.

From John to Elmer   *House of Commons*
                                        Leader of the Opposition
                                        Ottawa
                                        5 P.M., June 14, 1957

Dear Elmer,
[typewritten]
    I have just now had an opportunity to once again peruse your prophecy of June 2nd regarding votes in various polls and the general outcome in Prince Albert. How right you were! You are certainly a better political prophet than your brother.

[handwritten]
    Well Elmer, in confidence I shall be P.M. next Thursday (I saw Mr. St. L. today) and will be going to the Commonwealth P.M.'s Conference a week from Monday.

Elmer,
    Please keep this letter – it will be a memento of historical importance.
    You have been wonderful Elmer – and I have your letter of prediction of June 2nd.
                                        [unsigned]

From Elmer to John   *Saskatoon*
                                        June 17, 1957

JOHN DIEFENBAKER, QC PRIME MINISTER ELECT
HOUSE OF COMMONS OTTAWA

CONGRATULATIONS ON THE OCCASION OF A DREAM AT THE TENDER AGE OF SIX AT LAST COMING TRUE STOP YOU WILL SERVE CANADA WITH DISTINCTION I TRUST FOR MANY YEARS STOP LOVE TO OLIVE AND BEST WISHES TO THE FIRST LADY OF THE NATION WHO HAS DONE SO MUCH TO MAKE THE VICTORY POSSIBLE
                                        ELMER

From John to Elmer   *Office of the Prime Minister*
                                        [Ottawa]
                                        June 21, 1957

Dear Elmer,

Well this is the *1st day* of Summer and the 1st day of a new government.

Monday I shall be in London and I rather expect that I may be made an Imperial Privy Councillor, which carries the title of Rt. Hon.

I wish that you could have been here but *no one* is allowed to witness the ceremony of the "swearing in" as P.M. or as a Minister.

I expect to be back in Canada on July 6th. If you want to write me, you can do so by *airmail* (in one of those thin messages which can be procured at the Post Office),

  c/o Dorchester Hotel,
  London

So long for now and the very best to you.

                                        Sincerely,
                                        John

From John to Elmer   *Office of the Prime Minister*
                                        [Ottawa]
                                        July 7, 1957

Dear Elmer,

How are you anyway?

Olive and I got back yesterday noon and moved into the P.M.'s home last evening. It's a fairy place!

Will be in Calgary at the Stampede on Sat. next, then to Saskatoon.

I shall be phoning you to tell you the news later today – It's only 6 A.M. but being awake, I arose.

                                        The Best to you,
                                        John

From John to Mother   *24 Sussex Street*
                              Ottawa
                              September 17, 1957

My dear Mother,

When you receive this it will be my birthday and I'll be in P.E.I. and I'll be thinking of you.

62 years ago is a long long time and I have had quite a wonderful life – and all of it due to you and father.

I often think of how we would strut if he were living. He used to talk so much of those "stern, proud men" who were Ministers of the Crown when he was in Ottawa and saw them so close at hand from the Gallery.

But of all the years this last one has been the most unbelievable. Mr. Drew didn't resign until the 25th Sept. – so it isn't a year ago yet since things began to move and yet in a few days I will have been in office for 3 months.

But there are no more honors to acquire for me since the Queen made me an Imperial Privy Councillor yesterday – so now my job is to do well.

Well, Mother, you will be only 22 years older than me for the next 5 weeks. You are not so old, are you – or am I?

With lots of love and good wishes – and no words to express what I owe to you.

                              John

༄

From John to Elmer   *24 Sussex Street*
                              Ottawa
                              Saturday
                              5 Oct. [1957]

Dear Elmer,

We are ready to receive you and the Queen!

The following is a summary of things:

1. You have a morning suit "in toto" – my trousers are 38" at waist.

2. You will bring your tuxedo shirt, studs, etc.

3. You will be seated in the Governor General's box which will also have a seat vacant for Mother.

It's too bad she can't travel as she would have been the "Belle of the Ball" – the only mother who ever saw her son as a Prime Minister.
4. You will be at the dinner [for] H.M. [Her Majesty] at our place and I'll try to get you in on a reception too.

I suppose this will be a tough session of Parliament. Anyway, we will try to do our best.

Monday I speak to McGill and hope that I can think of something to say – day after tomorrow, whew! – and not one line of a speech as yet.

All the best and will see you soon.

John

∾

From Elmer to Mother   *24 Sussex Street*
                                            Ottawa
                                            October 14, 1957

Dear Mother,

This is the big day – your seat will be vacant in the Governor General's box and you better fly down today. So many ask if you are going to be present....

I spent my first night at No. 24 Sussex Street last night. It is a fairy castle, surrounded by beautiful grounds and overlooking the beautiful Ottawa River. Just now I am looking through windows on all sides. I was conducted through the entire place last night and that experience in time and things to be seen was [not] unlike going through a museum.

There is a large staff of servants who wait on you hand and knee – so that is something different for me....

This afternoon I change to the morning coat when the Queen reads the Speech from the Throne and officially opens Parliament.

Tomorrow night will be the big night, the Prime Minister's dinner, and I have my place at the end of the table....

Keep well....

Love,
Elmer

From Elmer to Mother   *24 Sussex Street*
                                                Ottawa
                                                October 16, 1957

Dear Mother,

This has indeed been a real week & I have enjoyed every minute of it. I have seen everything.

John & Olive left for Washington this evening and so I am pretty much alone in the big house. This is indeed a magnificent place with everything you could dream of.

Everybody has been wonderful and I seem to know everyone....

The big event was the Prime Minister's dinner last night. It was considered a great affair. The beauty of the whole set-up was indeed beyond words.

It was a tremendous job and it took six hours to set the table. I was shown the 14 pheasants, beautiful, fat and plump, before they were roasted. The whole menu was considered most unusual, prepared by the head cook in the King Edward Hotel in Toronto.

The Queen was most beautiful. She laughed gaily, totally informal and relaxed and the Prince a real man, just laughs wholeheartedly. He has a wealth of knowledge and I would say would stack up on any quiz show. He is just interested in everything.

After the dinner was over the Queen went into the drawing room with the ladies and the men were left with Prince Philip and he conversed about everything....

I could go on talking but it is getting late and I hope you are well....

                                    Love,
                                    Elmer

                         ✍

From John to Mother   *House of Commons*
                                                [Ottawa]
                                                October 22, 1957

My dear Mother,

You are getting close to *Oct 26th* which is the date of the birth of Canada's No. 1 Mother!

How does it feel to be approaching 85 years old – certainly your family has been a long-lived one! How I wish I could be home but there is no leaving here while the Liberals keep kicking me around. One of these days there will be another election!

This weekend the P.M. of England [Harold] (Macmillan) and the Foreign Minister will be here. That means an almost all-night session on Friday night for me.

I need not tell you that when I was a boy and saw my way to this position, I didn't know how much work there was (and worry).

Give Elmer Austin Cross' best wishes.

> Love to you,
> John

From John to Elmer   *Sydney, Nova Scotia,*
                                        February 28th, 1958

Dear Elmer,

I am attaching a copy of a letter I have just written to Mother [not included here]. I think that as soon as you can go into Prince Albert you should drive around from town to town and find out how things are. If there are any ideas that you pick up or suggestions you can pass them on to me.

I have been feeling very well and have not become too tired although the pace is rather a heavy one. However, that darned Executive in Hull put me in the skating rink the other night with the ice not removed and I am lucky that I did not catch a severe cold. It was a poor meeting. I should never have gone there and the failure of the meeting has been widely advertised.

On Tuesday we were in Quebec, at Rimouski and Mont Joli. There were six candidates on the same platform. We have only one member from that area now and we should have three more at least. Between ourselves, it was interesting that the Honourable Dr. Pouliot of the Duplessis Cabinet appeared on the same platform and made an impressionable speech on my behalf.

Things seem to be progressing well but there must be no let up. Prince Albert has to be watched very carefully. Overconfidence defeats more politicians than it has ever elected. Above everything else what must be assured is that arrangements be made in every poll for cars or sleighs to get out the vote on election day to guard against the vote not getting out and a storm taking place on that day.

I have decided if you want to do so that if I am re-elected that on the trip that I intend to take to India and the Far East, that you will be along as my assistant. It won't bother you to fly in the kind of plane that will be used because it is pressurized.

With all good wishes, I am,

> Sincerely,
> John

> ✍

From John to Elmer   *Office of the Prime Minister*
Moncton, New Brunswick
March 25, 1958

Dear Elmer,

I wrote mother today and attach a copy of the letter [not included here] which will save me saying the same thing twice.

The campaign has been a long one and everything would seem to indicate that things are going to be all right. I understand that the next Gallup Poll should come out on Saturday and will continue to show tremendous strength for the Conservative Party. What we have to fear, however, is a sense of complacency among the voters and if a storm took place on election day it would be anything but good.

I have been feeling exceptionally well considering all the circumstances but have been very sleepy today and yesterday which may be accounted for by the fact we are at sea level.

I am not sure when we will be arriving in Saskatoon on Sunday morning but will be wiring you to let you know.

With all good wishes,

> John

6

THE PRIME MINISTER

THE NEXT FIVE YEARS found John Diefenbaker's government almost continuously in hot water. There was intractable unemployment as the boom that had started at the end of the Second World War finally petered out. There was a nasty public fight with James Coyne, the stiff-necked Governor of the Bank of Canada, that resulted in the Governor's being forced out of office, and in heated charges that Diefenbaker's government was as arrogant as that of the Liberals before it. There was the decision to scrap the Avro Arrow, the Canadian-designed and -built supersonic fighter aircraft and the decision to acquire Bomarc anti-aircraft missiles from the United States. There were also purchases of Honest John surface-to-surface missiles for the Canadian brigade and of CF-104 strike-reconnaissance aircraft for the RCAF air division with the North Atlantic Treaty Organization's forces in Germany. All of those weapons systems required nuclear weaponry to be effective, and the decision to acquire them was unfortunately taken without much real understanding of the implications.

Through it all, Diefenbaker remained close to his family. His brother Elmer at home in Saskatchewan was a constant correspondent and a regular visitor to Ottawa. Elmer's letters provided local political gossip and reassurance of a kind that every Prime Minister needs to hear. There was Diefenbaker's Uncle Ed, his father's brother, who seemed to believe that the Prime Minister of Canada was just the man to sort out his land-tax problems. And there was John's aged mother, whose health was finally collapsing completely and who died in February, 1961. He had called her "Canada's No.1 Mother," and for him it was always true.

The hammer blows of politics and mortality must have worn Diefenbaker down. Certainly his performance in the 1962 election was disappointing, the rejuvenated Liberals reducing the great majority of 1958 to the minority government of 1962. There was little pause from politics for the Cuban crisis was soon on the government, followed quickly by the great dispute over nuclear arms. To many Canadians, the decisive Diefenbaker of 1957 had somehow been replaced by the hesitant man of 1963, and when the Cabinet split on nuclear arms and when the U.S. State Department issued a press release to correct some of the Prime Minister's comments on nuclear policy, the Conservative government was doomed to defeat in the House of Commons.

No one gave John Diefenbaker a ghost of a chance in the 1963 election. But the Chief, as he was universally known, staged the best campaign of his life, rallied a dispirited and divided party, and forced the Liberals into error after error. It was not quite a victory – Pearson took office at the head of a Liberal minority government – but it was far from the defeat it might have been.

From John to Elmer   *Office of the Prime Minister*
                                        Ottawa
                                        May 18, 1958

Dear Elmer,

I came out to the country place [Harrington Lake] which is almost 18 miles out of Ottawa, secluded in the hills of the Gatineau, late Saturday afternoon and spent Saturday night and Sunday as well. I went fishing and caught four speckled trout. I have never tasted anything better than those trout. They weighed from 1 1/4 lbs. to well over 2 lbs. and you may be sure I will be out fishing a great deal during the summer.

I spent the most restful day and a half that I have spent in over a year and a half for it is closed off from people and the only communication is through a phone which is known only to responsible civil servants and will be used only in the event of an emergency that requires my return to Ottawa.

This home consists of 10 rooms or more, very large living and dining-rooms, and is located on the side of a lake which is 4 miles long and about a quarter of a mile wide. There are some 9000 acres, all hills and dales and heavily-treed, and as it is a game preserve there are many deer frequenting its confines. In short, it is a wonderful place.

I suppose there will be some criticisms but as it is not being used to any extent and was to be the Prime Minister's summer home I cannot see how there can be any objection. It is owned by the Federal District Commission and the only reason it was not used by Mr. St. Laurent was that he preferred to be close to his home in Quebec City. It was a wonderful visit we had and I only wish that some of the succeeding weekends would allow me to stay there rather than to travel about.

This week we start again on the Speech from the Throne and should conclude it, and when it is finished we should really start to get work done. It is a hard thing to find everyone sufficient work for about 170 members who are not in the Cabinet or Parliamentary Assistants, but I think work will be found for all of them and they will be fully occupied.

All the Best,
John

I don't know yet whether I'll be in Saskatoon on Saturday en route to Edmonton to the Canadian Legion convention. I may have to stay here because of the serious International situation in France and Middle East...*

Will wire or phone you.

✍

From John to Mother   *House of Commons*
                                           [Ottawa]
                                           May 20, 1958

My dear Mother,

A new Quebec Member is giving me the dickens** so I can write you a short note. I am working very hard these days but things are going pretty well. I go home for lunch which breaks the day for me – but I am getting fat (FAT), having increased 5 pounds since I saw you – [now] weighing 176 lbs. as I rise in the morning.

---

* On May 13, 1958, riots in Paris marked the latest incident in the ongoing dispute over French rule in Algeria.

** Yvon Dupuis, Liberal member for St. Jean-Iberville-Napierville, in his address on the Speech from the Throne, criticized the government for its poor social programs and insufficient assistance for the unemployed.

Olive seems fine but is not sleeping as she should – too many teas she says.

All good wishes to you and much love.

John

♏

John's father, William, had two brothers, Henry and Edward. Henry died while John was very young, but Ed lived until 1961. In his memoirs John gives a brief description of Ed: "He was a born teacher and a most successful one. He taught school in Saskatchewan for many years. In retirement he lived in Regina. He never ceased his quest for knowledge, and when he died in the 1960s at the age of eighty-six, he was still wrestling with the philosophy of Kant and Schopenhauer. He was my teacher from grades seven to ten."

From Uncle Ed to John　　　　　　　*Regina*
　　　　　　　　　　　　　　　　　　　Monday
　　　　　　　　　　　　　　　　　　　September 29, 1958

Dear John,

Seems I can't get a proper receipt for my taxes paid on the farm. First receipt had discounts jumbled on *purpose*, I believe, and *Mrs.* attached to my name. I asked for a correction. Corrected copy addressed to Mrs. E.L. came, figures correct, and *enclosed** letter of apology addressed to Mrs. E.L.D. I received it at my address.

Is this a scheme of camouflaged fraud ultimately intended to defraud me out of my farm? Spite at Borden must be fierce. If I leave this alone, next fall if I'm alive I will be told farm is not assessed to one fox tail [?]. Your law experience & training may show you a danger signal. A *proper receipt* in my name with no fringes attached must be secured at once.

You are busy but can still be had for advice. Shall I obtain the help etc. of a lawyer who you select & he write the Sec. Tres., E.M. Hillhouse at Borden a stern letter and a proper receipt may be forthcoming? I may have to go to court to win my rights. What do you suggest? Either ----- Sr., Q.C. or ----- Jr. or Mr. Embury. If I explain all to one of these practitioners & he writes a registered letter, I may soon receive my proper receipt. You might write a line of explanation to him before I go

---

* Uncle Ed had received a letter dated September 23, 1958, from E.M. Hillhouse, Secretary-Treasurer of the Rural Municipality of Grand Bend, No. 405, addressed to Mrs. E. L. Diefenbaker.

see him and that may expedite matters pretty well. Do not lose my letter, return it to me & it may come safely.

Do not mention this to your mother or it might reach Borden. Ernest, my tenant, wrote me that their wheat No.2 turned out well on the farm, oats none too good.

I may send you a night letter this evening so as to keep you posted.

Glad you had a good time in Vancouver & lots at the Yukon [?]. You'll be home now.

I'm fairly well, but this excitement does not help things along. I do hope you can read my letter. Olive is having great times.

Please write soon. Love & best wishes to you and Olive.

> Affectionately,
> Uncle Ed

P.S. Do letters addressed to you in Ottawa require postage stamps? – I'm attaching one to make doubly sure.

From John to Uncle Ed   *Office of the Prime Mnister*
Ottawa
October 1, 1958

Dear Uncle Ed,

I am returning herewith your letter from the Rural Municipality of Great Bend. Outside of the fact that it is impertinent (as it is addressed to Mrs. Diefenbaker), the fact is that it doesn't do you any harm whatsoever and just shows that Mr. Hillhouse is a "smart alec." I wouldn't bother any more about it at all. There is no harm in any way and you haven't anything to concern yourself about in the slightest. Indeed, if you wrote him and pointed out that there was a mistake, you would give him some satisfaction. So I would forget the matter altogether. Next year, when you make the payment, point out in the letter for the benefit of the secretary that the receipt is to be made out in your name – Edward L. Diefenbaker – and no other. There is no purpose in going to a lawyer or giving the matter another thought.

Olive and I had a very good trip to the Yukon and found it most interesting.

Mother is far from well and the injury that she suffered from the broken vertebrae in her spine has added to her great discomfort from which she suffers much pain.

With regard to your mail, all you put on the outside is "Personal and Urgent" and address it to me and no postage is necessary.

With all good wishes,

> I am,
> Sincerely,
> John

ᔆ

In November, 1958, John Diefenbaker set out with Olive and Elmer on a world tour, which included fourteen countries in six weeks.

From Olive to Mother   *Hotel Königshof*
                                         Bonn [West Germany]
                                         Saturday
                                         [November 8, 1958]

Dear Mother,

This is the most wonderful place.

Today we visited the Beethoven Museum and if ever Elmer's face shone it is today. We saw the very room where Beethoven was born, his first piano, the manuscript of the Moonlight Sonata – so many things that are so familiar and so dear. John tramped around, only remotely interested, but this was Elmer's day. Lunch today with Von Breutans, the Foreign Minister, dinner last night Chancellor Adenauer, lunch yesterday with Dr. Heuss, the President. Both are dear, dear people.

John is doing a wonderful job, making a tremendous impression, not without some effort, but at the same time we are having a very interesting time.

Tomorrow we go to Soest where John reviews 3 brigades, then to Verdun for Armistice Day where John speaks. Carolyn & [her husband] Don [Weir] have been there and say that it is a very moving and impressive place – a beautiful chapel – and then crosses by the thousands in all directions.

After that – to Rome.

I wish you could see Elmer. He glows with excitement from morning to night. Everyone likes him. Everyone helps him....

> Love,
> Olive

From John to Mother   *Rome*
                                         November 12, 1958

Dear Mother,

We arrived in Rome last night amidst a terrific rain storm and we will be leaving here tonight.

Elmer is having a wonderful time and in today's newspaper is referred to as my "son Elmer." It provided me with an observation of how ancient I am becoming.

Last evening the Prime Minister of Italy gave a dinner in the most magnificent dining room I have ever seen.

I am enclosing a folder which shows some pictures of the hotel where we are staying here. From our window we can see one of Rome's beautiful fountains.

With all good wishes,

Love,
John

From Olive to Mother   *Lahore, Pakistan*
                                         November 16 [1958]

Dear Mother,

John was recounting today tales of your next door neighbor on the farm who had served in the British army in India, in Lahore, Rawalpindi & at the Khyber Pass. Well, here we are.

Lahore is a huge city – over a million – a mixture of great beauty & wealth & great poverty. It's so close to the border of India & feeling is so strong between Pakistan & India that soldiers are everywhere.

We are staying at the Governor's House. The place is full of red-coated turbaned servants ready to save you from lifting a finger. Last night our personal one knelt & untied John's shoes, pulled them off, pulled off his socks, and was ready to work on the trousers when John took over.

Elmer thinks it is a good life, thinks we should settle down here permanently – so he says. The fact is there are problems of course, lots of them. Everywhere we go we have 2 security men in our car, 2 jeeps full of soldiers with us, every street lined with soldiers. Elmer can have it.

Love,
Olive

From John to Mother   *En route Malaya*
                                            November 27, 1958

Dear Mother,

We are now on the way to Malaya and Singapore. Yesterday in Ceylon I went to a Baptist church where there were some 300. There were many official functions but yesterday was an experience of itself in that I went to the zoo for an hour. When they took a flash picture of the Chimpanzee, the Chimp was so annoyed and angry that he would have torn the camera to pieces if it had been able to get a hold of it. He spit and sputtered and jabbered away most profanely apparently....

                                    Love,
                                    John

From John to Mother   *Office of the Prime Minister*
                                            Ottawa
                                            May 8, 1959

My dear Mother,

Olive went to Montreal this morning on the private railway car and I am going down in a few moments to a dinner meeting to be held there tonight. I hope to make a reasonably good speech because there will be close to three thousand at the dinner. They have sold out all the tickets and it should be a big show.

I have been held pretty close to business all week and was not able to get out even for an hour's fishing. I had hoped that I would have been able to do so during the weekend but unfortunately I have to go to New Brunswick on Tuesday to receive an Honorary Degree from Mount Allison University and to make a speech there. What it will be about nobody knows.

I had a nice letter from Uncle Ed and as a matter of fact his writing is better than it has been in the last fifty years. I asked him to write a full account of the years we were on the homestead so that the material might be available for biographical purposes as the years go by. It was a good letter but it ended up on a strange note.

Last year he received a notice from the Secretary of the Municipality enclosing his assessment notice. It was addressed to Mrs. Ed. Diefenbaker. He was very annoyed about this and he wrote and told them that he did not like that type of conduct, so when they sent him the tax notice and it was still addressed in the name of Mrs. Ed.L. Diefenbaker he was really annoyed. In ending his letter of yesterday he says I wonder in whose name my assessment will be this year, and if it is in that same name again there is going to be the dickens to pay.

I thought you would like to hear this story because it really gave me a good laugh.

Sunday is Mother's Day and I wish I could be with you for, as you know, you have been a wonderful mother. However, I will be thinking of you and will be seeing you soon.

Roy Thomson, the head of all the Thomson papers delivered to me a beautiful jewel in the form of a pendant for your neck. Attached to it there is a St. Andrew's Cross of Scotland. It is about 1 1/2 inches in length and the Cross bar on the Cross is about 1/2 inch. It is very ornate. I will be bringing it with me when I come to see you for I know you will be very pleased with it. It is most unique and comes from the Highlands of Scotland.

> With much love
> and affection,
> John

S

From John to Elmer   *Office of the Prime Minister*
                                Ottawa
                                July 18, 1959

From John to Elmer

Dear Elmer,

I am in my office at the moment and it is now 3.00 P.M. and the House has been sitting continuously since 11 o'clock this morning and there is some hope that we may finish today. That is the expectation, but by the time you receive the letter you will know whether the objective was attained.*

Last evening we sat until after midnight, and as always near the end of the session the accumulation of work and the long hours make everybody short-tempered and bellicose. I am told that at the very

---

* The House did adjourn that day.

moment Pickersgill is charging me with political interference, but I am not going near the place.

Olive and I hope to go out to the country place tonight no matter whether the proceedings end here, and while tomorrow will be no rest it will at least be a change. I have two major speeches to make on Monday in Quebec and have not any new material, and for that matter no ideas. Three or four have given me their suggestions and when I throw the omelet together tomorrow morning I will have to unscramble it and come up with something.

Olive has not been so well again and she has to have some X-rays. She is having more and more difficulty in walking. It seems to be a continuation of the injury she received just over two years ago while we were en route to the United Kingdom.

I haven't told Dr. Baltzan* yet but I have recommended him as one of the Board to direct the awards under the Queen's Fund for Research into Children's Diseases. He wrote me recently that he might be going to Edinburgh to the Medical Convention and I haven't heard whether or not he did so.

The weather is abominably hot, humid and sultry, and I need hardly tell you I will be glad when the session is over to have some five months free from the House duties.

While I have pressing invitations from Italy, Turkey and the Union of South Africa, I am going to stay in Canada. I have quite a number of appointments in the next few months but intend to reduce them to a minimum. I would like to speak once in each province before the next session begins although that is a big prospect.

On Monday Joey Smallwood is going to bring a Motion before the Newfoundland Legislature asking for unanimous support for a resolution condemning my Government. Two Conservative members in the Legislature, Higgins and Duffy, will leave the Conservative Party and become Independents. The other two will not, and Joey has intimated that unless the vote is unanimous he will immediately go to the country. Under those circumstances I would not sincerely have a visit to Newfoundland in mind, although I did intend to spend three days there this summer.

I can't tell you yet when we will be coming West but it will not be long. I am glad to have your report that crop conditions are good and that the rains have brought about real hope for the wheat farmers.

---

* Dr. David Baltzan was the long-time Diefenbaker family doctor and family friend.

Incidentally, Ed Gerry has agreed to accept and will be appointed as one of the Tarriff Commissioners. I suppose when that announcement is made there will be more contoversy over the fact that he was my Official Agent.

With all good wishes,
John

P.S. I will phone you tomorrow. Please send me a list of the accounts I paid for Mother during 1958 — hospital, nurses etc.

ᔭ

From John to Mother   *Office of the Prime Minister*
                                          [Ottawa]
                                          Sunday
                                          [September 20, 1959]

My dear "Mudsy",

Sorry to hear of your accident, but glad to know as usual that you are full of grit. I will be seeing you later this week and will spend a day in Saskatoon.

Yesterday I was in the "Scottish Settlement" of West Gwillimbury (about 40 miles north of Toronto) and went to the Presbyterian Auld Kirk Cemetery and there found the headstones of your grandparents George and Christina Bannerman (when did the turn to the Baptists take place?). Do you know what Christina's maiden name was? You had a sister too of that name so it must have been a family custom.

All the Bannerman relationships were there down to the 10 year olds.

Well, I got lots of birthday wishes and messages myself this time, but nothing pleased me more than your present and your card which you signed yourself. That will go into the Archives as one from my mother in her 86th year!

I have to go to Cabinet today because most of the Ministers are absent and four are away at the Commonwealth Conference during the week.

On Friday night I spoke from the pulpit at the United Church to the Annual Council meeting. I told them we Baptists were not narrow in our viewpoint. We just knew the other churches were wrong! They enjoyed that one.

Much love,
John

From John to Elmer   *Office of the Prime Minister*
                                        Ottawa
                                        October 16, 1959

Dear Elmer,

Your letter reached me yesterday and I was glad to hear how things were. Mother's condition is of course very disturbing and I want you to keep me fully advised. There is really nothing that can be done and only today Bill Brunt told me that his wife's mother has had a terrible stroke and is unconscious. She is about two years younger than mother but of course has not been confined to her bed as has mother.

The problems connected with the credit situation are very heavy and trying and cause me much concern. Mr. Pearson last evening apparently made quite a vicious attack on me but I did not see the TV myself but have been told about it. One of these days I will take him and deal with him without the usual consideration that I show him, for if anybody ever was vulnerable he is the person.

The last couple of days have been heavy ones. I have had a visit from the President of Mexico. I couldn't stand these repeated dinners very long. Last night it was a dinner at Government House and at noon today we had him here at our house for Lunch. Tonight the President of Mexico gives a dinner at the Country Club for the Governor General and we have to attend. Next week it is the Crown Prince of Ethiopia as well as a trip to Winnipeg on Saturday Oct. 24th. If you would like to come down I would like to see you. I am going to speak to the Conservative Association there and it might do you good to get away for a day. However, I will call you in any event to ascertain your wishes.

The snowfall in Western Canada has added to our difficulties and naturally, Mr. [C.M.] Fines [Saskatchewan Treasurer], who is here in Ottawa for the meeting of the Provincial Treasurers, is screaming for assistance. They ask for help and no matter how generous the Federal Government is it gets nothing but condemnation from them.

I had a two hour interview this afternoon with Premier [Paul] Sauvé. He is a very good man and I think he will have no difficulty in winning the provincial election whenever he calls it.

The weather here is around freezing and it looks like snow too. Altogether it is the time in the Fall when everything is gloomy.

Incidentally I have read over Uncle Ed's summary of homestead days and found it pretty complete and also found that it contained information that I had long since forgotten.

I had a letter from Jim Wright of the Farmer's Union today and he told me that he liked your article in the Toronto Star.* To use his words – "I thought it quite well done with a homey touch, warm and with restraint."

> With all good wishes,
> As ever,
> John

~

From John to Elmer   *Office of the Prime Minister*
Ottawa
December 7, 1959

Dear Elmer,

...I had a very good weekend; got a tremendous amount of work done and am pretty well up-to-date. I had a lot of letters regarding the farm plan and the CCFers are mad because their government has to pay for a change, but by and large I hope I can iron out the difficulties. In any event they have learned they can't go on for ever suggesting that we pay the money and they provide the talk.

I have had no word from Uncle Ed and don't know how he is. It is strange that he would not write.

Tomorrow is our wedding anniversary. Olive summed it up yesterday morning when she said it just seems like a lifetime – the last six years. I don't know what she meant by that!

> With all good wishes,
> John

~

From John to Elmer   *Office of the Prime Minister*
Ottawa
June 13, 1960

Dear Elmer,

There have been all kinds of alibis for the outcome in Saskatchewan and no doubt there will be a number who will join with the Star-Phoenix in condemnation of me in connection with the deficiency payments

---

* An "as told to" article, "My Brother John," appeared in the *Star Weekly* on September 26, 1959.

decision. I believe that the medical doctors, by their lobby against the Medical Act, made that subject the issue to the exclusion of almost all others.

Now, of course, there are still two other provinces. New Brunswick looks alright, and as to the situation in Quebec I can only say that the members of the Government are very hopeful and seem to have no doubt as to the outcome, but if a party has been in power for 16 years, with two leadership changes in a few months, fissiparous elements are bound to appear.

I will be watching with a great deal of interest as I will have to have a number of by-elections shortly. I want to have them all about the same time. There will be one in New Brunswick, two in Quebec and two in Ontario. One of these will result from the reorganization of the Cabinet, and there will be others.

I spent a very quiet weekend and you will agree that I wasn't on the beam when I asked you on the phone on Saturday whether you were going to church!...

> With all good wishes,
> John

From John to Uncle Ed   *Office of the Prime Minister*
                                        Ottawa
                                        June 18, 1960

Dear Uncle Ed,

Elmer will be seeing you in Regina today. He was talking to me and told me of the Shrine celebrations there. Last evening the Shriners' had their ceremonial here and presented me with a portrait (three-quarter size) which was painted by Kenneth Forbes, the acclaimed Canadian artist, and which is to be exhibited in the Washington Memorial along with the Presidents of the United States who have been Shriners. It will be the first time that a portrait of a Canadian will be hung there and Mr. Justice Porter said it will be there for all generations to come.

This afternoon Olive and I are going to the Governor General's Garden Party and whenever I am there walking around Rideau Hall Park I think of father who used to describe the occasion when he played football there in the presence of the Lord Stanley who was then the Governor General. Incidentally, Lord Stanley's grandson, the Earl of Derby, told me when I was in London at the Prime Ministers'

Conference that his grandfather's records referred to the game. One of my major regrets is that father never saw the House of Commons in session after I became a member. Certainly he knew more about the House of Commons and the Senate than any person I have ever known that was not a member.

Elmer reports that you are getting along very well and I am glad to hear that as you must have lots of time to yourself I hope to hear from you soon.

> With all good wishes,
> I am,
> Sincerely,
> John

From John to Elmer   *Office of the Prime Minister*
                                        Ottawa
                                        July 23, 1960

Dear Elmer,

I had gone to sleep last night when you called and it was too bad that you couldn't hear but that apparently is not unusual when I am out at the country house. The man who substituted for you couldn't hear either, although I could hear both of you perfectly. Olive and I felt very sorry for you. Your way of starting the conversation was to ask me how I was feeling and how things were going, and then you didn't say anything more and I knew why that was so. Uncle Ed lived a long life and I am glad that he did not have much suffering.

Gowan Guest [John's Executive Assistant] went to work and between you everything seems to be in pretty good shape.

(1) The funeral is to take place at 11.00 A.M. on Thursday.

(2) I will be arriving early that morning.

(3) The burial will take place in our family plot. There is room in that plot for five. This will make four and no doubt you will choose to be buried there too when the time comes. Olive and I have to decide on another plot. There has been some suggestion that it should be in Ottawa for I must say that I would not think it should be in Prince Albert. This, of course, can be decided after we talk things over.

(4) We will have flowers sent from here.

(5) I tried to get Martin Pederson on the phone and will be talking things over with Donald Disberry.

(6) There should be some Conservative stalwarts acting as pallbearers and there might be some representatives of the Masonic and Oddfellows' Lodges of which he was a member for so many years. You have mentioned Tom Girvin and Ross Walker, and Olive has suggested Harry Hays. I will get some other suggestions.

(7) The minister of the Presbyterian Church should be spoken for. While I question whether there should be a sermon, a short one would not be out of place, but of course the minister did not know him as he went to his church in Regina through the years.

(8) You should pile together all his papers and documents from both locations and have them shipped to Saskatoon so that you can go through them at leisure.

(9) It may well be that his will may have been written out in longhand. Be sure you watch for all papers in which there is a disposition of his estate.

As other matters occur to me I will call you, and in the meantime I wanted to give you a general summary of things that needed to be done.

> With all good wishes,
> John

ᕳ

From John to Elmer   *The Waldorf-Astoria*
                                            New York
                                            September 29, 1960

Dear Elmer,

I haven't done very much today. We arrived at 10:30 this morning and I was present for Prime Minister Macmillan's speech to the [United Nations] Assembly. During the afternoon I had a discussion with Prime Minister [Walter] Nash of New Zealand and discussed the Hoover Commission terms with former President [Herbert] Hoover who, at 86, is as alert as can be.

After the morning session was over I came out in the corridor and Khrushchev with his phalanx of bodyguards started off in a direction away from me when suddenly Khrushchev reversed his course and came directly towards where I was standing. Our eyes met about twelve feet apart. I looked away and he passed by me at a distance of two feet.

I am reminded of advice given to a lovelorn maiden who communicated with Dorothy Dix. She was in love with a brakeman whom

she had never met and asked what could be done about it. The answer
was, "You just sit down on the track and he will run across you." K.
nearly did.

Tomorrow I will be in St. Thomas and will be back in Ottawa on
Saturday morning.

> With all good wishes,
> I am,
> Sincerely,
> John

From John to Mother　　　　　*Prime Minister*
　　　　　　　　　　　　　　　New York
　　　　　　　　　　　　　　　September 29, 1960

Dear Mother,

Olive and I are here in New York attending the United Nations
meetings. Today Mr. Khrushchev became very annoyed when Prime
Minister Macmillan was speaking and pounded his desk. This evening he
and Mr. Macmillan are meeting together and at 9 o'clock I am going to
see Mr. Macmillan and he will be telling me what happened at their
meeting.

Today I spent three quarters of an hour with former President Hoover.
He is eighty-six years of age and as bright as can be.

Tomorrow we will be in London, Ontario and tomorrow night back to
Ottawa....

> With all good wishes and
> much love,
> Affectionately,
> John

From Elmer to Olive　　　　　*Saskatoon*
　　　　　　　　　　　　　　　Thursday Morning
　　　　　　　　　　　　　　　December 22, 1960

Dear Olive,

Excuse me for writing in pencil. It is now 4:45 A.M. I am writing in
bed upstairs, while John is sleeping soundly (thank God), on the sofa in
the dining room. I don't want to sleep and as I wanted to reply to your

kind letter, I shall do so now, expressing my grateful thanks for the sincerity of its contents and John also expresses himself that way.

No, the reason I am lounging in bed, I am awaiting any eventualities that might occur momentarily. At about 1:45, Dr. Baltzan called on the 'phone. He went to the hospital after midnight and John & I went up immediately after the call. Mother had suffered a major stroke about that time & was unconscious. Dr. Baltzan was very worried. Mother may pull through the night but the end is inevitable and I trust and pray that it may be peaceful.

This has been extremely trying for John and I hope he will be alright. I gave him two aspirin and am pleased that he is in a deep sleep. He was not good this afternoon. You have been an inspiration to him, I may assure you.

Before I forget, I must add the observation, your extreme kindness at the Christmas season was appreciated. Mother was so elated with the priceless scarf you sent to her – my thanks.

Mother went to bed on Thursday, extremely fatigued. After midnight on Friday I heard strange mutterings & when I went into her room she was talking to the Budgie bird, which she imagined was beside her bed, and which I interpreted then as a nightmare. However, thereafter her mind wandered considerably and I called the doctor immediately. He said it was not necessary to hospitalize her and wrote out two prescriptions, which I had filled in the morning.

I kept close watch during the day (Friday) and after midnight she began talking to the Budgie bird and her mind wandered aimlessly from one subject to another. I called the doctor immediately. Fortunately he got a room in the hospital and we got her up there about 1:30 A.M.

During the day she rested quietly, but going back to the hospital 6:30 in the afternoon, I found she was in serious condition. That's when I called John and had difficulty in securing nurses. One was obtained for the night and they had nurses for Sunday. Apparently she had a minor cerebral hemorrhage and the messages in the brain were going over other channels.

It was so fortunate that John was able to make that flight as the weather ever since has been poor for flying.

John has had bitter experiences and I trust he will be alright. He is sleeping soundly however, and being fatigued I am sure he will sleep through to the morning.

It is now 5:15 A.M. and no further call from the hospital, so I shall rest quietly and we shall keep you informed.

Our thanks again, Olive.

5:45 A.M.

P.S. Please excuse this scroll, but I know you want to hear from me. I just phoned the nurse again and mother is quiet. The nurse does not know whether it is a result of the sedative or if she is unconscious. She will 'phone me if necessary and in any event at 7 o'clock. So we are keeping in close touch.

9 A.M.

This has become like a disjointed diary. I went up to the hospital about 8 o'clock and it is a very peculiar case. There is no doubt that mother had a stroke last night and I did not expect she would last through the night. However this morning she was having breakfast. Her face was very ruddy and her hands warm. She was laughing and the first thing she asked me: "Has John come home yet?" In the next breath she asked me how the Budgie bird was. Then she smiled and said to the nurse: "John said he got a good pick from the Budgie yesterday." It is very pitiable, considering that she was the same on Friday morning as she ever was.

John had a good sleep last night and he appears a little rested. He is phoning just now.

Excuse all this scribble, which is also disjointed, but I cannot take time to re-write.

The Best,
Elmer

∽

From Elmer to Olive   *Saskatoon*
                                           February 26, 1961
                                           5 P.M.

Dear Olive,

One week ago today about this time I left the hospital. Before doing so I asked my mother: "Do you want me to come back to see you?" The reply came back: "I want you to come back to see me – goodbye Elmer."

I was with Dr. Baltzan at his house that evening. He was tired and wanted to retire. I left about 11 o'clock and did some reading at home before I was ready to retire. Baltzan phoned me twice and finally got me at 11:15. He was at the hospital.

She went unconscious at 11 o'clock and remained so until 9:03 Monday night. Her respiration was bad and was breathing constantly with an artificial respirator which Dr. Marcel Baltzan had brought from St. Paul's Hospital. The breathing was cut off abruptly at 9:03 and it was all over.

I went up to the cemetery this afternoon and the flowers are still lovely. I took a number of pictures and if they turn out I'll send some along.

I just got back here and had dinner at a neighbor's. Dr. Bardwell is with the Chemistry Department at the University.

Isobel Orchard wanted me over there and I'll go over some other evening.

I was glad you and John bore up well as it is quite a strain.

I was with Dr. Baltzan the past three nights.

I went to church this morning and Mr. Elliot made a very fine reference. I was in a little difficulty for a few minutes but snapped right out of it. I got sleepy as I do in church (something like the Bonn incident), and in this case it was beneficial.

Beulah came over on Friday and Saturday afternoons so we got a lot of work done in the house.

I got a great many of these messages answered and it is a terrific job. If I had not started I should have been overwhelmed....

Now it is necessary to pick up a few odds and ends and I'll stay here tonight and get going tomorrow. Everything should be alright when these messages are answered.

I must get a few things straightened up now.

> Love & Best wishes,
> Elmer

P.S. Mother's funeral was televised again over CFQC-TV tonight.

From Elmer to John   *Saskatoon*
                                   February 27, 1961

Dear John,

I trust you are feeling well and not so tired.

I posted a great deal of mail today. The messages...keep coming. If I had not worked on them, it would have been quite impossible. I only have about thirty now to answer up to today's mail and I received quite a few again today. It's amazing the people who write you. Judging but what I have, you must be overwhelmed.

There are lovely editorials. Bill Algae of Toronto sent me one appearing in the Telegram and Ted Blair sent me the Fredericton Gleaner – nice editorial write-up....

I saw Dr. J.L. Gibson, head of the dairy dep't at the University today. He is a staunch supporter of yours and he gets furious if any derogatory remarks are made about you.

If you need a good agriculture man sometime, I think he would fill the bill. I'm just making that suggestion.

I note Thatcher's calculated estimate that the Tories won't elect five members in the West. As a rule, his estimates are reasonably fair. In the last provincial election he initially estimated he would elect 35 members, then he raised it to 42 and just before the election he confidently announced that he was certain to elect 50 members – he did not specify who the five opposition members would be.

After the election I saw Thatcher at the Shrine ceremonial in Regina and told him his estimate was reasonably fair. He laughed and said he expected to elect more than 18 members.*

At that Thatcher is very Liberal with his estimate of Tory re-election of 5 because the more conservative estimate of Liberals generally predict that the Conservatives will only elect three members west of the Great Lakes, and Howard Green is positively sure of re-election. Incidentally, they add that Howard will be the lone survivor in B.C.

Thatcher has not stated that one lone Conservative, John Diefenbaker, re-elected him once to the H. of C....

I was quite worried about the nurses. It was a terrible drain on you and I was quite helpless. When the final hospital account is paid this $400 should clean up everything.

It has been a great worry for all of us and it is a great relief, to say the least. Mother is now at peace and that is as it should be.

You will make a great contribution to the Conference and the Gleaner in its editorial stated that you made the greatest speech at the U.N. in its history up to that time.

By the time you receive this, you & Olive will be ready to depart.

> The very best,
> Elmer

---

* In the June, 1960 Saskatchewan election, Thatcher's Liberals elected 18 members to the CCF's 37.

From John to Elmer   *En Route Ottawa*
                                                  May 18, 1961

Dear Elmer,

I know you will be very interested in what took place in Ottawa and I am sending you both Ottawa papers for the days of the President's [John F. Kennedy] visit. The President and I had a private breakfast this morning and covered a number of important matters. We get along very well together. The opinion I formed of him when I first met him – a brilliant intellect and a wide knowledge of world events – was not only borne out but intensified as a result of our discussions in the last two days.

We had the Kennedys for lunch. I would like to have had you down but it would have been impossible for you to get away. Olive was able to have Hal [?] and his wife.

I am on my way back from Dalhousie and have no more speeches to make for three weeks when I will be speaking to the Greek Organization, AHEPA, which is holding a banquet in honour of myself and other Members.

                              With all good wishes,
                              Sincerely yours,
                              John

From John to Elmer   *Office of the Prime Minister*
                                                  Ottawa
                                                  July 5, 1961

Dear Elmer,

I got a great deal of pleasure out of the visit to Rosetown, Prince Albert and Batoche but the write-up in the Star Phoenix setting out what happened as you were waiting for the arrival of the aircraft was one that can only be designated as being "smart alecky." If you can find the issue and get the name of the person who wrote it, I will see to it that he will not get any information from me on the next occasion that I am in Saskatoon. I would not want that known by anyone of course....

                              With all good wishes,
                              John

From John to Elmer   *Office of the Prime Minister*
                                         Ottawa
                                         September 14, 1961

Dear Elmer,

I received your letter written from Kipling this morning. The President of Iceland has just concluded his visit this morning. These visits, however fine the people may be, and the President and his wife could not have been nicer, are upsetting to me as I cannot stand continued late hours and social functions....

When the letters I wrote to Mother come to me I will go over them and put them in a file. I have kept all hers although of course in the last year or so of her life they were few in number and indicated the difficulty she had in writing. I have a number of letters, too, from Father and Mother going back over the years which I will have to have sorted out.

The world situation is terrible and people not knowing the situation are loud in their opposition to Canada having any nuclear defence. It is an ostrich-like philosophy which, while adhered to by many sensible people, is most beneficial to the Communists and of course receives their support.

Everyone is pointing out that I am having a birthday on Monday which is getting close to 70.

                                         With all good wishes,
                                         Sincerely,
                                         John

From John to Elmer   *Office of the Prime Minister*
                                         Ottawa
                                         January 16, 1962

Dear Elmer,

The last few days have been trying because there has been so much to do in preparation for the Session. Indeed I have nothing ready for my speech next Monday and there is no immediate possibility of my being ready.

Alvin Hamilton went West to the [Jimmy] Gardiner funeral and I phoned him a few minutes ago and he is laid up with the flu, frostbite and infection in his ear. Mr. [Raymond] O'Hurley is very ill and Mr. [Ernest] Halpenny is in hospital with a heart attack. All of these things make it difficult and trying for the other Ministers.

I had a hearing appliance made specially for me by Senator [Joseph] Sullivan. It didn't work too badly but it was so fragile that the ear insert broke within a few hours after I had it. Olive said she thought it was helpful but I personally didn't notice any particular improvement. However I will try it again. If it would allow me to hear the low-voiced interruptions in the House it would be most beneficial....

Mr. Pearson must have been very angry at the unexpected publicity Olive and I received, otherwise he would not have had his stuffed teddy-bear labelled "Slap" although I don't know any better name to describe the general attitude of the Liberal criticism.

> With all good wishes,
> Your brother,
> John

ᗡ

From Elmer to John   *Lanigan [Saskatchewan]*
                                        March 30, 1962

Dear John,

Those babies got the book thrown at them and I imagine they are still licking their paws.

While driving I turned on my radio and it announced the Prime Minister had made his announcement on the final payment of 32 cents. When that news was finished there was the further news that they were warned if they did not behave like good children they would have an election thrown at them....

The announcement was made over the radio that there were various contributing factors like the devaluation of the Canadian dollar, the grain deals with Red China and other factors.

I was talking to the man in the beer parlor here this evening. He said there was real happiness in the beer parlor when some farmer announced what he had heard over the radio. Immediately one farmer stated he had always voted Liberal, but this time he would vote for [P.C. candidate, Reynold] Rapp.

You are really getting those lads in a very uncomfortable and embarrassing situation.

The radio said a few days ago that [Hazen] Argue was promulgating the Liberal farm policy – if he were fortunate enough to be elected, he would be able to complete his speech in the House of Commons in 1967.

Up to last week I think you had won over the Western farmers, but today the order of business is completed. The radio report said that never before was the final payment above 12 cents....

Rapp is even popular in the Melfort area, where in the last election they said, "he can't even speak English."...

I can't understand that report in the current issue of Time which gives the prophecy of various standings of the different parties in the H. of C. after the next election.* That report will require revision.

I don't think that the 3 Picksies – Pick, Haze 'n Chev,** will be very happy gnomes now. They will be misgnomers.

I got along fairly good this week and shall work back home tomorrow morning.

You'll be able to get on with the business now.

The Best,
Elmer

The election of June 18, 1962 put Diefenbaker's government into a minority position. The results were Progressive Conservatives, 116; Liberals, 100; Social Credit, 30; and NDP, 19.

From Elmer to John *Saskatoon*
June 20, 1962

Private

Dear John,

Harry Jones [P.C. M.P., Saskatoon] says you are alright and that you will come out stronger than ever. I think he is right.

I was afraid for awhile that Pearson would have the largest grins in the House and for the reason he hasn't he's a very sick man. Moreover, I would not be very happy if the SC and NDP were deeply in love with Pearson and the Liberals. As well, I am beginning to think that [Social Credit Leader Robert] Thompson's Alberta and B.C. Social Crediters are about as far apart from the same group in Quebec as West Pakistan is from East Pakistan.

* The April 27 issue of *Time* predicted that neither party would receive a majority.
** J.W. Pickersgill, Hazen Argue and Lionel Chevrier.

Pearson is most anxious to get into the House of Commons to howl, and the further the session is away the madder he'll get. You have handled the situation perfectly and the Grits are bound to make fools out of themselves.

I heard over the radio that the Americans want to keep the Canadian dollar steady. You will work yourself out of that. The Grits would ruin the country to get back into power and I think Canadians will realize that.

Everybody is jubilant that Tom was cleaned up*. They were all anxious that Tom would be defeated and the fact that it was done by a Conservative will indeed give prestige to the Party. It said on the news that Tom does not want to run in a by-election. He's not taking any chances of further defeats.

People don't care much about minority governments and when the time comes you will go back stronger than ever. The campaign was too long and it has been a terrific strain on you. When you get things reasonably levelled out you better turn the whole business over to Howard Green for a couple of weeks and get somewhere where nobody will bother you for two weeks. You need a rest. Let Pearson make a fool out of himself.

The whole thing will straighten out. The one time when you were in deep trouble was when you came back to Prince Albert. You were at that time in a very impossible position and you came through that in a big way. Nobody wants minority govt. and in a final analysis for selfish reasons, I think even Bay Street will come to the conclusion that they will have to support you. I think your slogan will be "Only the Conservatives Can Win."

It is discouraging that you have lost some good members but you will find that there will be other members who will have to take responsibility now.

I saw a funny little show in front of the Post Office this morning. There was a poor little mouse on the sidewalk in front of the Post Office. He was what you would call running scared. He went south, stopped every few feet, and contemplated. Then he about-turned and started back north also hesitating at intervals. The last I saw of the mouse he was still tearing like mad going all directions and he was completely confused. I thought to myself, "There is a very close analogy between that little mouse and the Pearson team."

---

* Tommy Douglas was defeated in Regina City riding by nearly a 2-1 margin by P.C. candidate Ken More.

It continues to rain and I think that will keep everybody happy in the West. This fast break in the drought period will certainly do you no harm.

I just called up John Hnatyshyn.* He thinks you should call Parliament in the fall, keep Pearson hollering, and he'll wear himself out. John thinks you should take a vacation, and when you get back you'll be in a fighting trim. I think he is right. As well, Olive needs a rest. She did a splendid job.

I wouldn't worry too much. In this race, the winner is the group that has the most seats in the House.

I have a few letters I must write. I've even forgotten who they are.

The Best,
Elmer

1. Mrs. Dorothy Sherick (Dorothy Peachy) Regina Leader: Says that the women are rallying to the P.C. cause. They are calling on the 'phone continuously and are carrying along their husbands with them.

Dorothy's mother, Mrs. Peachy, is living with her and she is still all out for John Diefenbaker.

2. Mrs. Hargraves, Regina, wants the P.C. Story put across the T.V. and have them fight it out.

3. Allan Sangster is all cleared for action and is going to fight.

4. Gordon Brown, Saskatchewan Hotel.

Son of former Lieutenant-Governor. Allan Sangster told me Gordon Brown is still out strong for P.C.'s & John Diefenbaker.

In his suite in the Saskatchewan Hotel he has framed pictures of John Diefenbaker, Alvin Hamilton and Roy Faibish.** He shows these to his visitors.

He is one of the big farmers of the South. The poor devil had a heart attack and was in the hospital for quite a long time.

---

* John Hnatyshyn was a long-time friend and supporter of John's, and a Conservative candidate in Saskatchewan provincial and federal elections.

** Roy Faibish was a special assistant to Alvin Hamilton.

Gordon is resting in his hotel suite but next month he wants to drive out to country towns and tell the story.

He has loads of friends who visit him in the Saskatchewan Hotel. He talks to them in a quiet, unassuming manner and he is most effective.

Gordon has a strong voice in the Wheat Pool. He says the Wheat Pool are not bitter as in the past and says they are beginning to come our way. This would corroborate the statement of Bob Taylor, Grain Commissioner in Saskatoon, who told me the Pool agents are changing their views. Bob told me he would call on a great many Pool agents in the next ten days. On my return to Saskatoon he wants me to visit him at his home and he will give me his report.

You should write a sympathetic, encouraging letter to Gordon Brown at the Saskatchewan Hotel. I know he would appreciate it. He will show it to his friends.

A young French Canadian farmer at Courval. He was a life-long Liberal and Gordon Brown swung him over. Gordon arranged for me to meet him. I praised a certain young French Canadian sky high, who was a merchant at Courval, and it turned out he was a brother-in-law of this fellow.

I saw this young farmer yesterday morning. He was most friendly and affable.

He is very mad at Thatcher because Thatcher asked support of P.C.s in the by-election in Weyburn and now he is mixing up in federal Liberal politics against the P.C.s.

This fellow told me they supported Argue last year because they thought that if the gov't changed, Argue would be Minister of Argriculture. On the other hand, one opposition member in Saskatchewan would not do much harm. I told him about Pearson calling up Syd Buckwold in Saskatoon, promising him the portfolio of Trade and Commerce if elected. They had not heard this here and I think it will spread.

Gordon Brown says the fight in this election is the "Public vs. the Press." He often refers to the "Bastards on Bay Street."

Mr. & Mrs. Bruce Campbell, Milestone:

I called on the Campbells and they are all out for the fight.

Opinion is that Argue will be defeated if Lawrence Watson is the candidate. There are two other candidates in the running – one is Bailey, a 30-year-old teacher of Bengough. Watson may not get the nomination, but pressure must be brought to assure that Watson will carry the hammer. Watson told me last fall in Avonlea that he might not get it.

An Incident at Kincaid:

Mel Peterson told the Campbells that Argue was holding a meeting at Kincaid and he brought along two Grits from Assiniboia. Those present at the meeting were not going to allow Argue to speak. One of these Assiniboia Grits got defiant and said Argue would speak. This bird got a real wallop on the mouth and it ended up by him receiving a few stiches on the lip – I suppose you would call that "Liberal lip service."

Kincaid incidentally is the district where Mervyn Woods was raised and he is a hero in this area.

Aitkin, farmer at Holbrite:

He is Reeve at Holbrite and I met him at the restaurant here in Weyburn last night.

Atkin was just out of the beer parlor and he was full of fight. He told me he had been CCF – an admirer of Reg Jones and the same type. He is bitter against Tom Douglas now. Being on the Holbrite Council he knows all about Tom's oil leases. He wants to meet Tom Douglas on the platform and if need be he says he will go all the way to Regina to meet him.

He is equally bitter at Argue. I told Ron Barbour about Aitkin. He knows him very well and is arranging to meet Aitkin.

The Story of the "Little Blond Girl":

I tell the women about the "little blond girl" in Saskatoon whose large staff where she works is 100% behind John Diefenbaker and Harry Jones.

This "little blond girl" had tears in her eyes when she told a friend of mine: "I don't know what it is all about – I don't know what they are trying to do to our Mr. Diefenbaker, who has done so much for Canada."

I usually ask the question:

"Is this little blond girl very important?"

The answer is invariably, "Yes."

Is she the most important girl in Canada?

The reply is "Yes."

Then you can add, "Do you realize that there are thousands & thousands of good people right across Canada like this "little blond girl?"

Women particularly like this true story. The Grits are always passing "stories," so I think something like this should counteract their chatter.

The object of this story, if the Grits start to ridicule this "Little Blond Girl" – it will make women ferociously mad. I told this story to Dorothy Peachy and she said it was wonderful.

Magazine - Newsweek:*
It was lousy, but I think it will make lots of votes.
I suggested the changing of the name of the publication – reverse the order and you change the name from "Newsweek" to "Weaknews."

The Winnipeg Tribune continues to hit hard.
I think the Chinaman calls the Winnipeg Free Press – "The Flea Press."

✍

From John to Elmer   *[Ottawa]*
                                        July 14, 1962

Dear Elmer,
    Be sure to look after yourself. You sounded so tired this morning when I phoned you.
    And when driving, one must be careful. If Bill Brunt had had his safety belts on he might still be alive.
    How about getting a front seat set installed?
    With my best wishes to a devoted brother.

                                        Sincerely,
                                        John

✍

From John to Elmer   *Office of the Prime Minister*
                                        Ottawa
                                        July 26th, 1962

Dear Elmer,
    Whenever I have any difficulty I can be sure to hear from you and I wasn't a bit surprised when I was told that you wanted to talk to me on the phone.

---

* A cover photograph in *Newsweek* magazine had featured Diefenbaker in a demonic pose.

What happened to me is that I stepped off the verandah on to grass soaked by an afternoon rain and turned over my ankle. There was a snap followed by severe pain and swelling. I will be in bed at home for the next few days and then for several weeks I will have difficulty in walking.

I am getting some work done although not too much although I have had a couple of Cabinet meetings. I propose announcing some changes in the Cabinet within the next couple of days and also the appointments of Parliamentary Secretaries. The Liberals with an assist from Eugene Forsey and the NDP and with the help of the Winnipeg Free Press, are contending that I have no right to make any appointments. The arguments they advance are sheer nonsense but they are going to make an issue of it. I am, as well, going to make a number of Senate appointments.

The reports I am getting are becoming more encouraging. People are just beginning to realize that the Liberal Party which had its lowest percentage of the Canadian vote in 1958 in 70 years, only had an increase in the 1962 election of 1% (ONE).

Furthermore, there was a feeling among some Conservatives that they should endeavor to equalize the membership in the House for they felt we had too large a majority.

I have committees of Cabinet Ministers working now to plan for the sessional programme. It will be difficult to keep our Members in the House although they will have to realize that being a minority their absence would lead to defeat.

The Liberals are beginning to understand that they are in difficulties in Quebec and one of the Ministers of Premier [Jean] Lesage is about to resign.

> Your aff. Brother,
> John

⌁

From John to Elmer

Office of the Prime Minister
Ottawa

Personal

October 24, 1962

Dear Elmer,

The International situation is very serious[*] and its implications keep me continually on call. Where things will lead no one knows. I was made

---

[*] The Cuban missile crisis.

aware of what was being done beforehand and two suggestions I made to change certain words in the President's draft speech were accepted following the view I expressed that they should be deleted. The situation is more serious than at any time since the end of the Second World War and all one can do is wait.

To deviate from the seriousness of the situation I thought you might be interested in a couple of pictures that appeared in last night's newspapers.

I will be calling you during the weekend. I have to stay here in Ottawa on Sunday to lay a cornerstone in a Baptist Church.

> With all good wishes,
> I am,
> Yours sincerely,
> John

ℐ

From John to Elmer   *Office of the Prime Minister*
                                        Ottawa
                                        November 15, 1962

Dear Elmer,

Yesterday the election took place in Quebec and it shows how uncertain is an election for with only one exception our Quebec Members were certain that Premier Lesage would be defeated.* For reasons that can be conjectured, in many constituencies the Social Credit were bedded down in the federal election. It will take some time to know what the important results will be but I would think that the next federal election would not be particularly affected.

I hope that we get some legislation passed in the next two or three weeks, and if we do I will then give consideration to a four to six weeks' adjournment over the Christmas season so that Members can get back into their constituencies, but this can only take place if we get some worthwhile legislation passed.

Today the Unemployment monthly record came out and it shows an increase over the preceding month of 23,000, or 4.3% of the Labor Force compared with 4.9% in October 1961, and 5.7% in October 1960, which is a very considerable improvement.

---

* Lesage's Liberals took 63 seats to Daniel Johnson's Union Nationale's 31.

Alvin Hamilton is in difficulty over one of his "famous" speeches which he delivered before the Saskatchewan Wheat Board. However, Pearson handled it poorly yesterday and Alvin did very well after I discussed the matter with him at length. It will now be out of the way for a while. I do hope sometime that he learns to keep his mouth closed on subjects for which he has no support other than in his own mind.

> With best wishes,
> Your aff. Brother,
> John

↶

From Elmer to John   *[Appended to a letter dated*
                                        December 2, 1962]

Did you hear about Tom Douglas during the by-election in British Columbia calling Regina on long distance?

On completion of the call, Tom asked the operator the price of the call. When she told him Tom answered: "In Saskatchewan I could 'phone to hell and back for that."

Replied the operator: "Why, sir, in Saskatchewan that is a local call."

↶

From John to Elmer   *Office of the Prime Minister*
                                        Ottawa
                                        December 4, 1962

Personal

Dear Elmer,

It is fine that you have been able to rent the house. I know that it will be much nicer for you to be in the YMCA in the meantime until you secure a suite. You will have more company there and more congenial surroundings.

Only a few minutes ago I telephoned Her Worship Charlotte Whitton [Mayor of Ottawa] to congratulate her on her re-election and she gave me full details of the campaign. One of these days we will have to decide on where to offer her a position. She would like to be an Ambassador and has her eyes on Ireland.

Olive has not been too well. As a matter of fact I am concerned over the fact that she doesn't take any rest. Last evening I called the doctor and while he told her to take it easy she was up and around this morning. We are approaching our Ninth Wedding Anniversary (December 8th) and I need not tell you that it has been a most happy nine years and she has done so much to make it so.

We are making arrangements to go to the Bahamas for my meeting with Prime Minister Macmillan. I will try and see what arrangements can be made so that you might accompany me although all arrangements would have to be made by you for your stay there. I should have some further information in a day or so.

With all good wishes,
Sincerely,
John

✑

From John to Elmer   *Office of the Prime Minister*
                                        Ottawa
                                        January 10, 1963

Dear Elmer,

Olive is undergoing her examination. She is in the Private Patients' Pavilion, Room 422, Toronto General Hospital and will be there until Wednesday. She has had her spinal examination and will have to wear a steel corset for her back. The neck injury she sustained on the aircraft is more serious than her back but no determination has been made as yet. She has Professor Dewar, the leading Orthopedic doctor in Toronto and he said that an operation would not be beneficial. She has had a great many other tests but no report on them as yet.

She is in very good spirits and apparently is writing scores of letters which she feels she should have written before.

I am glad that you are coming East for the Convention. I am informed that you are going to be a Delegate at Large. We are both looking forward to you coming here.

I have had a lot of worrying problems in the last week or so and if I believed in Gallup Polls the latest would be very disturbing. However, we would not have won the election in 1957 if the Polls had been substantially correct.

With all good wishes,
Your aff. Brother,
John

From Elmer to John   *[On board] Super Continental*
                                        January 31, 1963

Dear John,

I realize how you feel at the moment. It has been a most cruel ordeal to say the least. I also realized as I left that I should have stayed for at least the weekend.

It is a most lonely life and I know just how tough it is.

I think Dr. Rynard* gave you the right advice and at the earliest possible opportunity you must have this examination.

I have all the faith in the world with Dr. R. and right after I met him I felt he was my friend. In this I have never deviated. At least you know that you can place your trust in him.

Olive has been as strong as the Rock of Gibralter & is a most respected person.

I thought for the time being the best thing I could do was to slip along, but if you think there is anything I could do, let me know and I would go back to Ottawa again if necessary.

Everybody knows you have done an admirable job and you are doing that right now. If it does get too tough I would say to hell with it because you also have yourself to think about.

I thought the best thing I could do was slip away quietly in case any further complications were involved. I can assure you that I did not make any mistakes while in Ottawa.

I never did have any use for these damn Grits & never will. I have never had any use for the bastards and have never made any complimentary remarks in their favor.

You have staunch friends across the board and they know full well that you have borne the heat of the day. You can do no other than to win through, but I would say don't kill yourself. You have done more than your share now.

I enjoyed every minute of my visit and indeed I am most appreciative of the ear appliance which means so much. The only thing I thought that you and Olive had stretched the point.

You worry too much about me, but I want you to know that I am in the best of health. I take the best of care and I look after myself – I don't stint in that at all. Like yourself, I have an endless number of loyal friends and I feel that I can get along quite nicely without any assistance from Grits. You can never lose them as friends.

* Philip Rynard was a P.C. M.P. from Simcoe East, and John's Ottawa physician.

I think you are most fortunate in having Burt Richardson with you. He is a stalwart and that means everything.

Olive takes the philosophy that you are confronted with difficulties constantly and you are facing up to it constantly and you will come out on top. However, you must not kill yourself. There is always someone else who will willingly take over and make a mess out of it.

I'll call you when I get back home and you can let me know what transpires. I am no politician but I'll do what I can.

Elmer

∾

From Elmer to Olive   *[On board]*
                                         Super Continental
                                         Jan. 31, 1963

Dear Olive,

I know you are going through a very grim ordeal and I realize John's position. I realized after I left that I had done a very foolish thing not to have waited at least a few days longer.

It is a terrific burden you are carrying and I realize that I should have shared it at the time [but thought] that it might simplify things if I kept out of it. You may feel assured that I did not say anything that would involve the situation and shall keep perfectly quiet when I arrive home.

I have read the press reports and indeed I feel very sorry and concerned about you and John. Please keep me informed and if there is anything I can do don't hesitate to get in touch with me at any time. If I can serve any good purpose at all let me know and if there is anything I can do, if you think it is necessary, I would return to Ottawa at any time.

I am nearing Winnipeg now and shall post this note and shall call up on my arrival home tomorrow.

I enjoyed my visit so much and am very appreciative. It was so good giving me the ear appliance which I appreciate so much.

Take good care of yourself as you have had a tough time & I trust John will come through alright although the strain is so very terrible.

I am glad that Dr. Rynard is with him and he is indeed in good hands.

Now please let me know everything. I felt very badly coming away but as I said if there is anything I can do I should be glad to come back any time. In John's case and yours you are confined to secrecy constantly and if I can share anything at all I'll be glad to do so.

I know the strain John is under and that is shared by you alone. That is why I feel that I should have remained. I have written this in haste and have not had a chance to read it over as I am now in Winnipeg.

Here's hoping everything good.

> Love & Best Wishes,
> Elmer

On February 5, the Government was twice defeated on non-confidence motions, and on February 6, Parliament was dissolved.

From John to Elmer

> *Office of the Prime Minister*
> *Ottawa*
> *February 8, 1963*

Dear Elmer,

I have been thinking of you in the last few days knowing how you would be feeling in the midst of the difficult and trying circumstances that surrounded me.

Fred Hadley* was in touch with me and said Prince Albert was fine. I hope Saskatoon is in the same position for if ever a Member deserved to win Harry Jones does. He did well on the TV the other night and in the last few days has been most devoted and helpful.

It is impossible to describe the scenes that took place in caucus and outside but no doubt Harry will be able to tell you something of what took place. I will have the clippings sent from yesterday's papers both Grit and Tory so that you get something of the picture.

On Monday I am going to speak in Toronto to the Canadian and Empire Clubs. There will be some 2000 at the luncheon. I have no speech but will work on it for the next couple of days intermittently as I have so many other things to do. Then I must get my speech ready for London. I am going over just for a day. I will arrive in London Sunday morning and return Tuesday morning. At the moment I am thinking of suggesting that you might go along but have to consider whether if you did it would be subject to misinterpretation by the Opposition.

Olive has had a very hard and trying time but there has never been anything but words of encouragement uttered by her.

> With all good wishes,
> John

* Fred Hadley was a long-time Diefenbaker friend and supporter.

From Olive to Elmer   *24 Sussex Drive*
                                         Ottawa
                                         February 13 [1963]

Dear Elmer,

Your letter was a really good and cheerful one. Bless you for it.

Elmer, we too are fighting mad and I think there are a lot of others like us....

Elmer – *no more thanks necessary* re the hearing aid. If there is a refund – *put it in campaign funds!* – your private one.

Old Happy [the dog] has been a great comfort. He has been neglected for more pressing things but he seems to understand all. (If he "understands all" though, he's better than us humans!)

John is home this afternoon, working. Half a day up there is all he wants! Now the thing is to get this London speech under way. It worries him.

[Léon] Balcer is now resigning & well to have that settled. And poor Don Fleming. You know his son was shot – was involved with a young divorcée and has been very very ill. He can't face a campaign, and small wonder.

Now I must away and work.

"Be of good cheer," Elmer. We're away and running.

                                         Love,
                                         Olive

↜

From John to Elmer   *Office of the Prime Minister*
                                         Ottawa
                                         February 20, 1963

Dear Elmer,

I was in Toronto yesterday and received a tremendous reception attending the Ontario Progressive Conservative Association meeting. I faced the audience with some uncertainty but everything turned out well and I think we are on the way.

We will, however, face the sniping that goes on from those who left. I cannot understand Mr. [Douglas] Harkness. He agreed to the statement I made in the House of Commons on Defence, shook my hand after I delivered it, and then he went against me. Mr. [George] Hees is of course another of those who through history reached out for leadership too soon. He thought he was more powerful than he was. Mr. Sevigny has always been uncertain. I did much for him but he continued to get himself into difficulties.

It is too bad that Donald Fleming had to leave because of the difficulties created by his son, and that ill health removed Halpenny.

However, we shall fight on. Elections are not won except in the last week. I am the underdog now and that means that the fight must be strongly waged.

There will be any amount of money come in from across the line to help the Liberal party.

I had a full and complete medical examination over the weekend covering everything, and I now have the certificate which states that I am in excellent health. I thank God for this because no one but you and Olive have any idea of the terrible load that rests on my shoulders.

Earlier today I thought things were going along very well following my experience of yesterday in Toronto but I have just learned that Sevigny has rushed into print again with an attack on me. It seems impossible to fathom the mentality of such as Harkness, Sevigny and Hees.

I am also afraid that another will resign. He was lined up in the conspiracy with Sevigny and Hees but backed down at the last moment. I wouldn't put it past him that he might follow along with them. I can't do more than hope he will not do so.

I have just finished the first of the final draft of my major speech for the Guildhall and will try to finish it up tomorrow. Then I have a second one for London to be made at the Mansion House and no part of that is ready yet....

I had to go back to bed again today with my cold but hope that it will be better in a day or so.

> With all good wishes,
> Your aff. Brother,
> John

From John to Elmer   *[Ottawa]*
             April 2, 1963

Dear Elmer,

I went through Western Quebec yesterday. We had a very good reception with the exception of Quebec City. I believe we will win quite a number of seats in the rural areas through which I passed.

There was a bomb scare yesterday and while the incident was blown up there was nothing to be concerned about.

The Gazette came out this morning in favour of the Liberal Party and I am sending you the editorial. Most of the powerful papers in the east now are out against us.

I am going to end the campaign in Sarnia on Saturday night and will fly directly to Prince Albert. I could have landed in Saskatoon but it is a costly thing to land. I would suggest that you go on to Prince Albert Friday evening if you are free. However, if you have not voted at the advance poll then you will have to stay over unless of course the advance poll continues until election day. In the event you have to stay over you could vote in the morning and come to Prince Albert on Monday morning.

It is hard to make predictions although I am most hopeful. I am going into Ontario for the next four days and will see whether I can help in the election to assist several candidates who are putting up an exceptionally good fight.

I am just leaving for a luncheon reception at Dorion (Vaudreuil-Soulanges), and have an afternoon meeting in Montreal at Delormier Stadium. We then leave for Cowansville for a supper meeting with a couple of whistle stops en route, and then return to Montreal tonight and on to Toronto for the morning where I record a TV speech.

> With all the best,
> Your brother,
> John

On April 12, 1963, the election results gave the Liberals 128 seats; the Progressive Conservatives, 97; Social Credit, 24; and NDP, 7.

From John to Elmer   *Prime Minister*
                                        [Ottawa]
                                        April 12, 1963

Dear Elmer,

Olive and I are going to Church this beautiful Good Friday morning.

It will be the last time as Prime Minister, as everything points to the soldier vote being overwhelmingly Liberal.

We are going out to Harrington Lake for two days and final plans will be made for the change-over.

The Governor General [Georges Vanier] had a heart attack on the 9th just after midnight. I called on him yesterday, and while he must rest, he seemed in good spirits.

With all good Easter wishes.

Your brother,
John

P.S. Be of good cheer.
    These things too will pass away!

↶

From Elmer to John   *Box 1728*
                                        Saskatoon,
                                        April 12, 1963

Dear John,

You are most disappointed and indeed there are so many who share with you. Your fight will go down as the finest in history. It was a single-handed struggle, one that I had hoped would triumph.

You were not defeated by Pearson – you were defeated rather by a no good gang whom you dragged along, who would have got nowhere....

In almost each instance, prime ministers have retired a little less happy than when they assumed office. I had hoped that your experience would have been an exception to the rule. You may be disappointed, but how much more would you have been so if you had not reached the top?

I still think you will reach your highest stature if you are in opposition for one session.

Insofar as Olive is concerned, she has occupied her position unequalled in Canadian history and she will not be surpassed.

You will win through and you will receive even greater acclaim.

Your whole record has been clean and above reproach and that is one item that will go into the record book. To add to this, so many so often have repeated, "John Diefenbaker is the greatest prime minister Canada has had."

I have no apologies to make for myself either. So we are in the clear....

Pearson is the man who expects to step into the position that he and his gang degraded. Pearson is the man who gave himself "60 days." You

will be fully vindicated. You will be a free man. This job is too tough –
you are in the clear and I think you will be out of it in time.

> The Best,
> Elmer...

∽

From John to Elmer   *Office of the Prime Minister*
Ottawa
April 17, 1963

Dear Elmer,

I went by car today from 24 Sussex Street to Rideau Hall and at 12:05
noon I resigned as Prime Minister, effective Monday next at noon. On
that date I will have served five years and nine months.

Mr. Pearson will have many problems to face and will begin to realize
some of the responsibilities of office, and when he faces the largest Conservative Opposition since 1867 (excepting for 1925) he will have to be
more effective in the House than he has ever been before.

Olive is working hard getting the residence ready for the change-over.
It is going to be difficult in the Leader of the Opposition's home as we
will have to get a new staff, but after a week or so things will become
fairly routine.

I am not sure yet when I am going West but intend to do so before the
session opens on the 16th of May. As suggested by you, I have forwarded a personally autographed picture to Beulah and Harry.

> With all good wishes,
> Your brother,
> John

P.S. I should tell you a story I told the Governor General this morning
when I called on him. Mr. Meighen used to tell a story that when he first
went to Portage to open his law office in 1916 there was a bookstore
next door. He went in and received little attention from a clerk who did
not appear one bit interested.

While he was there a lady came in and she said to the clerk:

"Have you a 'Life of St. Paul'?" to which he replied:

"I haven't the life of a dog and am getting the hell out of here Monday next."

When I told General Vanier this he told me that the best example of humor he had ever heard was Howard Green's answer to the press men who asked for the reason for his defeat and his reply was:

"I have given the matter the fullest consideration and having examined the problem from all its angles reached the conclusion that it was because I didn't get enough votes!"

＄

From Elmer to John   *Box 1728*
                             Saskatoon
                             April 17, 1963

Dear John,

The news is that you will be calling on the Governor General today. So this will be the last letter to you as Prime Minister.

The whole thing is distasteful, but there is nothing that can be done. I know you will feel a lot happier with this great burden off your shoulders and you will be getting your full share of credit in the days that lie ahead.

The lousy press has been absolutely disgusting since the election. They have been so small that people will not trust anything that is contained in their sheets.

The Social Crediters are very happy. They seem to be very happy at the moment in their mutual activity of committing homicide. Our friend Thompson should not have been guided by Manning* in applying the axe to the Diefenbaker government. Sometimes questions are not very clear at the moment, but clarify themselves crystal clear later on.

I trust you are feeling fair & also Olive & that your success will increase in the future.

                    The Best,
                    Elmer...

* Alberta Social Credit Premier, E.C. Manning.

From John to Elmer   *Office of the Leader of the*
                                        Opposition
                                        Ottawa
                                        April 25, 1963

Dear Elmer,

Everything has been packed up now and the movers are here and are loading up the van.

I have been to the office twice this week. It was Mr. King's office and has murals that have never been explained. They apparently represent some mystical concept which came to him from his extra-terrestrial communications. There are knights in armour, there are goddesses, the God of Justice, angelic figures etc., under such words as Justice, Equality, Vision, Toleration, Truth, Struggle etc. I think I will have the murals covered up. While the main office is much smaller than the office I occupied since 1956, there are more offices forming part of the suite than I have had.

We will be moving into the home of the Leader of the Opposition ("Stornoway") tomorrow afternoon. I have only been in that house twice in George Drew's day. He furnished it, but before Mr. Pearson moved in, various businessmen, both Conservatives and Liberals, contributed to furnishing it from top to bottom.

You may recall that following the Convention in 1956 I was asked whether I was going to move into the official residence and I said we would not because if we did it would only be a short time before we would have to move again. It will be longer this time because of the support that the Opposition Parties will be giving to the new Government.

I had quite a good letter from Tupper McConnell who informed me that the reason for the antagonism to the Conservative Party of the Armed Forces overseas was that we had not made provision for extra salary to make up for devaluation of the dollar. He said the nuclear question received little or no attention except among very, very few of the higher officers.

It is natural that I should be very pleased that I received the majority of the service vote in Prince Albert, and a matter of comment that I was the only Conservative to do so.

I am hoping that Olive and I can go West in the next few days, but we have to arrange for passes and the like. It is quite a change from the private car to an upper berth, but such are the fortunes of life!

This morning a parcel was received from J.F.C. Wright of Saskatoon who sent us crocus plants in bloom and with soil attached. It was most considerate on his part and most pleasing to us.

> With all good wishes,
> Your brother,
> John

From John to Elmer

*Office of the Leader of the Opposition
April 26, 1963*

Dear Elmer,

We moved out of the Prime Minister's residence at 24 Sussex this morning and this afternoon we will be moving in to "Stornoway." Part of the staff we had stayed. The downstairs and upstairs maids will stay there for the time being. Flo Chausse hopes to get transferred to the Department of Public Works within a week or so. The second kitchen girl and one of the maids will go with us to the new location. Gordon McCartney will stay with Mr. Pearson as he did with me having started service with Mr. St. Laurent.

Last evening Olive made a discovery. We thought we had emptied every drawer and for some reason she looked at the desk in my room on which the TV was placed and found two extra drawers in the back of the desk which I had completely forgotten about which revealed quite a number of letters which would not have been fitting for our successors to read. With the letters there was also Uncle Ed's summary of the homestead days which he wrote in 1959. It is quite interesting although they are not very complete nor comprehensible. They do, however, give information that I did not have before regarding the comings and goings which occurred before we moved on to the homestead. One of these times when I have a little more leisure I will have a copy made and will send it to you.

> With all good wishes,
> John

7

IN OPPOSITION
AGAIN

THE ELECTION OF 1963 had toppled John Diefenbaker from power, but it did not destroy his influence in the Commons or country. The Pearson government quickly got into trouble as the "Sixty Days of Decision" that Lester Pearson had promised the voters turned into a botched Walter Gordon budget and a long series of political gaffes and scandals that kept Parliament in a continuous uproar for the next two years. At the centre, day in and day out, was Diefenbaker, the unchallenged master of the House of Commons.

As these letters to his brother Elmer and to his wife suggest, Diefenbaker was in good spirits through most of this period. Olive's arthritis, in evidence since 1957, had worsened markedly and she was in near-constant pain, something that tortured her devoted husband almost as much. To complicate matters, Elmer found himself involved in a long and abortive love affair that required the advice and counsel of his elder brother and that must have caused John Diefenbaker some exasperation and bewilderment. To his credit, little of this showed in his almost un-failingly kind letters. And there were also the iniquities of Peter C. Newman, whose book, *Renegade in Power*, exercised the Chief might-ily. *Maclean's* also drew the Chief's ire for a cartoon that portrayed him in Prussian uniform – the slurs about his German-sounding name still rankled almost fifty years after the Great War.

But it was politics, always politics, that continued to absorb Diefenbaker as he battled to obstruct and bedevil the government. There was the new Canadian flag, scornfully described as "the Pearson Pen-nant" by the Chief. There were problems with Quebec, bursting forth in the Quiet Revolution, and with the Liberal government beginning to press the cause of bilingualism and biculturalism. There were tussles over federal-provincial relations, particularly with Quebec over the Canada Pension Plan. There was the election of 1965 when Diefenbaker, with a miraculously re-united party behind him, blocked the Liberals' attempt to secure a majority government with one of his greatest electoral performances ever. The old Chief, an energetic 70-year-old, had seemed in amazing form as he stumped the nation yet again, blasting the Liberals for their scandals and sins. So successful was the campaign that some senior staff at party headquarters, working more for the party and to keep Conservatism alive and less for Diefenbaker, joked that if the party won, they would go on the radio, tell the nation it was all a joke, and then leap from the top of party headquarters in a suicide pact. The Tories didn't win, but it was closer than anyone had believed possible when Pearson called the election. The Liberals got their revenge after the election, however, when Pearson used the Munsinger case, a Diefenbaker government sex scandal, as the reason to establish a Royal Commission of investigation.

Pearson's ploy forced the Conservatives to draw their wagons into a tight defensive circle, but all was not well in the party, the temporary unity notwithstanding. There was serious opposition to the Leader in the caucus and in the party apparatus and, over a series of meetings that stretched into 1966, the dissenters gathered strength and became progressively more emboldened. Ultimately, Dalton Camp, the party president, led a successful revolt in 1966 and a leadership convention was called for the next year. What would John Diefenbaker do? His doubts and his waverings are reflected in his correspondence to Elmer, but there seems little reason to suspect that he truly believed he could win. Diefenbaker ran to try to stop the Conservative party from endorsing the formulation of "deux nations – two founding peoples" that had emerged from a policy conference in the summer. That resolution, the Chief believed, flew in the face of his "one Canada" principles, but he prevailed, and the offending passages were tabled, a conclusion satisfactory to Diefenbaker and his friends.

Even so, Diefenbaker's once fabled timing deserted him at the Convention. After a disappointing showing on the first and second ballots, the former Prime Minister's handlers failed to get a withdrawal statement to the Convention chairman, and the Chief's name stayed on the ballot for the humiliating third round when he attracted only 114 votes out of some 2200 cast. It was a long way from the cakewalk of 1956, and many Canadians believed that John Diefenbaker had passed into history.

From John to Elmer   *Office of the Leader of the*
                                        Opposition
                                        Otttawa
                                        April 29, 1963

Dear Elmer,

Olive and I moved into the Leader of the Opposition's home on Friday. It was a very trying situation and no attention was paid to leaving the house in a state of even approaching cleanliness. There was very little furniture and Olive is away this morning making purchases, including even dishes, kitchen utensils, cutlery, etc., none of which there was any.

Yesterday, we had the Ed Gerrys over and I talked over the situation in Prince Albert with him.

I have just read the Winnipeg Free Press article by Norman Ward which clearly indicates that the Liberals are afraid that we are going to nominate candidates provincially. The article states, "there is growing speculation in Saskatchewan that the only way to reduce the number of seats in Saskatchewan may be to legislate them out of existence."

Confidentially, I am very much concerned with the condition of Harry Jones. He is still in hospital and one can only hope that he will be alright. Under no circumstances should you mention this. If you visit him at any time, don't give any indication indicative of such a feeling.

Thank you for your letter and observations which came to me yesterday.

                              With all good wishes,
                              Sincerely,
                              John

From John to Elmer   *Office of the Leader of the*
                                        Opposition
                                        Ottawa
                                        May 1, 1963

Dear Elmer,

The work is still going on at home. Olive is trying to make the residence comfortable and she is of course assisted by my advice!!

Herb Caldwell of Brockville telephoned me and used the phone number we had at the Prime Minister's residence and asked for me. He was answered by the voice of one of the new maids who said: "He ain't here any more." Whoever she was, she knew what she was talking about.

I am hoping that we can go West because there is quite a bit of furniture that should be shipped down here as "Stornoway" is anything but equipped. We have had to buy a washing machine, dryer and all the kitchen equipment and there will be about $1000 in odds and ends of furniture that we will have to purchase. The only room that is properly equipped is my office and library which Olive has fixed up most attractively.

I must start to work on my speech for the Opening of Parliament. So far all I have done is to think about it but have come up with nothing that has been helpful.

The Toronto Telegram has been trying to explain how it was that it opposed me and I have just had sent to me a letter written by the editor to a Mrs. Carr who has been a subscriber to that paper for fifty years. I am attaching a copy [not found] and you will note that I was anti-Eastern Canada. That of course is a falsehood although some of the big interests interpreted my desire to equalize opportunites in Western Canada with those that existed in the Central Provinces as contrary to the old princ-iples of the Conservative Party.

[Handwritten]
Note – Every other day during the last election had stories on the front page saying they were through with the West, especially Saskatchewan.

[Typewritten]
It is almost six years since I had my hands on the wheel of a car so I will have to take some lessons before I get a licence. I simply can't exist by depending on taxis. It is three miles to the residence and the course followed takes me by 24 Sussex Street, our new home being one mile further. We are only about a block and a half from Millie's [?] home. I have only seen her once and that was over two years ago, although I think Olive had her on one occasion to tea.

I will try and let you know in a day or so what day we will be West, but I don't want you to put yourself out to meet with us, as this is the time when you should be out doing your own work.

> With all good wishes,
> Affectionately,
> John

From John to Elmer　　　　　　　*Office of the Leader of the*
　　　　　　　　　　　　　　　　　Opposition
　　　　　　　　　　　　　　　　　Ottawa
　　　　　　　　　　　　　　　　　May 16, 1963

Dear Elmer,

The first hurdle is over. Mr. Pearson and Mr. [Lionel] Chevrier proposed the name of Mr. [Alan Ayelsworth] Macnaughton as Speaker and I spoke in support of the Motion, as did the leaders of the other parties.

This afternoon the Speech from the Throne will be revealed and I am sure will contain nothing beyond what has already been referred to in detail by [J.W.] Pickersgill. I know one thing, however, there is not going to be any cut in income tax for Pearson answered me immediately and took it seriously when I suggested that the Speaker of the House in the United Kingdom was exempt from income tax, and possibly this Government in its "days of decision" and in a spirit of benevolence might bring this into effect here. It took him about 15 minutes to see this and he was out of order when he referred to it, but he certainly cleared everything up when he said there was no possibility of this as they inherited such a large deficit! I think this is the first time there has ever been such a revelation of a budget in advance.

I met Paul Martin this morning and complimented him on the fact that he had fallen down in the Liberal hierarchy, and he said that whatever position he was in wouldn't affect him when it came to the choice of a Leader.

Tomorrow there will be a short session and then on Monday the debate will begin. I will send you Hansard daily so that you won't have to wait for your regular copy.

　　　　　　　　　　　　　　　With best wishes,
　　　　　　　　　　　　　　　Your brother,
　　　　　　　　　　　　　　　John

                         ℐ

From Elmer to John　　　　　　　*National Hotel*
　　　　　　　　　　　　　　　　　Prince Albert
　　　　　　　　　　　　　　　　　September 7, 1963

[Appended to a letter of this date]

"Believe it or not! – This fall John Diefenbaker will be Prime Minister of Canada again."

This is what *all* Canadians are saying.

Croyez-le	In	In	In
ou non	German	Greek	Italian
John D. etc.			
In	In	In	In
Ukranian	Chinese	Japanese	Hebrew
In	In	In	In
Polish	Cree	Russian	Icelandic
	Indian		
In	In	Czecho	Yugo
Norwegian	Swedish	Slovakian	Slavian.

The above cosmopolitan group are all Canadians and there is a unity of sentiment expressed by Canadians regardless of race or creed – by each one in his own spoken tongue.

∽

From John to Elmer   *Office of the Leader of the*
                                              Opposition
                                              Ottawa
                                              September 24, 1963

Dear Elmer,

I am in the midst of clearing up the backlog of work that piled up during my absence. Yesterday I gave a Press Conference and am attaching hereto a clipping from this morning's Montreal Gazette.

Emmett Hall talked to me today and said he had been in Saskatoon over the weekend and saw Harry Jones who appears to be desperately ill. He wants to come East next Monday and I hope he is able to do so.

I am glad that you are going to get your work finished up in the southern part of the province in the next few days and when you have completed it it will be a welcome relief not to have to drive these long distances again for some months.

I heard a little story today which you might pass on to Ed Wright. The President of the United States was shocked one morning when outside of his office he heard little Caroline singing: "I'm going to marry a Negro,

I'm going to marry a Negro" – she sang as she marched up and down. As always in time of trial and difficulty the President called his brother, the Attorney-General. The latter was shocked, and turning to the President said: "This is a very serious situation, an unbelievable situation. Do you realize," said he, "that nearly all Negroes are Baptists?"

With all good wishes,
Your brother,
John

ↄ

From John to Elmer   *Office of the Leader of the*
Opposition
Ottawa
October 22, 1963

Dear Elmer,

    There has not been very much doing in the House the last few days although yesterday on the Supply Motion I moved an amendment but the reports in the press are very limited.

    Those who are operating to remove me have Mel Jack as their self-appointed co-ordinator. He was in the Rideau Club on Friday and advised that I would be put out and thereupon George Nowlan or Senator McCutcheon would take over temporarily and a Convention would be held in the spring of 1964. He said his group have everything in good shape to bring this about. He further stated that when I was in Alberta I endeavoured to have a motion introduced condemning George Hees. It was never discussed and I never thought of such a thing and did not speak about it by inference or otherwise. He also stated that at the Executive Meeting being held this weekend that the Annual Meeting would be arranged and when that took place his group would ask that the vote on the Leadership would be by secret ballot his view being that if I refused the group would ask what I was afraid of. Altogether he talked loudly and completely revealed all the plans.

    I will speak to the Executive Meeting on Saturday morning and in the afternoon will leave for Winnipeg where I will speak to the Annual Dinner of the Conservative Association in Manitoba....

With all good wishes, I am,
Yours sincerely,
John

From John to Elmer   *Office of the Leader of the*
                                        Opposition
                                        Ottawa
                                        October 25, 1963

Dear Elmer,

As the days pass by the control of Banks* over some of the members of the Government becomes more apparent. We had a longer Question Period than ever today, mainly concerned with the Seaman's [sic] International Union and its leader, the uncrowned king, Hal Banks.

I am going to meet with the Executive tomorrow morning and then go on to Winnipeg, arriving there at 8:45 tomorrow evening, and will be at the Marlborough Hotel Saturday night and will leave there Sunday morning. I will be calling on Sunday morning.

The conspirators are still working hard. The Mickey O'Briens are going to have dinner with us tonight. Mickey called me last night and told me that Fulton and his people are trying their best to bring about a change in leadership. I am more definitely set than ever before against resigning no matter what they may do. It is going to be a big fight and when these great and powerful financial interests determine on a course of action they exert a tremendous influence. I beat them before and intend to do so again.

The summer weather continues here. It is 75 degrees today. There has been no rain for six weeks and the dairy farmers are finding a pronounced reduction in milk production.

                                        With best wishes,
                                        Your Brother,
                                        John

∽

From John to Elmer   *Leader of the Opposition*
                                        Ottawa
                                        October 31, 1963

Dear Elmer,

Things have been moving along very well this week and more and more the government is showing weaknesses.

---

* Some Montreal Liberal M.P.s were found to have taken contributions from Seafarers' International Union president, Hal Banks.

However, the publishing of the book by Peter Newman* is a terrible piece of muckraking and slander. I am considering commencing action for libel. It is full of falsehoods. I am told that some wealthy people in high places provided the finances for its publication and there is some evidence to support this fact....

> With all best wishes,
> I am,
> Your Brother,
> John

↶

From Elmer to John   *[Saskatoon]*
                                        November 4, 1963

Dear John,

So many were impressed with your speech on T V. They say it was the best yet and that means a lot.

I don't think that book business means too very much. It should work in your favor as Newsweek did. Give the public to understand they have an opportunity to buy another magnificant publication like Newsweek, but this one is a superior publication. Probably national distribution should be under The Truth Squad** that did such a fine job distributing the coloring books. There's a lot of coloring in Newman's book also.

I just phoned Harry Jones' wife [Eloise]. She was so very pleased that you phoned her this morning.

Just now I'm leaving town & shall be out around Kelvington, Wadena, Wynyard, etc. The weather gets better each succeeding day.

You told me to give you some data for the true story of John Diefenbaker. I jotted down some ideas the other night, and I can send you some more, if this is what you want. This is only for the intro-

---

* *Renegade in Power* was a bestselling account of the Diefenbaker Government from 1958 to 1963. The book was singularly unromantic in its depiction of John.

** The "Truth Squad" was comprised of Judy La Marsh, M.P. for Niagara Falls, Fred Belaire, a researcher, and Jack Macbeth, a journalist. They were to follow Diefenbaker through the campaign, catching him in inaccuracies and exaggerations. According to Peter C. Newman in *Renegade in Power*, "the technique came to grief the first night, when Diefenbaker laughed the 'truth squad' out of a hall in Moncton, N.B." An equally unsuccessful strategem was the distribution of coloring books ridiculing Diefenbaker, which Newman described as "neither funny nor in good taste."

duction. I cannot report on your court cases & debates in H. of C. That is something you know.

Well, I must get going. I gather that you will be going to Nova Scotia this weekend to receive a good reception. You are gaining every day.

Now I must get along and keep going.

> Best of luck & in
> haste,
> Elmer...

First sentence in Chapter 1:

A teenager was seated in a rear pew of the church one Sunday evening among his young friends. The key note of the preacher's sermon revolved about the context wherein "Abraham told Jacob to go to Bethel." In his inimical mode of self-expression the minister placed emphasis on the words: "Abraham told Jacob to go to beat hell."

There was a momentary degree of disorder, when these young men reacted in a very positive manner to this plain statement of fact.

These words could be interrupted [interpreted?] as being a most suitable slogan for the young man who was to be the future prime minister of Canada.

His mind, his movements were ever mobile. At all times he inevitably was in the lead. He had very little sympathy for those whose movements were slow. He planned and set up his objectives, that he resolutely determined to attain with no waste of time.

As public school pupil, secondary school student, college student, young Lieutenant in the Canadian Army in the First Great War, law student, barrister-at-law, outstanding student of politics, brilliant parliamentarian, his clear thinking, methodical plan of approach, were always in the forefront. Any extraneous material was immediately eliminated and his mind was immediately focused on a job he was determined to finish.

His alert mind was always very closely associated with speed in all his aspects. During the homestead days he was a horseman of no mean ability. He loved to jump on the horse's back and in light-hearted vein he galloped away.

He was endowed with a keen sense of humor, he could at all times hold the attention of people with his well-chosen repertoire of amusing stories and anecdotes.

He had two favorite stories that he recounted in the course of his political speeches and invariably received a hearty response from his audience:

He had addressed an audience in a small town in a rural area in Saskatchewan. After the meeting he shook hands with a man standing on the sidewalk asking him:

"How did you like my speech?"

The reply: "I guess your speech was alright, but a half-inch of rain would do a lot more good."

The other:

At a political meeting, the speaker spoke interminably over a wide range. He covered his subject matter. The hour was late. Said the speaker:

"In conclusion, I would like to touch on the subject of future generations." A voice came from the back of the hall: "You better hurry up, or they will be here before you finish your speech."

In his boyhood days he translated his humor into practical pranks.

On the Diefenbaker homestead near Borden, Saskatchewan, there was a frame barn with a hayloft, and here one day an act of juvenile drama was portrayed wherein all present were highly amused with the exception of the dog who was the centre attraction of the act. The dog was taken up the building and interned in the mow [the place where the grain is stored], a ramp erected from the door of the mow to the ground. Tippy was securely roped to a little wagon. During the ascent, the feelings of the dog were not unlike those of a condemned man mounting the gallows, the descent similar to those of the last conscious moments of his life.

Where did John receive his inspiration? He was only dramatizing an act he had remembered in Toronto as a young lad. On that occasion his father took him to the Ringling Circus where one of the world's most thrilling acts was enacted – it was loop the loop on a bicycle. John never forgot this thrilling experience and the whole drama was re-enacted on the homestead with an equal degree of painstaking precision.

The other act with dramatic coloring was "featured" in the Opera House, the Empire Theatre, in Saskatoon during his student days at the University of Saskatchewan. Each year the students observed a University theatre night. The night selected by the students was invariably when the top-billed show of the season was featured.

During the recess between acts, the students enacted their own show, giving their college yells, throwing paper darts, and thus and so. During the student show John Diefenbaker and his college chums had secretly smuggled into the gods two live roosters. The birds were suspended by strings and in mid-air engaged in internecine combat. The two promoters in the student show were forceably removed from the premises and the main show went on.

From John to Elmer   *Leader of the Opposition*
                                        Ottawa
                                        November 5, 1963

Dear Elmer,

Newman's book is being widely advertised by the Liberal Party. It is very obvious that he is their hireling and that the purpose of writing it was to destroy me by smear and character assassination. I heard him as he appeared on TV last evening being interviewed by a young woman. (I don't have the name at the moment.) He said the reason he called me a "Renegade" was that I was a "Robin Hood" who robbed the rich provinces to help the poor. That of course is not true. What I tried to achieve was to equalize opportunities for all Canadians wherever they lived. What the effect of the book will be I don't know but the last couple of days have indicated that a reaction is setting in. The Toronto Telegram spreads it out in detail and accompanies the articles with frightful pictures of me.

John Bassett[*] demands that the vote in February at the Annual Meeting shall be by secret ballot which shows that he and the others that are with him are afraid to stand up and be identified....

Olive is going to make a speech today to the Conservative Members' Wives on her trip to Israel. I wish I could get the notes but there is no encouragement in this regard! I would like very much to hear what she has to say but that is out.

                            With all good wishes,
                            Your brother,
                            John

The Neatby book on Mackenzie King[**] quotes a letter to Mr. King from

---

[*] The owner and publisher of the Toronto *Telegram*.
[**] Neatby, H. Blair. *William Lyon Mackenzie King, Volume II, 1929-1932: The Lonely Heights*. Toronto: University of Toronto Press, 1963.

T.C. Davis after he defeated me in June, 1929. Davis wrote, "This defeat will give Diefenbaker 'a final blow' this time which will put him out of the running for all time to come."!!

∾

From Elmer to John   *Retailers' Trust Company*
                                        Saskatoon, Sask.
                                        November 11, 1963

Dear John,
    ...As you have rightly said it is a straight case of "assassination of character." Those I have spoken to already are unanimous in their opinion that the whole thing will lack fire.
    Newman said he interviewed 1000. [Senator Grattan?] O'Leary said he got his information in the cocktail bars, Newman said he did not imbibe in the cocktail bars, so the logical conclusion is – Newman is a Coke sucker....
    [The wife of the principal of Wadena school] heard about Newman's book & wanted to know where to get it.
    I told her, "It is $7.50 and that is too much to get for any book. This book is all slander, untruths, and assassination of character. It is published by the Liberal Party as vile propaganda and the proceeds are to be used as campaign funds for the Liberal Party. I don't want you to waste your money."
    She said, "I am so glad you told me that. A person might as well fight back all the way."...

                                        [Elmer]

∾

From John to Elmer   *Office of the Leader of the*
                                        Opposition
                                        Ottawa
                                        December 3, 1963

Dear Elmer,
    Olive is most anxious for you to come for Christmas. She feels that you will be very lonesome and that it would do you good to have a break. If it is possible to do so I think it would be a good idea. Arrange-

ments can be made later about your attending the Annual Meeting if you so desire.

It is impossible to get you a Christmas present but if there is something you would like do not be afraid to let me know as that will be helpful.

Olive and I celebrate our Tenth Anniversary on Sunday and I haven't the faintest idea what I should get her. The Tenth Anniversary is an aluminum one and that is out. I will be home for the weekend and will call you at that time.

> With all good wishes,
> I am,
> Your brother,
> John

From John to Elmer   *Office of the Leader of the*
                                        Opposition
                                        Ottawa
                                        December 17, 1963

Dear Elmer,

You will be arriving in Ottawa on Saturday and Olive and I will be in Chicago. If you will let us know at once the train you will be on, I will have Mr. Patzer, the chauffeur, at the station to meet you.

I am going to Toronto tomorrow to meet with John Bassett. It will be the first time we have met in a year. We are going to have dinner together. Senator Walker and Ted Rogers arranged for this meeting to take place at a dinner party at Ted's home. I am not looking forward to it in sweet contemplation. However, if I see him and there is no change in his attitude I will feel that I have done everything possible.

Thompson, the Social Credit Leader, made a speech in the House and plagiarized almost every word without giving credit to the author. I am enclosing a reference to this which is most interesting.

We had a nice visit with Dr. Baltzan on Sunday and as always I was most impressed with his wisdom and common sense.

I think we should have a good Christmas with you and Olive's grandchildren – and Happy too.

> All good wishes,
> Sincerely,
> John

From John to Elmer   *The Four Seasons Motor Hotel*
Toronto
January 4, 1964

Dear Elmer,

This is the morning after the meeting with John Bassett and it turned out very well it seems to me. Time will tell but I am hopeful that after the Annual Meeting the Telegram may decide to come back to the P.C. party. If it does it will be beneficial.

Your visit was a most enjoyable one and I was glad to see you in such good spirits. It may be that you will come to the Annual Meeting – that will be for you to decide.

I had a letter from Martin Pederson enclosing a vicious letter [not found] of the leader of the P.C./Lib. alliance from Regina (Armstrong always against me with Leslie and that ilk).

Of course, much of the trouble is due to failure to get candidates in the field as should have been.

It is very warm here today.

Hope you have a good trip home.

With all good wishes.

Your brother,
John

ᗌ

From John to Elmer   *Office of the Leader of the*
Opposition
Ottawa
January 25, 1964

Dear Elmer,

...I am no clearer as to the prospects at the National Meeting than when I was in Saskatoon. Any change of the rules for a secret ballot at an annual meeting however small the percentage in opposition it would be a continuing source of weakness for any leader now or in the future. That being so, I have decided what I will do. If there is a majority in favour of a vote taking place on a secret ballot my course will be clear and will be followed immediately. I do not intend to be the Leader of a Party and be subject to continuing sniping from the minority.

It begins to look as though there will be a tremendous turnout. Charles Lynch last evening dealt with the Meeting in his usual manner and I am sending you the clipping from the Citizen. There will be quite a number who conscientiously believe in the secret ballot not realizing that it has never been used on a vote of confidence motion and I realize fully that taking this stand may mean a tremendous change for the Party and me. I will keep you advised how things are going and hope that your initial business trips for 1964 have brought you worthwhile and satisfactory results.

Sincerely,
John

℘

From Elmer to John   *Box 1728*
                                        Saskatoon
                                        January 26, 1964

Dear John,
    ...I just received a card from Paul Lafontaine on board the ship Bremen, presumably on a Carribean cruise. He urges me to be present at the P.C. meeting & asked me to reply. I had to answer "no." After talking the thing over with Olive, I think she is right that I should not attend. I have so many friends who would like me to attend but then you can't tell. If one of these bastards were to catch up on me innocently it might have very disastrous results. Olive's opinions are always sound. Olive "has the answers" – not the Liberals.
    I know you will get an outstanding ovation. I am sure the bastards will depart in peace – but rather with their tails between their legs.
    Pearson is in trouble now as you can see by the Tribune. De Gaulle wanted to make a big man out of himself – so did Pearson. The result, President Johnson put thumbs down & said no recognition of Red China. You were so right when you withheld – you & Eisenhower were right. There is trouble already in South-Eastern Asia & in Africa....
    The weather has cleared & it is fine again.
    I'll be back over the weekend.

Elmer

From Elmer to John   *Saskatoon*
                                        March 4, 1964

Dear John,
    ...You have too many worries of your own and I should not bother
you with my stuff. I had not intended mentioning it to you, but I am glad
I did so as I have the matter cleared up once and for all. That settles it for
good and all and my mind is made up now.
    I have known her for thirty-five years and we had everything in
common, being a fine musician, organist, professional photographer,
etc. For years she has been crazy about me and she cared for me like a
child. She is endowed with great sense. I have always been very fond of
her. I had a misunderstanding with her and this other fellow came into
the picture. She was not interested in him, but he insisted. So that was the
trouble. Now I have a clear picture and I have the whole thing off my
mind. She still is on the most friendly terms with me, so that is the main
thing. I have a perfect argument now to withdraw very graciously so the
thing is not serious at all.
    As far as Jane ------- is concerned, I cut that short. She is far enough
away now, so I won't have any more trouble there. I have not written
her at all and I'm keeping out of that completely. So now I shall be free
from all of that. I hesitated weighing you down with any more worries
because you have enough, but it is a good thing I did because I have now
every[thing] cleared up and I can get down to business....
    I'll slip along now and have lunch.

                                        The Best,
                                        Elmer

                          ∽

From Elmer to John   *Saskatoon*
                                        March 4, 1964

Dear John,
    ...I have some good news as well. I decided to 'phone my friend to-
night and I broke the tension. She is happier now and so am I. She is
most loyal. She is one who would stick with you through thick and thin
and she has done a great deal for me. I told her it was a necessity to be
rational and I had made up my mind. So with no acrimonious feelings,
we're still friends. I'm keeping away now so there will be no trouble at

all. I have the thing off my mind now and it will not be necessary to give you any worry about this. Under the circumstances I think it was the right thing to do letting you know about it and when I got your answer, that settled the whole thing. She does not know that answer and voluntarily withdrawing on my own initiative, she has now a higher regard for me. That is the way I want it to be. So now I've burned all the bridges behind me....

> The Best,
> Elmer

From Elmer to John   *Saskatoon*
                                        March 8, 1964

Dear John,

It was good to see you for awhile, even under the most extenuating of circumstances.

Mrs. Brooks [?] just called me up. She was at the funeral and told me she got a glimpse of you. She is the real staunch friend of the family.

I sent you the [Saskatoon] Star-Phoenix giving an account of your interview. That covered the ground all right.

If [Paul] Hellyer did not get drunk over the weekend I think you would be able to accept it that he is not human. [*]

Ross Walker's analysis of [George] Hees was absolutely right. When I recommended Hees to speak to the R.M.A. Convention, he told me then that Hees was no good, but I persuaded him to accept Hees. He was absolutely right.

He doesn't love [Walter] Gordon any more than Hees. Gordon is a child. It's a little too late now in life for the Grits to have an official "coming out" party for Gordon – I mean a "coming out" party from the nursery. I cannot conceive of any grown-up man sending out such childish rubbish. He must be completely nuts to reveal to the public that his chronological age is absolutely at variance with his mental age.

Gordon Brown is absolutely right when he says the next move is to whittle [Mitchell] Sharp down to size. When Gordon gets back he should

---

[*] In March, 1964, Paul Hellyer, Minister of National Defense, tabled a White Paper which proposed the unification of the Armed Forces. There was also at this time controversy over whether Canada would send troops to be part of the U.N. peacekeeping force in Cyprus.

be feeling better and he will be starting on Sharp immediately. Gordon always wanted to meet poor old Harry Jones, but I guess it's a little too late.

Harry is going to leave a tremendous impact in the minds of men. If [Syd] Buckwold were as popular as Harry, then I would be afraid. You know the answer to that question now and I think everyone else knows the answer – Feelings are too bitter just now in the light of what happened last year. The true meaning of "truth" was not interpreted right by the "Truth Squad." Even the word "Pravda" means "truth."

We just have to win this Saskatoon seat. I am glad of your intentions to come. One good speech from you would settle the whole thing. I was quite surprised today when Jim Chronas [?] asked me: "Who do you think would be a good candidate?" I asked him and he replied: "Harry Jones' widow." You see that is just his personal opinion and I think that idea would gain momentum. Jim said: "I would like to see her sign her name 'Mrs. Harry Jones, M.P.' " That is very human appeal.

You should make a special effort to see Jim when you come to Saskatoon next time. He has wanted to see you so much for a long time. He saw you at the funeral. He has done a great job for you among Greeks across Canada. He is writing an article now and will send you a copy. He can't get over the passing of his wife. He said he had a bad dream about his wife last night. He got up at 3 o'clock this morning and started writing his article.

I phoned Lorne Connell last night and explained things. He is quite happy so that is alright. I'll likely be in Prince Albert this week.

I trust you will be feeling better.

> The Best,
> Elmer

The Pearson government is full of:
contradiction, confusion, contention and contrition.

⌒

From Elmer to John   *Box 1728*
                                   Saskatoon
                                   May 11, 1964

Dear John,

I moved into a suite on 6th Street, near Buena Vista School, and it is a very good one and newly decorated....

You told me to let you know about Helen ----. It is now too late. I mentioned that thing so often and I wanted to marry her. I have known her for 35 years and I knew I could have everything. I couldn't put the idea across and I told Dr. Baltzan to raise the question but he could not get the opportunity. There is no use bothering about it anymore....

The new telephone book is coming out and it will show my address as the YMCA, but fortunately I shall be able to retain my old number 653-7176.

I expect to be going out tomorrow morning and shall let you know where I go.

Good luck,
Elmer

ᗌ

From Elmer to John   *Moose Jaw*

May 14, 1964

Dear John,

...I don't want you to do any worrying about my love affairs, as I have decided definitely that I am going to satisfy myself that things are going to be as they are as I cannot change the situation.

I called Helen ---- on the 'phone and she has definitely given me an answer that she is going to marry this other fellow and so I am not going to worry myself anymore about the matter. I'm just going to get it out of my mind and that is it.

I have definitely made up my mind not to make up my mind to do anything that is foolish and I'll get myself straightened around. So don't worry about this.

I am very glad that I got the suite business cleared up. I am quite well satisfied with it and there is no chance of me being moved out. It is comfortable and different than being at the YMCA.

I am glad that my medical report was very good and that means a great deal.

I don't want you to worry unnecessarily as you have enough of that. I want you to keep on working seriously, hoping that you will be back at 24 Sussex Street before the end of the year, and I think things are very hopeful at the moment....

I'll call you on the 'phone.

The Best,
Elmer

From Elmer to John   *Box 1728*
                                        Saskatoon
                                        May 24, 1964

Dear John,

...You asked me about comment on the flag issue. I sent you some papers under separate cover. I note most of the comment in favor of a new flag are teenagers and of course they like to get their names in print.

I called up Eloise Jones [Harry Jones' widow] and she has been getting opinions on the street and her assessment is that opinion is pretty evenly divided.

I called up Kay Pederson and she says there is much bitterness against the new flag.

An argument I have heard is that there are serious questions to consider these days and there is no time to bother about Pearson's flag business. That will spread further disunity in the nation. I noticed Tom Douglas made a similar statement and he may have had his ear to the ground.

I was talking to Roy McGregor [?] and he indicated that there was division of opinion among veterans here, however, he is a Scotsman who loves to argue.

Since writing you I called George Bateman [?], who says the local branch has been active for two years to preserve the Red Ensign and opinion is unanimous.

George Bateman just arrived back from the Legion Convention in Winnipeg and he says all Legion members are incensed. He said that Legion members all across Canada stated that they had voted Liberal all their lives but they made it very emphatic that they would never again cast another Liberal vote. George said that this thing would not hurt you. He further said that as Prime Minister, had Pearson made a short speech, conveying warm greetings to the Convention, he could have gained great respect, but when he introduced this flag business, his respect went right down the drain.

He said every other private home in Winnipeg was decorated with the Red Ensign....

I did not want to go into this pension increase in detail over the 'phone, but when I arrived back yesterday, I received a communication from the Pension Commission in Ottawa. It said the pension was increased to Class 15, effective Dec. 2, 1963, and the disability is now increased to

30%. A cheque was enclosed for $214.84, at a rate of $36.00 per month from Dec. 2/63 to May 31/64 as an adjustment at 54. It also says that the monthly amount payable now will be $54.00 per month.

I could certainly use that now, but if I accept it, I certainly hope that it will not stir up trouble. You may let me know of your personal views on the subject.

I know my hearing has been very much impaired. The disability is only 30%, but I recieve sharp noises that mean nothing to me. I can understand you over the 'phone but others I cannot follow at all. I am told nothing can be done about correcting this condition, but the only thing I can do now is to use stronger & stronger hearing aids.

You may advise me if I should accept this cheque of $214.84 and I'll receive your reply when I arrive back over the weekend. If you think it is advisable I'll...[two lines crossed out here]....

I'm going to see Helen ---- tomorrow. She is still very friendly and that would have been the most ideal set up if complications had not set in. I'll talk the thing over with her and if there is no change, I'll drop the whole matter....

I must close now and if I get any further information will send it along.

> The Best,
> Elmer

From Elmer to John   *Canora, Sask.*
                                        May 26, 1964

Dear John,

...The other matter to report, I saw Helen ----. She told me this other man is very much in love with her but she is holding back on him. She said she likes me as much as she ever did and she wants to see me. So I am allowing her to decide the question for herself. That's about all I can say.

Any other political information I get I shall pass on. I do feel that politically in the West you are stronger than you ever were.

> The Best,
> Elmer

From John to Elmer   *Office of the Leader of the*
                                        Opposition
                                        Ottawa
                                        May 28, 1964

Dear Elmer,

I had just arrived in the office this morning when Olive phoned and advised that her brother Don had passed away. He had been ill for some months but nobody had expected his death. You remember him as a little boy in Saskatoon.

Olive as always is like a rock. This afternoon she and I were to go to Toronto to a Variety Show in memory of the late Mayor Summerville. I do not think she should go although she feels she should.

Last evening we went out to a Women's Conservative meeting in Carleton and from all appearances there that is one of the constituencies that will be won back.

It is impossible to follow the mental processes of Mr. Pearson. He was going to have a distinctive flag. Now he is going to have two flags and two anthems. Having already established the principle of two nations in his speech at Murray Bay, Quebec, this latest step is a further divisive and disruptive force.

French Canada in not satisfied now because, while he is going to abolish the Red Ensign, he is going to reinstate the Union Jack.

I hope I will be able to unite the Conservative Party in the House and really put on a fight.

This man more and more is showing signs of egomania. After having seen the film on me over the CBC the Liberals decided they ought to have one on him and they spent $35,000 of the Canadian people's money. While the CBC wouldn't let me see or know of any part of the film they were going to produce they provided a preview for him, Paul Martin, Sharp, [Maurice] Lamontagne and some of the Liberal organizers. Five runs were provided. I have often seen people who have enjoyed a picture stay for the second show – the entertainment value of the Pearson picture must have been in a class by itself if after they had seen it and re-seen it four more times, the CBC decided not to produce it! According to the press it showed him to be too petulant and would leave a bad impression. What has happened reveals him in a truer light.

I will be away on Saturday and will call you on Sunday on my return.

                                        With best wishes,
                                        Sincerely,
                                        John

From Elmer to John   *Empire Motor Hotel*
                                        "Meadow Lake's Finest"
                                        Meadow Lake, Saskatchewan
                                        June 2, 1964

Dear John,

I'm scribbling a few lines while having breakfast in the hotel whose ownership is shared by Fred Hadley.

I left Saskatoon at 3 o'clock and arrived here at 8 P.M. It is a long drive and I thought I might as well get it over this week.

I might as well keep going and have a lot of driving, so that is the main thing.

You told me to write you but I did not seem to get an opportunity.

This experience I have had is a rather unhappy one and the only thing I can do is live with the situation and I am the only one who can right things as they are. I'll have to satisfy myself that I shall have to live with myself.

I knew this girl for over thirty years and after her husband died she made a dead set. This Jane ------- business came into the picture and when this woman got married Helen thought everything was alright again. A silly woman called Helen up on the phone telling her I was chasing around with Jane ------- in Regina and that was the hitch. At her weakest moment this other bird barged in and took over. She was sick at the time and everything happened from then on. I lost control. She wanted to marry me but procrastination just ended things. I don't see much hope now. She had everything & we were very close for over three years until all these incidents came in and the both of us were happy.

She knows how I stand now. This other bird has been pressing for marriage, so if he wants it he is to go right ahead.

It's not a good situation for me but I'll live it down and as I have said I'll learn to live by myself from now on.

The election is fine in Saskatoon. Everything points to the election of Eloise Jones.

This is a short note and I shall write you later on. I have to get an early start here this morning.

I shall drop you a line later. Pearson is in a mess.

                                        The Best,
                                        Elmer

From John to Elmer   *Leader of the Opposition*
                                        [Ottawa]
                                        June 19, 1964

Dear Elmer,

Our heart-to-heart talk early Wednesday morning was worthwhile and I hope that you will do whatever you feel is best.

If Helen means so much to you as you said, for your own well-being and happiness your course should be clear.

Whatever you do, don't put off your decision indefinitely. That would not be fair to either her or you.

Olive and I want you to do what you want to do.

Yours very sincerely,
John

⌇

From Elmer to John   *Elrose*
                                        June 29, 1964

Dear John,

...It is getting late now but I have the final report on Helen ----. I finally got her on the 'phone this afternoon before I left. She did not have her mind made up the last time and she said that there was a possibility that she would come back and she wanted to see me, but this other fellow must have turned on the heat.

I asked her if she would go out with me to Pion Era as she did in previous years and take pictures. She said she could not as she was going up north for three weeks and admitted that she might get married any time. She told me she could have changed her mind before but now it is impossible.

So now I am glad I finally got her on the phone and I can forget all about the whole thing and I shall get down to business. It is a bit difficult as I was with her for over 3 years and that was the last thing I thought would ever go flat. However, that is a closed issue now and I'll forget all about it and I'll keep busy from now on. I know that this thing has been on your's and Olive's mind also but you must also forget about it. I can't fight that sort of thing and it is just as well that I did not. Under the circumstances if I had married her and something else cropped up I would be in a lot of trouble. I have never seen this fellow, I don't know his name, but I'll just keep away....

So long,
Elmer

∽

From John to Elmer   *Leader of the Opposition*
                                               Ottawa
                                               July 3, 1964

Dear Elmer,

Since writing you earlier today I have received your gift of the very fine pencil, but I wonder what the meaning of the epigram is, which reads:

"A little more praise and a little less criticism please" !!

The implication in that message would seem to indicate that you are being influenced by the Winnipeg Free Press and the Saskatoon Star-Phoenix!

With best wishes,
John

I still hope that something may turn up so that your affairs will turn out well. However, the fact that Helen is going away would not leave much upon which to build much hope. However, don't worry.

∽

From Elmer to John   *Box 1728*
                                               Saskatoon
                                               July 15, 1964

Dear John,

...I saw our friend Helen on the street yesterday and for a change I turned on the heat. This fellow Martin is hanging on and the only thing she has said, "he is a nice fellow." She said she would call me on the phone and see me next week. So that is the situation. This is the first time

I really talked business and she knows now how it stands. I had decided to drop the whole matter but apparently it is open still. I'll let you know what happens....

> The Best,
> Elmer

From Elmer to John   *Box 1728*
Saskatoon
July 22, 1964

Dear John,

...You were asking me again about Helen ----. She did not get in touch with me as I anticipated. I did call her today and got her on the phone. I asked her why she did not call me and she said she could not. That bird is there constantly and he won't leave her alone. She said she would try to call me next week. However, I think my best bet is to drop the whole thing. She told me she is not making any moves at all. I think my wisest plan under the circumstances is to drop the whole thing cold....

> The very best,
> Elmer

From Elmer to John   *Box 1728*
Saskatoon
July 23, 1964

Dear John,

I saw Helen ---- today and I turned on the heat. This bird is there constantly and she says he will be here in Saskatoon for a month. I was most definite and tried to force the issue. I told her that I would not bother her during the next month but thereafter I expect to meet her out of town for a couple of days and I told her we would arrange everything. I said that I would under no circumstance take no for an answer. She did promise that she will try to meet me but even so I have little hope. She said when she does get married it will be fast and all over before anybody knows about it. She gave me to understand she is still holding off for a couple of months and I told her I definitely wanted to see her for a couple of days before that time. I was more than positive today. If by chance she takes me up on this I'm in for it and that will be it. She said she is not married yet and I do think she is holding off deliberately. I saw her during the week and she told me the thing would have to be settled one way or the other shortly. She said she can't have two men and I informed her in that case you better settle for me and finish it up. So there is the story.

I know she does not want to lose my friendship. I told her [I'd] definitely come to a point when I can't do without her. That is the way it stands. She has intimated different times if we could meet out of town that would settle it....

The Best,
Elmer

෴

From Elmer to John   *Rosthern*
                                        August 11, 1964

Dear John,
   ...I received your letter before leaving Saskatoon and am sorry that these stupid people have caused trouble again. I can't understand the stupidity of some people. For once in thirty years they had everything in their favor and they will find that they will land up with nothing at all.

I told you last year that I heard Sally [?] was mad because he was not appointed Speaker of the Senate. He was given one of the finest appointments any man could get and if I were in his place I think I would go out of my way to please. He has nothing to worry about but the rest of these jokers are going to be out on a limb in time.

It is most unfortunate that a fellow like Fulton, with all his brilliance, should make such a complete fool of himself in his B.C. provincial politics and then in a city like Montreal to have a paltry 80 turn up at the Canadian Club. That would break anybody's heart. He had everything in his favor. When you start at the top and drop to the bottom, you are out.

In your case it was the converse. It looked as though you would never get the start but you did finally get the start and you went right through to the top. That would give any man satisfaction.

Birds like [Leon] Balcer have no conscience at all and he has just killed himself. He will land up in the gutter and he will have only himself to sympathize with.

I would make no hasty decisions as this thing might work out alright as it has been in the past. In geometry sometimes a theorem leads to an "absurdity" and then a new approach is necessary. This might well happen and then probably the mountain will come to Mohammed. You have a great many staunch friends and they will fight any time. You beat them at the Convention and you can do it again....

The general opinion I have had lately, people don't bother to discuss the flag issue anymore because they are completely fed up with it. They feel that world conditions are more than serious at the moment and they conclude that Pearson is a child to restrain himself with baby talk about something called a flag. I do think he could be made a complete laughing stock worrying about such paltry things. You have a very powerful group of serious thinking Canadians with you and you found that to be true in your past election experiences. You are stronger than ever. What you hear today regularly is that the Liberal Party ruined itself by taking Pearson instead of [Paul] Martin and I think St. Laurent can take full marks for putting Pearson there. I think he can do a lot of good for you....

You were asking me about Helen ----. I had lunch with her today and she was very friendly. She said she would marry this fellow, but it might not be for a year. I notice she is not wearing his ring but has her husband's rings. He talked her into buying land and settling on the farm. They looked at farms but they are not available by reports at any price now. The farmers won't sell.

She told me she thinks of me often. She has relatives visiting her at the moment and when they leave she is going to get in touch with me. I know that she regrets that things got out of hand and she says she was very foolish. I'm not going to worry myself about it. I'll let the thing ride along and see what happens. I'm not making any foolish moves but when she is ready I'll see her. I know she would be fanatically loyal when she does get married....

I do trust things will improve and that everything will work out alright as I know it will. I wouldn't worry too much. Everybody knows you are doing a good job. Do you recall, on the Sunday night before your last Federal election in Lake Centre, I returned to Saskatoon. I was alone and I drove through that blinding rain. I was very doubtful of getting back even on the gravel. Strange things went through my mind that night as I drove. I was not sure of anything and I thought things could be very serious. When I finally arrived home you were at the front door. You said: "Well, it's finished now." I did not tell exactly what you would call the "truth," when I said: "You have nothing to worry about." It worked out with a thumping majority. You have since proceeded from one difficulty to another and at present the score is almost 100%. The last chapter has not been written yet. A condemned man is never hanged until the noose is around his neck.

The Best,
Elmer

✍

From Elmer to John   *Box 1728*
Saskatoon
August 23, 1964

Dear John,
    I am very sorry that you are experiencing so much grief but sometimes it happens that everything goes wrong. It will work out some way. I notice in Reader's Digest's [Norman] Vincent Peale says, "The way out is the way through," and you usually reach that objective. Your troubles at that are not as great as Pearson's. He knew he was in trouble when he took over after making all his spurious promises.
    Abraham Lincoln said: "I am a slow walker, but I never walk backward." You were cursed for not making decisions fast enough, but Pearson can heed these words after all his backtracking. The word "slow" is nevertheless applicable to his pace in getting legislation transacted....
    You and Olive have been concerned about Helen but you have enough troubles without bothering about that sort of thing. Naturally I have missed her, but as I told you, I'm not bothering about that humbug. I'm going to ignore her completely from now on and if the urge on her part becomes strong enough, I might discuss things but I won't be at least anxious. I think she would like to come back by observation. I'm feeling fine now and am keeping out of this business completely....
    I trust everything will turn out OK. You'll find you have tremendous support. It's developing into a fight between Quebec & the rest of Canada.

The Best,
Elmer

On July 22, the Conservative party initiated a filibuster over the adopting of a new flag. The issue was to preoccupy John for months to follow.

From John to Elmer   *Leader of the Opposition*
                                        [Ottawa]
                                        8 P.M.
                                        August 27, 1964

Dear Elmer,

I am in the House this evening – the first for a week as I have been staying at home with Olive.

Dr. Rynard saw her today and said she was getting along pretty well and should be able to be out for a car drive next week.

I hope that you are having fair success at least, when you are about your business.

There will be no holidays for us this fall but I will be out for sure for a hunting trip – and will want you to be along.

Today there was a great storm in the House over a letter written by the Minister without Portfolio regarding car stickers of the 3 maple leaf flag which he offered to supply at 2 1/2 cents each. He suggested they be turned over to garage owners for distribution so that there would be no political overtones.

Every day the Pearsonites find themselves in difficulties – it is an amazing record of ineptitude.

The P.M. cancelled the trip to the U.S.S.R. because he is very annoyed with the fact that we won't give him "his pennant" (J. Hnatyshyn, Mike Starr and others were going on the trip), but it is out for now.

While the Grits spread the news that I am old and decrepit, I am fortunate to be in better health than for 10 years. I take a 1 1/2 mile walk each morning before breakfast accompanied by Happy II.

When you visit us this fall or at Christmas I will give you a tryout on this course!

Well, I must get back to work.

With all the Best – (and I haven't forgotten that you have a promise to let you have a loan).

                                 I am,
                                 Sincerely,
                                 John

Olive was in hospital in Toronto being treated for her spinal problems.

From John to Olive   *Charlottetown*
September 17, 1964

My darling,

I am now on board aircraft enroute to Ottawa (7 A.M.) after a wonderful meeting here. Yesterday I had a press conference at Moncton – this morning one is scheduled for Halifax. There is a new spirit in the party reminiscent of 1957!

Many asked about you at the meeting. The porter at the Charlottetown Hotel, Hilton McInnis, spoke of you in such a kindly way. He too suffers from spinal troubles – a fact that he shared with you when you visited here some years ago. A letter to him thanking him for his solicitous words would please him.

This morning at 5:45 I went for a walk by myself – and met the early birds or some who had not been to bed yet!

I hope Helen [Brunt] is enjoying herself and that there isn't *too much* gossip.

All my love,
John

I coined a phrase while speaking at the meeting last evening.
"Mr. Pearson says he will have his flag by Christmas."
"By Christmas! He won't!"

From John to Olive   *Office of the Leader of the*
Opposition
Ottawa
September 21, 1964

My darling Ollie,

We had fun today. The Liberals thought I was going to move an amendment on the Motion to go into Supply. I decided not to, and the other Parties were all in a disturbed state. The result was we got the

Motion through and the Government had to introduce legislation, otherwise the day would have been a complete loss.

[*Ottawa Journal* reporter] Dick Jackson came in this afternoon when I was out of the office and delivered a couple of articles which I am sending you herewith.

I called Ken Thomson today and raised strong objection to the false articles that are being written by [Patrick] Nicholson. In one of them he quoted Senator Brunt as having raised many thousands of dollars for me, and added that $182,000 had been given to me in 1956 as an inducement for me to take the leadership. I told Ken that this was all completely false and I would have to sue for libel. He wrote another article that is equally libellous. Tomorrow morning we are going to get in touch with one another and decide on what is to be done. I assured him that I had no objection to criticism, but unadulterated falsehood produced by a malicious person will no longer be tolerated.

There is a big fight on in South Waterloo for the nomination but I think that Jim Chaplin will win. Dr. Macdonald has acted foolishly. He has quite a bit of support but because he does not like the way the organization is operating has threatened to give a statement to the Toronto Star. He should learn that that kind of candidate never achieved anything but disillusionment for anyone so indulging.

I hope that the sun will shine for the rest of your stay and that all hurricanes will give Bermuda the widest possible berth.

All my love,
John

I know that you will be learning a lot from association with Helen. She is a wise woman – politically none better.

✍

From John to Olive   *Office of the Leader of the*
                                        Opposition
                                        Ottawa
                                        September 23, 1964

My darling,

Your letter written Sunday came to me this morning and with much pleasure to me. When it arrived I was having a long interview with John

Bassett who informed me he is going to give full support to me from now on, and expressed his affection for you.

Mr. [Walter] Gordon is very angry at me over what took place on Monday and even the Globe & Mail had an editorial on the subject, and Lynch had an article which expressed his views in unmistakable terms. I will have the pages from Hansard enclosed so that you will know what was said. I was full of warmth and understanding of the Minister of Finance. He started to say something and after he bellowed about for three or four minutes he decided to read into Hansard a speech he had delivered three or four days before in Hamilton.

Dr. Rynard was just in and finds things are favourable in his constituency, as do all our Ontario Members.

Yesterday Mr. Pearson had to deny an interview he gave the day before in Newfoundland when he said (under Joey pressure) that it wouldn't be long before the two flags, the maple leaf and the Union Jack, would be flying over Parliament Hill. His statement that he never said such a thing was untrue and even his best friends in the Fourth Estate could not understand why he should have done so.

I will be looking forward on Sunday to seeing you but again would point out that if staying longer would benefit you I wish you would stay. That does not mean that I am pressing you to do so, though!

With all my love,
John

⟳

From John to Elmer   *Office of the Leader of the*
                                      Opposition
                                      Ottawa
                                      October 13, 1964

Dear Elmer,

The enclosure is a very good picture. I think it was taken somewhere in the Okanagan Valley. I seem to remember we went out walking one morning. It is worth preserving.

The Queen left this morning. Olive and I were at the dinner given by The Queen last evening. It was a very nice affair. The disgraceful conduct in Quebec City* has been commented upon all over the world.

---

* A separatist demonstration.

Last evening Mrs. Lesage tried to tell me what took place was the action of a few ill-mannered Russians and some Americans. I said, well, that might be a good alibi for some people but did not go down with me when I consider that on the whole route The Queen travelled there were no more than 1500 people.

Yesterday here in Ottawa it was a very good show and around the Cenotaph some 25,000 were gathered. I occupied a standing position on Parliament Hill in front of Sir Wilfrid's monument and like Pharaoh's daughter "stood afar off to wit what should be done."

I had hoped to be going West the day after tomorrow but that is out now and I cannot say when it will be.

The Government with transparent generosity offered to give us two weeks' holiday providing we would give three months' Interim Supply. Our answer was no. If we ever did that we would be tied up completely on the flag debate and they would get what they want.

One particularly happy result of the visit of The Queen was that Pearson was not able to fly his troika flag. He had it all worked out that this is what he was going to do and had even produced a large flag with silken ropes which apparently was to be flown over The Queen during the visit. I suspected as much; now I know what the Government's plans were.

Premier [Ross] Thatcher* was there. I asked him about the story he was alleged to have told in Prince Albert about Pearson and he gave me a repeat performance. He is very proud of the story. I don't know whether I told you the story or not. The one that I am referring to had to do with a recommendation Pearson made to the Pope for the appointment of Lesage as Cardinal. The Pope was very surprised to have the recommendation and asked what the reason was for this most unusual request in these days. Pearson replied that "After you appoint him Cardinal I will only have to kiss his ring"!...

> With all good wishes, I am,
> Sincerely,
> John

---

* Ross Thatcher had run successfully for the CCF federally in Moose Jaw - Lake Centre after John vacated the redistributed riding in 1952. As Leader of the Saskatchewan Liberal party, he was elected Premier of the province in 1964, ending 20 years of CCF rule.

From John to Olive   *Leader of the Opposition*
                                        [Ottawa]
                                        Monday, 6:30 A.M.
                                        October 19th [1964]

My sweet one,

Before taking my morning walk I rush to report "progress."

First, if you were to see your bed you would ask the question of the 3 Bears – "Who slept in my bed?"

That is what I did last night!

Comfortably too!

I must get some speech material ready today for that awful program for the next ten days.

That won't prevent me from thinking of you. I do hope the doctors can find something helpful to diminish the pain in your back. I don't know how you stand it. If I had the same affliction, you can be assured that I would be as quiet as you! I *fooled you* by that statement, didn't I?

Helen [Brunt] and I had a chat about the circumstances connected with the February 1963 Cabinet resignations – some things that seemed to surprise her.

I told you about Davie Fulton having to leave the aircraft when the passenger who had a confirmance of her flight arrived at the aircraft just as the doors were closing. He will be seeing me today. I suspect that he is here to arrange Dr. W's [Dr. Charles Willoughby's] resignation.

Do call me whenever you feel like doing so. I really shouldn't go to Edmonton Friday, but as you insist I should, I shall.

With so much love, my darling,

John

ᧃ

From John to Olive   *Leader of the Opposition*
                                        [Ottawa]
                                        4:30 P.M.
                                        October 20, 1964

My darling,

Your note posted this morning at 5:30 A.M. has been delivered to me – wonderful speed in service. Too often it takes two days from Toronto!

I am thinking of you constantly, sweet one! Salt or no salt!

I shall be so relieved tomorrow morning when I learn that you are back in your ward.

And I shall be seeing you at suppertime, but only for a short while (less than one hour) as I will have to come back to Ottawa on the 8:50 P.M. flight.

This afternoon little Lester let the cat out of the bag – I knew it was there – when he told me it was the Government's intention to move confirmation of the Flag Committee Report. He thinks that will limit us to two weeks of debate at the most. He has not realized yet that he must get Supply for another month – we can talk that out and in to an election if we rush to do so. We shall still be in the House at Christmas time!...

All my love to my wonderful wife,

> John

ᔕ

From John to Olive   *Leader of the Opposition*
    [Ottawa]
    1 P.M.
    October 23, 1964

My darling,

I am just leaving for the aircraft and decided to send you the enclosures [not found].

The Flag Committee is about to report.

Here it is *Confidentially.*

The new flag which will be forced on us will be:

and they will try and trick the people by having the Red Ensign as a secondary flag for Commonwealth purposes.

The report will come in Thursday.

> With so much love,
> John

From John to Elmer   *Leader of the Opposition*
                                        Ottawa
                                        December 9, 1964

Dear Elmer,

I am back in the office today but won't be staying too long. I have to speak on the flag question and will do so tomorrow. It may well be the last speech on this subject, as we have exhausted every avenue to stop a flag without the Union Jack on it.*

The Government is in trouble over the purchase of furniture by two ministers, Lamontagne and Tremblay.** There were big headlines yesterday in the [Montreal] Gazette and the Globe and Mail. I am sending you the same herewith.

Balcer made another dig at me yesterday and when I brought it up in Caucus today, he left.

There was quite a lot of comment over Pearson's prologue on patronage. Moses was able to preach a code of morality in 10 lines; the Prime Minister took almost the same number of pages. It might well be said that, with all the difficulties he is having to describe the situation arising from the fact that these ministers bought furniture on credit, and with no time limit for payments, that the Prime Minister "is now paying for the Cabinet which was sold him some time ago!"

You seemed to be a bit down when I talked to you this morning. Always remember at times like these, how much worse are the conditions of others of your acquaintance.

With all good wishes.

                                        Your Bro,
                                        John...

---

* At 2:15 A.M. on December 15, the House of Commons voted 163 to 78 to adopt the new Canadian flag. During the filibuster, the Conservatives had made 210 speeches, the Liberals 50, the NDP 24 and the Social Credit 15.

** Liberal Ministers René Tremblay and Maurice Lamontagne were accused of using their positions to make purchases of furniture on very favorable terms. John picked up on it with his customary vigor. "The situation has all the appearance of political upholstery," he said on December 18. "Furnish us with the facts!" cried a Conservative backbencher.

From Volume 3 of *One Canada*:
"I met with caucus on 5 February. It was a rousing meeting.... It was with the support of caucus that I met the National Executive the next morning.... My leadership was affirmed. Balcer was defeated."

From Elmer to John   *Saskatoon*
                                        February 9, 1965

Dear John,
    You did some pretty fast work and flattened that group out. The Entomological department of the Conservative Party received a real setback – I refer to the so-called "termite" branch of that department. You scored a complete victory in an impossible position and even if you don't get your rich rewards at the moment, you will in the future. These "termites" were starved at the meeting and it is logical to think that they will be fighting among themselves in the future for self-preservation.

    Using the word "termite" is the strongest condemnation that could be hurled against members of this gang. I did not understand the full significance of the term until I heard of examples.

    I recall an incident at Canton Island on the world tour. The captain of the crew was a very fine chap and was decent throughout. However, he was in charge and he gave me orders to throw away the few pieces of coral I had collected. He told me these corals might contain termites and if that was so, it might ruin the whole aircraft. I threw them away.

    Bob McKay, who spent all his life in construction work, told me today that in his experience he has seen buildings completely undermined and collapsed through the activities of termites. He agreed that your comparison could not have been any more suitable. If any of that gang studied entomology at the University of Toronto, they know exactly what you mean.

    The people must know the facts that Balcer is just a hireling working in the Termite Community. I think he has given the public enough evidence that he is a hireling.

    Jim McDonald [?] could well be mad because he knows the role he and [Ontario Lieutenant-Governor] Earl Rowe have always played in the termite cell. The press reported that you had addressed Senator McCutcheon as a "termite." In reply, that amounted to advising you that he asked you to resign last fall, amounted to fact that he was commissioned to do so by the Supreme Council of the Grand Order of Termites.

    You brought these predatory insects out of their dark and parasitic chasms into the broad daylight. They came out with their bellies full and they received an additional bellyfull.

I noted last night one of the members of the Supreme Council of the Order of Termites had his say. That was Illustrious Brother Insect [Douglas] Harkness. He said Diefenbaker had to go. I know from conversations with Alberta members what they think of Harkness. They wanted him out in the last election and he will be out this time. D.H. are the initials of Douglas Harness but in the next election "D.H." will also mean "Dump Harkness."

You did the right thing throwing the book at these bastards and you can feel assured that the public can also be cruel and relentless when a man is condemned without reason. They have come up with the slogan "Dump Diefenbaker" but I notice not one has come up with any reasons for doing so and they won't.

It is a most embarrassing position for anybody to be in for no reason at all. I don't know what the answer is, but I don't think I would be too hasty. I think you are quite capable of trapping all this gang of pisces in the same net and depositing it on the beach, where they might be known as sons of beach.

If the worst comes to the worst and the story is told, you could become one of the Great Canadians. At any rate, the story must be told. In any event, you have the satisfaction of having been prime minister and you yourself made yourself the Prime Minister.

The way things are today, I would not be at all surprised if you were P.M. again. The pattern is so crazy today that anything can happen....

> Best of luck,
> Elmer

&

From John to Elmer   *Office of the Leader of the*
                                        Opposition
                                        Ottawa
                                        February 25, 1965

Dear Elmer,

Last evening I spoke to the Brotherhood Meeting at the Jewish Synagogue, Beth Emeth Bais Yehuda Brotherhood in Toronto. There were about 500 present. As with Laurier, so with me, they turn out in numbers but vote against!

I have not made any progress in regard to the question of leadership. Yesterday I outlined my views to the Members in Caucus on the national picture and stressed the need of a united front on amending the Constitution. If my views are not acceptable to them then the course I should follow is clear.

Fulton is manipulating again. This morning the Honourable Michael Starr called on me and said he had received a phone call from Neil Crawford in Edmonton and during the course of the conversation Neil said that Mr. Fulton had been in Edmonton and was most anxious to help the Conservative Party [and] would need a request from me asking him to come back to Ottawa. Neil felt that this would be a fine thing to do and would bring about the addition of many young people to the Party. It strikes me as strange that Crawford should have taken that course instead of phoning me direct, but apparently this was a suggestion of Fulton's.

It is of interest that Monte Monteith [M.P., Perth], some weeks ago, advanced a similar suggestion, and one or two other private Members have done the same.

Olive is far from recovered and will have to stay at home for another week or so. I feel most keenly for her and in last night's Telegram [Lubor] Zink wrote an article entitled "Olive Diefenbaker" which is a nasty piece of work.*

Olive and I were supposed to go to a luncheon for General Greunther today but that is out of the question under the circumstances.

Carolyn and the family went home the day before yesterday and apparently Happy became lonely and he disappeared yesterday morning.

> With all good wishes
> Sincerely,
> John

P.S. If you look at the first February issue (15th) of Maclean's you will find a cartoon about which I am going to sue them for libel.** I have been waiting for a really good case and I think I have got one now.

---

* In an article entitled "For Better, For Worse," Zink blamed Olive's support of John for his failure to step down as P.C. leader.
** The cartoon depicted Diefenbaker as a Prussian soldier fighting Pearson's British soldier.

From John to Elmer   *Office of the Leader of the*
                                        Opposition
                                        Ottawa
                                        March 4, 1965

Dear Elmer,

We had a hullabaloo in the House yesterday and as it will be some days before you get the issue of Hansard I am sending you a copy herewith.

I suppose when Rivard walked out of the jail in Montreal that he would not say "au revoir" but "au Rivard".

There has been no change in my personal situation this week. I went to Caucus yesterday and there was little or no decision made and I am very much concerned that I am going to be placed in an impossible position. I think what I will do today is have a number appointed from the Provinces where we have Conservative Premiers to interview those Premiers as to the attitude they are going to take. If we oppose the formula for amendment of the Constitution – the stand that I insist on – if the Caucus does not go with me on it then of course there can be no argument as to the course to be followed.

I have not had a word from Dalton Camp since the Executive Meeting on the 6th of February. I think I told you earlier that he did not even notify me as to the result of the vote which was against having a Convention and left the idea that there was only a majority of two whereas only 41% voted in favour of a Convention.

Olive is fast getting well and on Friday night will go out for the first time for many weeks. We are going to attend a performance of the boy singers from Vienna.

I will be sure that Happy is not taken along as I don't want a repeat of what happened in Prince Albert when Max let out a wolf howl as soon as the boys started to sing. I will never forget the piercing wolf howl that rent the air at St. Paul's Presbyterian Church when the Welsh lads struck some high notes. Max outdid them!

Mr. Walter Dinsdale took my place yesterday to meet with the students in Sir George Williams College in Montreal and so that you will be able to get the full benefit of his remarks the report in this morning's "Gazette" is attached.

The weather is fine. Spring is on the way and this puts me in very good spirits.

My only concern is that I have not been able to make the announcement that I intend to make.

> With all good wishes,
> Sincerely,
> John

* formula*

From John to Elmer   *Office of the Leader of the*
                                        Opposition
                                        Ottawa
                                        March 5, 1965

Dear Elmer,

Events are moving very rapidly. I don't think it will be too long now before I will be able to take definite action. The Caucus has been meeting this week and Balcer has again revealed what has taken place in Caucus. The Montreal Gazette this morning contains a report and also last evening's Montreal Star.

A letter has been received by me from a lady in British Columbia who wrote a letter of criticism to Davie Fulton. In his reply to her he says I am in disagreement with many Members of the Party and it is difficult for him to keep silent. I quote his words: "I am sorry about it but it is becoming increasingly difficult to be silent." If he makes one of his speeches then I will have something to say about him and the way in which he tried to become Prime Minister in 1963 by joining McCutcheon, Nowlan, Halpenny, Balcer, Hees and Sevigny to put me in as Chief Justice of Canada.

There is also an article today by [Arthur] Blakely [in the Montreal *Gazette*] regarding Pederson of which I am sending you a copy.

> Sincerely,
> John

From John to Elmer   *Office of the Leader of the*
                                        Opposition
                                        [Ottawa]
                                        6th March [1965]

Dear Elmer,

I don't know what course to follow – but must do something one way or another soon.

I am suing Maclean's [magazine] for that *damnable* cartoon on its Feb. 20th issue, page 4.

Olive is better.

Last night we went to hear the Vienna Boys Singers Choir (22 members). Wonderful.

All good luck to you.

John

From John to Elmer   *Office of the Leader of the*
                                        Opposition
                                        Ottawa
                                        March 13, 1965

Dear Elmer,

I am sending you herewith the story of the flag in pictures as it appears in this morning's copy of the Globe and Mail. I will be 'phoning you tomorrow, but in the meantime, the debate goes on.

You will have heard on the CBC this morning of rumours of my resigning because of the pressure from Toronto. It also said that a fund was being raised for me, which is a complete falsehood. However, this is in keeping with the attitude of Senator McCutcheon who gave me until the 26th of March to be out.

Fulton has stated that if there is no vacancy in the Party leadership by April 1st, his silence will have to end. I have not particularly noticed that there has been any silence on his part.

The Editor of Maclean's magazine has written to me offering his personal apologies for the cartoon which appeared on February 20th. The letter says that "there was not the slightest intention on the part of the Editors to convey any reflection on the part of yourself.... The artist himself envisioned the drawing, but neither he, nor we, envisaged the invidious construction which could be put upon it."

That, of course, will not conclude the matter. David Walker has given notice of my intention to take out proceedings for libel action.

I am dictating this in the presence of Senator [Arthur] Pearson, who, as always, is around when I need help and council.

> With all good wishes,
> I am,
> Your aff. bro.,
> John

From John to Elmer

Office of the Leader of the Opposition
Ottawa
April 6, 1966

Dear Elmer,

I am attaching hereto a copy of a letter written to Ron D. McLelland, M.P., our Member from Rosetown-Biggar, who had asked me to be an honorary pallbearer at the funeral of the late Tim Cooper. It is impossible for me to get away and you will observe that I have designated you to take my place and be my representative. The funeral is arranged for Saturday at the First Baptist Church, Saskatoon.

The vote on Capital Punishment took place last night and I was disappointed in the support from Western Members. You will see in Hansard that with five exceptions, Saskatchewan Members all voted against abolition.

Olive is quite a bit better than at any time during the last six months. She has been going to an osteopath and can now walk with less stiffness and she is freer from pain than she has been.

The trip to the Far East is off as I told you. Justice Spence* is calling the Commission for the 19th of this month. His attitude, if it is measured by the observations he has already made, is anything but judicial.

---

* Justice W.F. Spence of the Supreme Court of Canada was appointed to look into the "Munsinger Affair." The Conservative Minister who had been primarily involved, Pierre Sevigny, was cleared of any serious breach of security, although Diefenbaker was censured for not dismissing him anyway.

Hugh Arscott sent me a literary masterpiece which is going the rounds, and I am attaching a copy. You will note that it has picked up some of the literary gems of the past beginning with Moses and has translated them to apply to the present.

> With all good wishes,
> Affectionately,
> John

Dear Sir or Madam,

We have the distinguished honor of being members of the committee to raise fifty million dollars to be used for placing the statue of Ross Thatcher in front of the Parliament Buildings.

This committee was in quite a quandry about selecting the proper location for the statue. It was not thought wise to place it beside the statue of the late Arthur Meighen who never told a lie, and not beside that of Mackenzie King who never told the truth, since Ross Thatcher could never tell the difference

After careful consideration we decided that it should be placed next to the statue of Christopher Columbus, the greatest Liberal of them all, in that he started out not knowing where he was going, and arriving did not know where he was, and returning did not know where he had been, and did it all on borrowed money.

Five thousand years ago Moses said to the children of Israel, "Pick up your shovels, mount your asses and camels, and I will led you to the promised land."

Nearly five thousand years later, Bennett said, "Lay down your shovels, sit on your asses, light up a Camel, this is the promised land."

Now Thatcher is stealing your shovels, kicking your asses raising the price of your Camel and taking over the promised land.

If you are one of the few citizens who has any money left over after paying taxes, we expect you to send a generous contribution for this worthy cause to:

LEADERSHIP SOLIDIFICATION COMMITTEE
c/o HAZEN ARGUE
ASSINIBOIA, SASK.

From John to Elmer   *Office of the Leader of the*
                                        Opposition
                                        Ottawa
                                        April 22, 1965

Dear Elmer,

We are leaving in a few minutes for Halifax. There will be a short stopover in Montreal. Tomorrow evening I will speak to the St. George's Society in Halifax and Saturday, to the Executive of the P.C. Association of Nova Scotia at a luncheon and at a public meeting at Kentville at night.

A few days ago the photographer from the Chronicle Herald of Halifax took a picture of the recent presentation of the earliest Sir John A. photo study that I have. It is dated in the late 1850s. Following the publication of this, I received an invitation today to speak to the Cape Breton Highland Society on November 30th next. The picture and write-up is enclosed herewith.

I still have a cold on the chest but am feeling pretty well again. I am sorry we did not get west for Easter and I am hoping now to arrange to do so about the middle of May.

Today I agreed to go to Frobisher Bay sometime in May. The Eskimos are holding a big celebration and Olive is looking forward to a feed of blubber and R. R. and R. (it is made of rabbit, reindeer and 'rat). Olive has less time for reading now than she ever had because her hours are spent either playing the piano or doing needle-point for the piano stool.

                        With kind regards, and
                        good wishes,
                        Yours sincerely,
                        John

From John to Elmer   *Office of the Leader of the*
                                        Opposition
                                        Ottawa
                                        May 4, 1965

Dear Elmer,

Mrs. Wagner is trying today to secure the help of the local

photographic experts so that I will be able to operate your camera without too much grief.

You have been talking about being overweight and I have decided to send you the menu of "How to Eat and Grow Slim," which is being followed by a number of Conservative Members.*

> With best regards,
> Yours sincerely,
> John

♒

From John to Elmer   *Office of the Leader of the*
                                               Opposition
                                               Ottawa
                                               May 29, 1965

Dear Elmer,

I am sending you a page from The New York Times regarding coins and stamps. I haven't heard from you recently that you have been able to secure "coin finds" of value. If there are any particular coins that you would like to have to make up your Canadian 50¢ collection, I will try to secure them for you.

The Globe and Mail in today's issue, again predicts my retirement, so it can be expected that there will be another burst of press and radio propaganda in this regard. I have not changed my stand, and do not intend to. I make my own decisions, and will not be subject to controlled intimidation.

During the week I spoke to a couple of Conservative Associations including the Association of West Ottawa and West Middlesex. Both meetings were very encouraging. This morning I received a letter from the Halifax Conservative Association which was most favourable, however, one can expect the McCutcheons, Fultons, and Hees to continue their work.

On the afternoon of the meeting at Strathroy, the Toronto Star had an article from an unidentified Conservative from London, Ontario to the effect that the leading Conservatives would be staying away from the meeting that night. It was obvious that this was the work of Mr.

---

*The diet was a no-carbohydrate, high protein diet created by Dr. William D. Howe, NDP M.P. for Hamilton South.

Halpenny who happened to be in Ottawa that day. I brought him to the Cabinet as Minister without Portfolio and an extra-marital involvement took place which brought about his decision not to be a candidate in the 1962 election. He then wanted to be a member of the Senate where he would be less subject to effective criticism.

Sevigny is writing a book on political revelations;* I wonder whether he will include some of his extramural activities. I am told that he is going to have the book carefully examined by his solicitors to guard against possible libel action. It might be better for him not to publish the book at all as the Prime Minister knows of his proclivities.

As I told you earlier, I am going to be in Weyburn about the middle of June, and will then go on to the Coast for a couple of days.

> With best wishes and
> kindest regards,
> I am,
> Yours sincerely,
> [John]

From John to Elmer
                                    Leader of the Opposition
                                    [Ottawa]
                                    Sunday
                                    September 5, 1965

Dear Elmer,

I am pleased with your report as to political matters in and about Nipawin, Codette and Shipman.

Without any indication (other than his B.C. and Alta. trip remarks), there is little to indicate what L.B. Pearson intends to do.

He is afraid of a recession in 1966; of Parliament in September, 1965; of another scandal in connection with the big bankruptcy case in Quebec City.*

He counts on division in our party – *but* fears me as a campaigner according to some press informants.

---

* Sevigny, Pierre. *This Game of Politics*. Toronto: McClelland & Stewart, 1965.
** See footnote to John's letter of December 9, 1964.

He let the cat out of the bag when in Edmonton eight days ago he blurted out that it was in Edmonton that during the election of 1963 he received a telephone call from the White House. His aides have explained since that it wasn't from Pres. Kennedy. Who but the janitor would call him! It's becoming clearer with the passing years that Washington did everything it could to help him in the elections of '62 and '63. Will Johnson do it this time? I think not.

Tomorrow may reveal the thinking of the P.M.* He is out at Harrington Lake – It's been renovated again ($6000 for the bathroom, $8000 for painting).

It may be that I shall go to Medicine Hat and Lethbridge for Friday and Saturday this week. Tomorrow I will have to decide and will let you know the decision.

If there is no election called – I shall go to Viet Nam in a few days – but no plans can be made so long as uncertainty exists.

> With all the Best,
> Your aff. Bro.,
> John

ᔐ

From Elmer to John   *National Hotel*
                                             Prince Albert, Sask.
                                             October 24, 1965

Dear John,

Fred Hadley told me you had called him up this morning and that you were very happy the way the campaign was going...

Ed Jackson took Dick Spencer, George Klein, Jim Martin and myself today to Sandy Lake Indian Reserve. We all gave speeches, the Chairman of the meeting being the Chief.

When we concluded the Chief delivered an address on citizenship as an elder statesman. He stated that he attended all political meetings and emphasized that all Indians should attend every political meeting in order to determine which candidate they should support. The Chief concluded his outstanding address with the memorable words – "That Pearson – his face makes me sick."

---

* The election was called on September 7.

All reports indicate the Indian vote will be pretty well solid....

I have heard it said quite frequently of late that you will take 175 seats. I do not know where this estimate originated. I would be quite happy if you could live up to 140 seats. Then Pearson would not have to worry anymore about Hal Banks & [Lucien] Rivard.

I must retire & get up in the morning.

> The Best,
> Elmer

✍

On November 8, 1965, the election results were: Liberals, 131; P.C.s, 91; NDP, 21; Créditiste, 9; Social Credit, 5; and Independent, 2.

From Elmer to John   *Box 1728*
                                        Saskatoon
                                        November 13, 1965

Dear John,

I was glad you 'phoned me and that you were in good spirits after a most gruelling campaign and the disappointing outcome.

I was most disappointed, to say the least, because I thought you would finish up with the largest group. I mulled this thing in my mind over and over. It became more difficult and finally one night I came up to 120 seats. I did not expect you would come below that level.

Regardless of some of the trash you read even now, you carried on a brilliant campaign and no one could have done better.

Nothing could be more ridiculous when you consider that Pearson got almost his whole count in 2 or 3 provinces. Out of 131 seats, he got 105 from two provinces, and 112 in three provinces. That means the rest of Canada is represented by 19 members.

I think it would be appropriate now that Pearson should sign all his correspondence as "Prime Minister of Ontario, Quebec and Newfoundland."

These people must be pretty thick in the head when they imagine Canada is in Confederation. They will say it is right because they all have a maple leaf flag.

Walter Gordon has offered himself on the alter of Sacrifice. Nevertheless I think there is more behind that and probably the sacrifice might have been more real if it were offered up before the election.

I don't know which paper it was, but awhile ago in one of the Eastern papers it said President Johnson referred to them as "bastards." He referred to Pearson and Gordon. Probably after that he wrote Pearson: "You tell the other bastard to resign."

I think you finished the Gallup poll for good & all. Von Ribbentrop[*] was bidding against himself and his final bid was up to 150 to 175 for the Grits. I imagine that is the last political auction sale Ribbentrop will attend.

On election night Mayor Cole and [Robert] Smellie came face to face. Lewis Brand said they were not very happy in each other's presence. There was a lot of growling and snarling in this Kennel Club and there was no need for Tom Douglas' heel-biting hound. These two got their lessons and I don't imagine Cole will be depending on Herb Pinder from now on as his spiritual advisor. He knows now what the meaning of politics is.

I have not heard very much about the election. Probably I'll hear more. As a matter of fact, I haven't talked to very many.

You will note from the enclosed news item [Mitchell] Sharp wanted a fall election so this is one instance where there is unanimity between the former and the present Finance Ministers.

There is a lot going on behind the scenes at present and the Grits are not not at all happy.

Sharp seemed to think that by spending 13 1/2 million to get a few Prairie seats was well worth the money spent. Be Sharp! Look Sharp!

I may have some other material later but I think you could well use this item. Ministers of Finance are good at voting money.

I got this registered letter from the Land Titles. I have done nothing about it.

My cold is much better but I'll see Dr. Baltzan on Monday. I'm not worried about it.

I expect to go to Regina on Tuesday and shall be away for a few days.

You better get lined up on Viet Nam, etc. It will get you & Olive away for awhile & if you don't do it next month you will be all tied up again.

The Best,
Elmer

---

[*] This was the Diefenbaker nickname for Peter Regenstreif, a political pollster.

From John to Elmer   *Office of the Leader of the*
                                            Opposition
                                            Ottawa
                                            November 24, 1965

Dear Elmer,

    The Caucus meeting of the Members was an excellent one and every-
body was in good humour. Lynch's article summarizes the situation.
The Tories are full of fight and the Grits are full of remorse and recrim-
ination. Hees and Fulton were there and Hees took the limelight. The
cartoons in this morning's Toronto Globe and Mail, and the Montreal
Gazette tell the story.

    Tom Van Dusen just came in and said the newspapers and pundits can't
get over it, that the Conservative Party is now a "happy" Party.

    Olive and I are getting ready to go to Nova Scotia for three days and
we will be returning to Ottawa on the 3rd of December. On the 10th we
will go to New York for the ocean cruise of ten days. The ship,
"Empress of Canada," calls at three ports – San Juan in Puerto Rico,
where a day is spent; St. Thomas in the Virgin Islands; and at Kingston,
Jamaica. Everything is going to be done to make our trip an enjoyable
one. I am told that Mr. Crump of the CPR is even interested because, as
he says, the ship having been launched by Olive – "belongs to Olive."

    I just received word this morning that Lewis McK. Robinson, father's
old friend and mine through the years, passed away yesterday in Regina.
You knew him too from the days when we lived on 9th Street, when he
was the City Solicitor. If you want to write a letter of condolence to Mrs.
Robinson, her address is 2348 Robinson Street, Regina, Saskatchewan.

                                            With all good wishes,
                                            Sincerely,
                                            John

                              ℘

From Elmer to John   *Robert E. Lee Hotel*
                                            Jackson, Mississippi
                                            February 25, 1966

Dear John,

    I had an interesting day. I arose about 6 o'clock, at the Buena Vista
Hotel in Biloxi. Caught the 7:30 bus to New Orleans. It was lucky I got

the bus. The owner of the taxi line was driving his own cab this morning. He said four of these young bucks, taxi drivers, did not turn up for work this morning & did not even bother to communicate with him. The boss just found that nobody turned up. He said these young squirts don't bother. They got money in their pockets and they are liable to take off any time. I was lucky the boss had to deliver somebody to the Buena Vista Hotel this morning and I grabbed the cab and got to the bus depot.

It poured rain this morning all the way into New Orleans. I would have come into New Orleans yesterday, but I was tired after Mardi Gras and took it easy. I lay on the bed and went to sleep. I am fine today.

I got into Jackson at 6:00 P.M. and decided to stay over here and go on to Memphis, Tennessee at 1:20 tomorrow.

I heard that Jackson is a beautiful city and it is. I'll browse around in the morning. The restaurant keeper told me to see the City Hall, that was renovated last year. He said the City Hall is actually the Masonic Temple & the lodge rooms are on top and it was built during the Civil War.

The old State Capitol is quite a building & there is a museum there.

The "new" Capitol was built in 1903. It is a most imposing building about 2 blocks away from the Robert E. Lee Hotel – the latter is next to the bus depot.

The Capitol is beautiful illuminated at night. I saw it illuminated and wandered over there. It was open and the squad was cleaning up. The foreman was a nice chap. He told me to take my time and wander around. I was very much impressed.

In front of the main entrance inside is a lone statue of your good friend Bilbo who amused you. He is of Tom Thumb stature. The foreman asked me if I had heard of Bilbo. I told him everybody knew Bilbo as he was a most controversial individual. This Baptist Church preacher-man Bilbo turned loose about 100 Negro prisoners from their prisons to make sure that he would be re-elected and was blame near impeached on the floor of the Senate. I understand he died right after that, which served as a delaying action. I told our friend that you had followed Bilbo's career. This fellow knew about you.

Across the street is the First Baptist Church, a magnificent stone church that extends right along the whole block. I don't know whether Bilbo preached there or not.

Incidentally, wherever you go you see a "First Baptist Church." The name "First Baptist Church" is not confined to Saskatoon.

Leaving New Orleans you cross the 24 mile bridge across Lake Pontchartrain, built by your other friend, Huey P. Long in 1935. This concrete structure is now considered inadequate and they are now talking about rebuilding it. They also have 2 1/2 mile long bridges across Tampa Bay in Florida. I thought we were crossing the Atlantic.

I had to go to the Bank in New Orleans. I showed the young fellow your letter. He told me John D. was defeated three years ago and was succeeded by Pearson. I was quite amazed because he was the only one so far who knew Pearson's name.

I hurriedly had something to eat at Woolworth's and just got my bus to Jackson.

By that time the bus was pretty well filled. I grabbed the first seat, sitting next to an attractive woman, who had just come back from Florida and said she was going back to Canada. I asked her where she lived and she said Camrose [Alberta]. Her husband is office manager in that cereal plant in Camrose and she knows Smallwood. She said she was tied up when you visited Camrose during your election and said your party was late arriving in Camrose. She knows the Chester Ronning family and says they are spending the winter in California. This Mrs. Bradley went on to Memphis, and staying on the bus to Wichita, Kansas. She was born and raised in Portage La Prairie and knew Arthur Meighen. She is going to stop off in Winnipeg for a week.

She was in Ortona Beach in Florida and tells me Ortona is filled with people from Ottawa.

I wish I had been in Florida about two years ago. Through my short experience, I realize a fellow could have carried on a most extensive election campaign here in Florida.

You say I talk too much. I listen to what they have to say but I find if you can give them about two good ideas, they'll carry the ball. I told Mrs. Bradley that it was difficult to stomach Grits in Canada, but when you came down to Florida to find grits on the menu, that's the straw that breaks the camel's back.

Our friend Mrs. Wilson from Ottawa told me that she could not stomach grits, either in Canada or in Florida. Grits are on every menu in Florida.

I had to take a taxi today off Canal Street in New Orleans to get my bus. A bird parked in his car on the street was holding up the traffic and for the first time I heard some first class swearing on the part of the taxi driver, in the southern drawl. It was most refreshing. After that a colored boy got in the way. The taxi driver called out "Move on you S.O.B."

I sent a card to Bob McKay. I told Bob, if a Scotsman with his Gaelic or Scotch brogue were to come face to face with a Southerner with the Southern drawl, and both of them started talking together, they would soon stop talking and just look at each other.

My friend from New Jersey has a slight Southern drawl, but she tells me she can't understand anything these colored people say. I can't understand a word and all I say "You seem to be right." They are all the same whether they come from "Ailebama" or anywhere else.

I leave Jackson at 1:30 & will be in Memphis tomorrow night, then on to St. Louis & Chicago. Everybody keeps going "for $99 for 99 days."

I must get along and get up in the morning.

> Affectionately,
> Elmer

ℐ

From John to Elmer   *Office of the Leader of the*
                                        Opposition
                                        Ottawa
                                        March 17, 1966

Dear Elmer,

Your birthday is Monday and we will celebrate it a few days later when Olive and I are in Saskatoon.

It is just a week today that I arrived on the northwest corner of Vancouver Island and was informed of the [Lucien] Cardin press conference. Much has happened in the intervening days in which has been included the mysterious breaking in at "Stornoway" last Friday night or Saturday.

No one can predict what will happen in the investigation. There is no limit to the ferocity of the Liberal Party. For years they have attacked me personally by everything at their disposal. Nothing has ever held them back. Slander and falsehood are the weapons. The Munsinger woman certainly made it clear in the TV appearance that she owed no debt to the Russians who attacked her over and over again when she was a little girl. There is nothing that I have ever heard that there is anything in the file to indicate that she was a spy and she has denied that. Without evidence the plan is to smear by innuendo and suggestion. There seems a widespread demand for the Prime Minister's resignation among most Liberal newspapers. However, they also add my name as a counter weight. Their demands for my departure from public life will have the same effect on me as any such suggestion over the years!

Today is St. Patrick's day and it is a year ago today that I was very close to hanging up my running shoes. What a difference a year makes!

Affectionately,
John

∽

From John to Elmer

Private & Confidential

House of Commons
[Ottawa]
April 22, 1966

Dear Elmer,

I am busy preparing for the Spence Commission. It's a problem to know what to do because what is being done in that Pearson-Cardin Commission [is] destined to destroy me.

Monday it will begin again and will continue through the week except for an adjournment on Tuesday.

It is apparent that the Commissioner is trying to find grounds to damage the Conservative Govt. and me in particular. It is an indication of Pearson's attitude that he applauded Cardin when he was attacking me in the course of his Munsinger charges.

Things will turn out alright I feel sure.

Newspapers are challenging [the] Spence secrecy decision and they must have been effective as I heard today that on Monday the session will be open to begin with. I shall keep you informed as to progress and if you are out of Saskatoon you might call me on the phone.

I hope you are getting along successfully with your endeavors to get membership to the R.M. [Retail Merchants] Association.

Olive is feeling somewhat improved. I am well and full of energy.

John

∽

From John to Elmer

Office of the Leader of the
Opposition
April 27, 1966

Dear Elmer,

As we approach the end of April it becomes necessary to make an income tax return. I did, and while all of my deductions for indemnities as Member and Leader of the Opposition were made on cheques issued to me, I still had to make up almost $3000.00. I would be better off if I did not have any money on deposit in banks and trust companies!

Pearson has bought himself a house. It is about two blocks from the Leader of the Opposition's home, and according to Pat Nicholson its maximum value is much below what he paid for it. Apparently he was very annoyed with the Caucus some weeks ago and decided to resign and the house was then purchased, at a price of $70,000. Since then he has changed his mind. The annoyance arose out of the attitude and actions of Cardin in the House, and when all the French members of the cabinet decided to resign unless Cardin received the consideration they believed he should, retreat by the Prime Minister was the order of the day.

I was talking to Ed Topping this morning and he gave me the news of Prince Albert. He said Jack Cuelenaere is holding meetings all over his constituency of Shellbrook which would seem to indicate the possibility of an early general election in the province.

In conversation with certain leaders of the Government party in the province, there is great fear of the NDP coming back into office. Indeed, the Premier informed me that if anybody else but [Woodrow] Lloyd was leading them it would be a pretty difficult task to meet the challenge. This conversation is of course, confidential, and took place a couple of weeks ago when the Premier called on me.

The Spence Commission resumed this morning. Counsel for Fulton and I demanded production of the police reports and it adjourned for 10 minutes to look into them, but it was more than an hour later before the sittings resumed.

The Commissioner is very arbitrary and very much one-sided, but he is doing a pretty good job in threatening the press. Indeed, he advised them that he might have a security investigation made into some of the revelations that have been made recently. This attitude on his part does Davie and me no harm.

Fulton will go on the stand either in the late afternoon or tomorrow.

I am quite lazy these days and haven't been doing much in the House. However, the matters that are being discussed are not those that require any participation by me.

With all good wishes,
Your brother,
John

From John to Elmer   *Office of the Leader of the*
                                        Opposition
                                        Ottawa
                                        May 20, 1966

Dear Elmer,

I sent a telegram to Ross Walker in regard to the awards to be presented to the various Saskatchewan merchants and referred to the fact that you had brought this to my attention.

Yesterday I was in Montreal and spoke to the American Publishers Association. They gave me an excellent reception.

Today the Toronto Globe and Mail has a long article on the Munsinger affair and a vicious editorial against me. I am sending this to you.

Pat Nicholson, who is once more in a friendly mood, wrote an article which sets out what is behind the investigation. It is obvious that the findings by the Commissioner will be condemnatory but I don't fear the effect because the reports I get, to use your expression, are that people are "fed up with the whole matter."

Many Members of the House are greatly disturbed about the bomb scare and the consequence will be that some additional security measures will be taken. I am opposed to this being done as I think it will remove Parliament from the people. The bomb-carrier intended to blow up the House of Commons and if it had not been for the premature explosion he would have been able to throw the bomb over the gallery, closest to the washroom, and it would have been right over the heads of the Opposition third parties. This is another example of the uncertainty of life!

On Wednesday evening I spoke to the Teacher's College Dinner Meeting and there was close to one thousand present. The Principal recalled that Father went to that school but reported that there were no pictures of the Class of 1891 as far as he knew.

I hope that the Convention was a success.

                                        With all good wishes,
                                        Affectionately,
                                        John

P.S. I am going out fishing tomorrow to spend the day about 40 miles from Ottawa.

On Sunday, Jack Bigg, M.P. has convened a dinner of former Prince Albert people and Olive and I intend to be present.

From John to Elmer   *Office of the Leader of the*
                                        Opposition
                                        Ottawa
                                        May 31, 1966

Dear Elmer,

Originally it was intended that Olive would accompany me but now, in view of her condition and her agreement that it would be foolish for her to take the trip to Prince Albert, she will not be accompanying me.

Attached is a summary of my itinerary so that you will know where I will be. If you will take me to Prince Albert you might be able to work out of there during my stay.

I am informed on pretty good authority that Commissioner Spence has had his report written even before the evidence was in. However, it is something one cannot prove, although he did state at the Governor General's Ball three weeks or so ago that he had it ready. He had joined generously in the consumption of whiskey and he spoke with non-judicial irresponsibility.

Brigadier Wardell in the Fredericton "Gleaner" has written an editorial on the Spence Commission which is sent herewith.

I haven't been in Saskatchewan since the 26th of March and am happy at the prospect of the meeting.

                                        With best wishes,
                                        Your brother,
                                        John

ᔪ

In early July a reporter from *The Toronto Star* contacted Elmer and elicited comments from him on the Spence Commission.

From Elmer to John   *Box 1728*
                                        Saskatoon
                                        July 11, 1966

Dear John,

I understand now I should have ripped into Spence, but I suppose I am a bit too cautious. If I had spoken my mind it would not have done Spence any good.

However, I had the same thought that you had that Davie Fulton was talking out of turn again, thinking that his statements would remain unanswered.

The report was that it was "Someone *high* up in the Conservative Party." He will be in a sort of a mess if he made those statements.

I just told him you were "over & above board" in everything.

They can't pin anything down on what I said but probably Fulton will get a fast ride. He should be in the House of Commons where he belongs.

I don't think there is anything to worry about, even though I did not express any of the opinions on Spence that I should have.

Nobody has any respect for this fellow Spence & I suppose I should have told them that Spence dragged the Supreme Court down to a very low level and should run as a Liberal candidate. There are two openings now with two Members going to the Senate.

If Fulton made these statements he will be rather embarrassed. At no time did you discuss resignation as a result of Spence's report. I do think someone should make an announcement that Spence should resign immediately from the Supreme Court of Canada because he has done the court no honor. He must be dragged through the mud.

I am glad you are taking Olive west. This should improve her condition.

I'll see you when you arrive & hope everything goes well....

I must get this letter in the mail & hope everything will be alright.

> Your Brother,
> Elmer

From John to Elmer

*Office of the Leader of the
Opposition
Ottawa
July 12, 1966*

Dear Elmer,

You don't want to be concerned about your conversation with the Toronto "Star." The fact that you said nothing is possibly better than to have launched into an attack on Commissioner Spence. The suggestion made to you that Spence will condemn me and I will then resign, and that this information has been secured from a Conservative in high places, would indicate that Davie Fulton was the source from whom the hoped-for announcement originated. I have not had an opportunity of asking about this but will very soon....

I will be seeing you shortly.

> With all good wishes,
> Affectionately,
> Your brother,
> John

ɔ

From John to Elmer   *Office of the Leader of the*
                                         Opposition
                                         Ottawa
                                         July 12, 1966

Dear Elmer,

I keep warning you not to buy things for me but you continually do so. The latest is the Funk & Wagnalls Dictionary. Thank you very much. It is a very handy dictionary and will receive lots of use.

Olive and I had a letter from John Weir [Carolyn and Don Weir's son], who is now 8 years old, and this is how he produced one word – "mis-chuffe"! That is the most unusual spelling and I sent him a pocket dictionary, and almost simultaneously your presentation arrived. I am beginning to wonder what word I mispelled in my last letter to you! Thank you again.

> With best wishes,
> John

ɔ

From Elmer to John   *Box 1728*
                                         Saskatoon
                                         July 16, 1966

Dear John,

I'll drop a few lines this morning. I trust everything is going alright and that Olive will show great improvement.

I think I took the right course when I got the telephone call from Toronto. Probably I should have lashed out at Spence because these silly Tories, with the exception of [Erik] Nielsen, keep their peace.

When they asked me questions I suspected this fellow Fulton. My answers were direct and if he gets into hot water, some of these Tories, in the future, might be more careful what they say.

This bird asked me if the humiliation of such a report would cause you to resign. I told him you had nothing to worry about because you have been over and above board in everything. He agreed with me.

If I had been on the bit at the time I could have brought comparisons of two Grit politicians. One walked the Valley of Humiliation and was alone when he was on the tramp. All these characteristics are common to Grit worker Spence. Now that the humiliation issue is raised you might give an interview on this issue yourself.

Spence has to be sweared completely and I don't think he will be able to take it....

> Affectionately,
> Elmer

From John to Elmer   *Office of the Leader of the*
                                        Opposition
                                        Ottawa
                                        August 16, 1966

Dear Elmer,

We had a good trip back and Olive and I should benefit by the rest.

This morning I am busy as can be trying to get some of my correspondence answered. Ottawa is in an uproar over the failures of the Government and even the most worshipful of the press are beginning to wonder.

There was an article in the "Globe & Mail" on Saturday which among other things stated as follows:

"Among the world's tattooed are such prominent figures as Opposition leader John Diefenbaker, with a double eagle on his left shoulder..."

I wonder sometimes where their false and even libellous statements come from and I am going to write a letter to the "Globe & Mail", although the danger always is that one would advertise something that would otherwise not be referred to. However, I cannot allow that type of thing to go unchallenged. The reference to the "two eagles" apparently is to do with the 33rd Degree in Masonry.

I am attaching my cheque for $45.00 to cover the advance you made to me, and also the expenses to which you were put.

> With best wishes,
> Your brother,
> John

∽

From Elmer to John   *Star City*
                                        August 18, 1966

Dear John,

It was a long vacation for you and Olive for a change although you did not get too much rest in Prince Albert.

Olive was feeling pretty miserable before she left and I do hope she is feeling better now. She appeared much improved and I trust her stay in B.C. will have beneficial results.

I trust you will be able to get away to Formosa [Taiwan] and now it is possible to do so. I know you have worried about relinquishing the leadership. Indeed if you did take this trip, if Olive's condition is alright, you would be out of the country on the occasion of your birthday, so it would not be necessary to make the announcement on that date that you have been worrying about. I thought it was the wisest thing to give the Toronto Star an emphatic "no" when they called me. They got no information out of me that they wanted and so they cannot quote me.

Insofar as Spence is concerned, he is now a dead duck. He took a flying chance but has lost the respect of everyone.

Neil Crawford told me that a judge of the King's Bench in Alberta, who has been on the bench for years and who was appointed by the Liberals, is very much disgusted with Spence and he told me that is the general opinion.

Pearson is too much beset by rail strikes and other matters at the moment to bother himself about Spence. Whatever the findings of the report he will be in hot water and it would have been much better if he had left his fingers out of that. Nobody wants to worry about that kind of trash, when the world is in such a mess.

I thought Hazen Argue would say something about $2.00 wheat or something of that nature, but the strange thing, he was not even mentioned in the press as being present.

The public is very suspicious of Thatcher with his new party talk, as being a complete hoax. He is not liked at all and he has lots of trouble.

You managed to become Prime Minister at the right time. That can never be taken away and your record was good. You were very disappointed that you did not make it again, but then you would have been so much more disappointed if you had not made it at all. There are going to be real disappointments among real ambitious people who would be prime ministers, and things have come to such a mess at home and abroad that I don't think there is any man who will be able to come up with the right answers.

Pearson has made such an awful mess out of everything that he makes you stronger every day.

I can't tell you what to do, but I think you and Olive should go to Formosa when you have the opportunity. I know it is very difficult to make decisions as there are so many strings attached,

When I look back into the past and think of all the difficulties that beset themselves, it is indeed a miracle that you did reach your ambition. Olive did a great deal to get you there. You must remember that those who have personal ambitions are in fear all the time and they never reach their goal.

I was talking to a fellow in Nipawin today, who played hockey with Simpson at Flin Flon, and he told me that they know around Flin Flon that you and Simpson were the ones who gave them the Hanson Lake road.

I was at Choiceland last night and they are very much pleased with your speech.

They are fanatically loyal in Nipawin and they are behind you 100%.

Everyone in Prince Albert was happy because you were there. I saw Fred Hadley for a minute and he said so many mentioned that they were very happy that you were at the fair.

Neil Crawford told me you got a tremendous ovation at the Stampede. He said Calgarians have no use for Kennedy [?] and he did not know why Kennedy was invited.

Neil told me he expects to be a candidate in Alberta in the next provincial election.

I am going to Melfort in the morning and shall work back. It is difficult to get people in now but I am doing alright.

I enjoyed thoroughly getting away for the two weeks but was disappointed that the rains came in the middle of the fishing. You did well landing the Rainbow trout.

It has been raining and thus the harvest has been delayed. I hope it clears.

I dropped in at Mrs. Cameron Lytle's. She was away at the time visiting her brother the store keeper at Alingly. They gave me supper and her son-in-law took me out to see the crop. It is terrific and he told me one field was ready for combining this week but the rains are holding everything up.

I visited the travel agency in Saskatoon, but they know nothing about the China tour. It is a U.N. Chartered tour. I think Ariel Sallows knows about it and I'll see him one of these days.

Among other things there is a special C.P.R. cherry blossom tour by luxury ship at the end of February to Japan and, if you wish, you can return by air and visit wherever you wish.

When I get things straightened around I think I'll take your advice and start spending and see things. My pension will start at the beginning of the year so I won't have much to worry about. I might have four years with no strings attached like Fred Hadley.

Everything goes well and trust everything will work out alright.

Affectionately,
Elmer

∽

From John to Elmer

*Office of the Leader of the
Opposition
Ottawa
August 22, 1966*

Dear Elmer,

Your letter writing from Star City is quite a masterpiece. I was touched by your references to Olive and the tremendous contribution that she has made.

The house on Acacia is a cold and damp one and she is already beginning to show the detrimental effects of living there. While it may be misunderstood, I think there is only one thing to do and that is to move into an apartment for the winter. She feels that she must carry on as we have but that is not my view. When winter comes it will assuredly mean that her trouble will be greatly accentuated.

I am glad that you decided that you are not going to spend your winters in Saskatchewan and that you are now planning a trip to the Far East. I will have Miss Pound make inquiries as to the trip to Communist China which is being arranged under CIIA [Canadian Institute of International Affairs] auspices for next March.

This morning the announcement was made that the railway strike of the non-operating trades will begin on Friday morning. Even [with] a Government that will not act until things become of crisis proportion, the Prime Minister can do no other than call Parliament together.

Your brother,
John

ℐ

From Elmer to John   *Saskatoon*
                              September 11, 1966

Dear John,

I must drop you a line as I called on old lady Doerksen this afternoon. The old lady said: "That is Elmer – Elmer and John were little boys." She was so happy.

Mrs. Doerksen had so often talked about Mr. & Mrs. Diefenbaker, John & Elmer over the years.

The relatives called on her yesterday to celebrate her 95th birthday. She received a great many cards, but the thing that really pleased her was receiving your wire at noon. Her daughter and son-in-law, Stobbe, said she was just thrilled to get your greeting and she has spoken of you so often.

The old lady said: "Just to think that I received a telegram from John Diefenbaker."

That really set things off, and they could not figure out how John Diefenbaker knew the date of her birthday.

Last night John Doerksen phoned her from B.C. They asked him if he had written John Diefenbaker to give him the birthday of his mother and he said "No." So they were all baffled. Anyway, I just wanted you to know the old lady is in seventh heaven and the family very much pleased.

Her mind is perfectly clear. She fell down and broke her hip but she was only in hospital for four days and it is completely mended. Her doctor was amazed.

She said John & Elmer slept on the floor of their house for a week, when the shack was being built.

She told me a great many neighbours got together to build the shack. In a few days the shack was up. We moved into it in a few days and after that the interior was finished.

The Doerksens had always spoken of the Diefenbakers as good neighbors.

Mrs. Doerksen said they came from Russia in 1905 and neither she nor her husband could speak a word of English. She said [Uncle] Ed, being fluent in German & English, would interpret and this pleased old Doerksen very much.

After Ed left the homestead he went back there to take applications for loans and to sell land and he got his meals at Doerksens'.

They are quite a family and have done well. The old lady has about 140 or 150 great grandchildren....

It is an amazing thing after all these years to call on this old lady who has all her faculties, and to learn that after all these years speaking so often of the Diefenbakers, that she should receive your wire on her 95th anniversary. It was very refreshing.

The old lady liked mother very much.

The Stobbes told me one day you were out with Gerhard snaring gophers. A fight ensued. Gerhard threatened to spank you. You ran off and that ended the incident.

The old lady told me one day you told her that you were going to be a lawyer....

A good many P.C.'s are as innocent as babes in the crib, however, the day you retire, they will elect about the same number of members that the P.C.'s elected in Newfoundland last week.

Indeed you will celebrate another anniversary a week from today. It is a bit difficult for me to look back through the mists of time to the homestead days. About the only thing I can recall clearly, Tip got a fast ride from the mow in the stable to terra firma.

I have a lot of pictures, but I wish I had started taking pictures on the homestead. I wish I had some pictures of the building of the shack. It was quite interesting when Mrs. Doerksen told me the shack was up in a few days. She also told me the name of the man who dug the well. She remembers everything.

The Best,
Elmer

From John to Elmer   *Office of the Leader of the*
                                        Opposition
                                        Ottawa
                                        September 21, 1966

Dear Elmer,

We are on our way and I thought you should read what is going on. Mr. Camp wants to be leader and he thinks he will get a lot of publicity. He has been working ever since the last Convention to make trouble.

A few minutes ago John Bassett of the Toronto Telegram, who personally and as owner of the newspaper opposed me in 1963, phoned me that tomorrow the Telegram will have an editorial condemning Camp, and also a cartoon showing me inviting him into the office and when he steps inside the office he will fall into a bottomless pit. The editorial says that anyone who has opposed me through the years has ended up in defeat. I am not worried although I am concerned over the fact that as soon as the Party gets united there is always someone to throw monkey wrenches.

The speech I make tomorrow evening in Toronto will not of course be published in any way. It will have nothing to do with leadership.

After you have read these newspaper clippings you might send them on to Ed Topping in Prince Albert.

                              With all good wishes,
                              Affectionately,
                              Your brother,
                              John

                              ✺

From John to Elmer   *Office of the Leader of the*
                                        Opposition
                                        Ottawa
                                        September 26, 1966

Dear Elmer,

Olive and I returned late Saturday night. We drove up from Montreal and Tommy Van Dusen was able to brief me on what had happened when I was away.

Olive had a wonderful time at Plymouth and it is rather a unique experience for any descendant of the Pilgrims to see that two of the six houses that have been reconstituted were those of her ancestors, Elder Brewster and Richard Warren.

You have told me of the feeling shown to me in the United States. It was as you stated. On every hand people stopped and shook hands and this was so not only at Plymouth, where naturally it became known that Olive and I were around, but in Boston. At Plymouth the President of the Conservative Association of Sudbury, who introduced me to a meeting in the campaign in that city, had a great surprise when he ran into me. Yesterday morning, as Olive and I stood and looked at Old Ironsides, the American battleship of the Civil War, a woman came over to me and said: "Did anyone ever tell you that you looked like John Diefenbaker?" She was from Toronto and it was not long before we understood each other.

The Consul-General and his wife could not have done more for us. Olive's greatest pleasure was to visit the home of Louisa M. Alcott, the writer of "Little Women," which Olive can almost quote from beginning to end.

The political storm which followed the publication of the Spence Report is, I am told today, receding and there is a strong reaction in my favor. There will be an article today or tomorrow in the Fredericton "Gleaner" that Camp, who was a Liberal supporter and on the staff of Premier [John] McNair, the Liberal Premier of New Brunswick [from 1940-52], became so ambitious that McNair thought he was trying to take over. He is front man for Davie Fulton.

On Saturday in Vancouver there was a meeting of the Conservative Executive and amongst those who fought for me were Gowan Guest, Stuart Fleming, Buzz Matthews, Howard Green and George Chatterton [M.P. Esquimalt-Saanich]. Howard pointed at Davie and said: "Being a traitor will never make you leader and I tell you you will never be leader." Fulton lowered his head.

For several weeks I have known that J.M. Macdonnell has been in communication with Martin Pederson and I learned a day or so ago that he had joined with Camp. He has been complaining that sufficient money has not been made available to him to run Headquarters and apparently he is satisfied that there is going to be a change in the money supply. I informed Dr. [Lewis] Brand that Pederson had been approached to make a settlement by Dick Spencer, and while he was loud in his appreciation of me, said he was not going to make any statement but the Annual Meeting would decide the course to follow. Lewis was greatly surprised and has already wired me that he will do everything he can to help when he comes back from the United Nations at the end of next week.

Spencer told Pederson that the decision will not be made in Ottawa but will be made at the Saskatchewan Convention on October 14th.

I have a couple of appointments for early in October, one of which I am very sorry to have to turn down now. That was to debate at Hart House in Toronto on the 6th of October on the subject of Parliament, and the other to speak to the Law Students of Osgoode Hall on the 12th. I have to cancel out the first for to do otherwise would be to invite every Liberal and NDPer in the forum to clobber me.

These things blow over and later on it would not really matter but to attend so soon after the Munsinger Report would not be helpful to me.

On Thursday evening I spoke in Toronto to the Albany Club. The place only holds 125 diners and after, dinner being over, another 50 came in. With the exception of 5 or 6 at the outside, there was general and very warm support.

Olive developed a bad cold on the trip and I showed signs yesterday of having one coming on so stayed indoors and took pills.

I cannot tell you yet just when I will be in Saskatoon but it will not be too long.

> With all good wishes,
> Your brother,
> John

P.S. Ken Banks called me this morning and he said that he was agreeably surprised at the reaction to the report. Generally speaking, it was favorable. Your answer to the "Star" was alright. Next time tell them to go to a hotter climate!

∽

From Elmer to John   *Box 1728*
                                        Saskatoon
                                        September 27, 1966

Dear John,

I was glad you called me yesterday and am very pleased with Howard Green. Howard was a man who never did support you, but after you formed the government he has been loyal.

I like the stand of Howard Green. He told Fulton a plain statement of fact and if there were a few more like him it would be a lot better for all concerned. In the cartoon in the Winnipeg Tribune, it showed a bunch of mice bringing up a big bell to bell the big cat. Howard Green was not among these mice – Fulton was.

It just takes one or two in each province, like Fulton, to ruin the P.C. Party in each province. Balcer performed this service well in Quebec and [James] MacDonnell has worked very hard in Ontario.

In Saskatchewan not very much is known about the activities of Pederson – nobody has seen him for weeks – I have not seen him in months.

I phoned Agnes Kinear, but she is out of town for a couple of weeks. I imagine she would have some information.

As soon as I got the story of a petition being circulated on Saturday, I got in touch with John Hnatyshyn and I phoned him at the house on Sunday morning before he went to church.

John immediately got in touch with his son Ray, who began investigating immediately very quietly. He got no information on the activity of Pederson.

He (Pederson) did announce that he wanted to be confirmed in his leadership at a leadership convention and that was in the press at the time.

If I know anything about it he will be fired out. This thing has been brought to my attention regularly but I have never mixed up in it in any way and have never expressed any opinions on this subject.

Jack Wilson has always attacked him in a vile manner, but I never expressed any viewpoint.

Probably the best way to find out before his Moose Jaw Convention where he stands would be to force him to make a public announcement in Davidson, as to where he stands, and then fire him out at the Moose Jaw Convention. I think he will be thrown out in any case, because everyone realizes he will get nowhere.

You mentioned to get in touch with Arscott, but John H. thinks Ray can dig up this information much better.

As soon as Hnatyshyn gets some definite information on his activities John will take positive action.

John told me he has not been in touch with him for months. He says Pederson knows he has no use for him and I guess they don't get together too much.

I haven't been out with the R.M.A. for a couple of weeks or more. When I was out actively I was able to get the odd bit of information....

> Anyway,
> The best of luck,
> Elmer

From John to Elmer   *Office of the Leader of the*
                                        Opposition
                                        Ottawa
                                        November 8, 1966

Dear Elmer,

   This morning's Globe and Mail indicates that Elmer Bell, President
of the Ontario Association, is going to support Camp. This will be interpreted to mean that the Ontario Government will be of the same view.
The clipping is attached.

   Yesterday's Globe and Mail had an article regarding the Ontario
Convention and it showed Camp's Headquarters was a "boozorium."
That clipping is also attached.

   I am concerned that a terrific fight is shaping up which can only do
harm to the Party for years to come. Olive and I are concerned about
you. You always feel everything so keenly and I hope that you will not
get into controversies personally, and whatever is said in criticism of
me, whether inside or outside the Convention, will be listened to by you
without comment. I know it is going to be hard to do but for your own
sake it will be best. You are so devoted that whatever is said or done
against me hurts you personally.

   I have nothing ready for the meeting and I must take a day off and go
to work. I have to speak to the Women's Meeting on Monday morning
and to the Association as a whole on the same day – all of this of course
depends on whether the National Executive reverses the programme
which was sent out by Dr. [James] Johnston, the National Director. He
phoned Camp about the middle of September and asked him to come to
Ottawa. He wrote him twice after – the purpose of the suggested meeting
being to get the organization ready for the Annual Meeting, but instead
of coming to Ottawa he launched the attack on me.

   I will be calling you on the telephone.

                                        Affectionately,
                                        John

P.S. I am sending you under separate cover by first class mail, the
speeches by Camp in 1963-64-65. I think it would be well to hand these
to John Hnatyshyn for study and use.

From John to Elmer   *Office of the Leader of the*
                                        Opposition
                                        Ottawa
                                        November 9, 1966

Dear Elmer,

I am disappointed at being informed by Ed Jackson that he is not coming. He makes a patent excuse that he has lost eight days recently, but his wife told me when I talked to her on the phone that he still had a couple of weeks of vacation time still available. It is the one time that he was needed and could have been very helpful. However, I have already written him and impressed on him the need of being here and will do no more.

The unification debate still continues and will go on next week. I think what the Government will try to do will be get it wound up when the Members are at the Annual Meeting.

I don't know whether I sent you the cartoon on the "Dump Dief" programme, but you will note in the cartoon that he is waiting. The other cartoon is also a Western one. An article by Lum Clark in the Windsor City Star is beginning to represent a viewpoint. These cartoons you might return to me. I do not know what the papers will do when I finally leave!

We will be able to talk things over after you arrive in Ottawa. On your trip East have a good time and don't worry about things. I am not going to be concerned. If things turn out badly for me that will be the end for me.

Fulton is continuing his undermining operations and seems confident that he is going to succeed. I have never been able to predict the result of these things.

I have not taken part in the debate in the House on unification but the Members of the Party have. Both groups, those who are for and those who are against, have been holding up Supply and if it continues it will mean an early election. Conservative Members have no intention of giving up their opposition.

                                        With all good wishes,
                                        Your brother,
                                        John

From John to Elmer   *[Office of the Leader of the*
                                        Opposition]
                                        Ottawa
                                        November 23, 1966

Dear Elmer,

I went over to Caucus today and there received an important call and when I got through with the call Caucus was over. All of the Fultonites were there in force. They apparently thought I was going to make an announcement.

Any final decision will not be given to them but to my friends and supporters, and then to the Nation as a whole.

I am going in the House today for a short while but am not sticking around. The Estimates are up in Committee and there is really no need for me to be present.

Alvin Hamilton debated with Tommy Douglas before the student body on Saturday afternoon. Alvin really went after your friend "Tom" and showed that he had departed from every principle and denounced him as a renegade from Socialism. When he finished Douglas had a two-minute reply and all he said was for "the life of me I can't understand why Mr. Hamilton made such a savage attack on me, I'm not a Conservative!" From there on it was not Alvin's meeting.

For no good reason Olive decided to clean up house yesterday and she was pretty well all in last night.

I hope you found everything all right when you got home.

I have pretty well decided not to send out Christmas cards excepting to a few personal friends, and instead of spending a tremendous sum as normally we do on cards and postage, feel the right idea is to make a contribution of a couple of thousand dollars to the Crippled Children's Fund, or something of that kind.

                        With all good wishes,
                        Affectionately,
                        John

P.S. No decision has been made yet as to when I will go West but I don't anticipate going until the strike is settled and I can travel by air.

From John to Elmer   *Office of the Leader of the*
                                        Opposition
                                        Ottawa
                                        December 2, 1966

Dear Elmer,

When you write Tooke [Foster] you can tell her how much I appreciated her letter to you regarding the National Progressive Conservative meeting.

I see a reference in the press that I have not been taking much part in the House and that it has been very dull. Dr. Rynard has been in charge of the debate on Medicare but Fulton tried to take over which annoyed the doctor no end.

It is interesting to watch Fulton these days as he meets with people whom he had never even noticed before, and also with the press. He is doing what he described to me at one time, and which his wife said no one excelled him in, and that is "cultivating" people.

I just learned of an incident that took place in the 1962 election when Fulton spoke at Melville on behalf of Jim Ormiston. After the meeting he decided to meet with people and after he would walk up to people and introduce himself. Standing by himself in the background against the wall was an individual poorly dressed and obviously keeping out of the way, and Fulton walked up to him and said: "I am Davie Fulton, the Minister in Ottawa. You look an awful lot like Drum Clancy. Did anyone ever tell you that?" He said: "I am"!

There is also a great deal of pressure on me now to make an announcement of what I am going to do. I have determined on that but have to choose an appropriate time. It is rather too long to wait until the 14th of December which will be the tenth anniversary of my election as leader, but that might be the best.

All of this, of course, is dependent on when I can go West. As yet there is nothing. My pal Mike Crammond, the Sports editor of the Vancouver "Province," informs me that the fish are out of sight because of recent heavy rains but as soon as the salmon and the steelhead decide to be around and about again he will let me know.

I had a letter from a lawyer in Brockville, Albert B. Henderson, and in that letter he says: "I am personally proud that my son spent three days in Ottawa during the convention working for Arthur Maloney and in

your support. The work of your brother, Elmer, was especially notice-
able. He made many friends on your behalf."

I will be in touch with you over the weekend and you may be sure I will
let you know well in advance of my trip West so that if you want to come
along to the Coast you may do so.

> With best wishes,
> Your brother,
> John

∽

From John to Elmer   *Office of the Leader of the*
                                        Opposition
                                        Ottawa
                                        December 8, 1966

Dear Elmer,

It begins to look now that we will be sitting on Saturday because Mr.
[Gilles] Gregoire, M.P., the separatist ally of the Liberal Party refused
to consent to the legislation to put an end to the Vancouver Longshoremen's strike.

There has been no word yet as to any improvement in the fishing
possibilities on the Pacific Coast, but as soon as things improve Mike
Crammond will be notifying me. It is fortunate, however, that I am here
at this time, because my absence could not be justified during the debate
on the Longshoremen's strike. From all appearances now, I would say
that the earliest date for leaving would be a week from today, and that of
course will depend on the circumstances then existing.

Next Wednesday will be the Tenth Anniversary of my Leadership of
the Party, and it will be necessary for me to be here that day.

Today is our 13th Wedding Anniversary, and Olive has a very busy
day with three different gatherings, one of which is the meeting of the
wives of the Conservative Caucus.

The number of Christmas cards sent out has mounted year by year
until last year we sent out some 28 thousand cards. The cost is very high,
and for postage alone it amounts to $1,300. Therefore, we have decided
this year we are not sending out cards excepting to a limited number of
about 2000. Instead of the tremendous expenditure of some $23,000 for
cards, which is additional to the cost of the postage, Olive and I are

going to make a contribution to two funds – the Crippled Children's Fund, and the Fund for Muscular Dystrophy.

Many of my own consituents will be disappointed but to take the place of the card we are placing an advertisement in the Prince Albert Herald, and the Shellbrook and Nipawin papers, accompanied by a photograph of the picture on the card.

We are looking forward to having you here for Christmas if you can arrange it, and you should then decide to go South for a month or so. I wish I could go to a sunny climate too!

I haven't heard from Ed Jackson for weeks. I tried to get him to come to the National Meeting but he offered the excuse that he had to take his wife to the coast for a holiday, but that was not what she said when I talked to her on the phone. At any event, he has now moved to Vancouver.

All the best,
Affectionately,
John

From Elmer to John   *Saskatoon*
                                        March 14, 1967

Dear John,

It said over the news this morning questions were asked in the H. of C. of the International Savings & Mortgage Corporation.

I sent you along the report in the Financial Post Year Books. Camp was a director it would seem of this small company in Wpg.

Directory of Directors says Dalton Camp was a Director and apparently when he was in Wpg. at the Great Luncheon he must have been making an assessment of the leadership of Coin [James Coyne, former Governor of the Bank of Canada] & [Sinclair] Stevens....

It looks as though Camp was mixed up with all these bums, which seems to be Rockefellers' Trust Company in Winnipeg or at least it seems to be the same bank.

If you can get the evidence of this Trust Company in Winnipeg I would say you should give Stevens, Coin and that gang a real blast and that is the reason Camp went to Winnipeg....

The Best,
Elmer

From John to Elmer   *Leader of the Opposition*
                                    Ottawa
                                    April 6, 1967

Dear Elmer,

It is bitterly cold here again today and I hope that you are having lots of sun where you are.

Yesterday morning I spoke to a group of high school students and had a busy day. The TV men came for my comments on the new Cabinet Ministers – Trudeau and Chretien. Walter Gordon is back as President of the Privy Council and looks happy about it....

As I want you to receive this in Beppu this letter is brief today.

                    With best wishes,
                    Sincerely,
                    John

Hoping that you are having a fine time. Your cable said you were. However it is well to rest and not to overdo it.

By the way, Senator McCutcheon is in the field for leadership and has appointed Dick Thrasher (of all people) as his campaign manager! I wouldn't have believed it without proof.

Mike Starr declared his candidature today.

Stanfield last night in Wpg. said he was not *seeking* nomination.

Camp has stated that he has decided to get in the race. (It is now clear that he started the trouble with this in mind.)

His financial backer (Sinclair Stevens) has been fired out of BIF [British International Finance] and the Bank of Western Canada.

Things are moving rapidly – Ça va bouger!

∽

From John to Elmer   *Office of the Leader of the*
                                    Opposition
                                    Ottawa
                                    April 17, 1967

Dear Elmer,

Olive and I spent a quiet weekend. I worked without stopping for hours on end only to find that my dictating machine was not working. This may be described as a case of love's labour lost.

I watched the hockey game between Toronto and Chicago on Saturday afternoon which Toronto won by the score of 4-2. They now hold an edge in the series of three games to two. Montreal defeated New York in four straight games and will play the winner of the Toronto-Chicago series.

The big event today is the Inauguration Ceremony of the new Governor General, Roland Michener, which will take place this morning. Olive has a new outfit which she bought at Blanche Buchanan's and it is very attractive.

Spring has been slow in coming although the snow is gone in most parts of the city. It is quite cool again today with the temperature around 38° above zero which will mean that when the Governor General and Mrs. Michener return to Rideau Hall after the swearing-in ceremony in the Senate Chamber, they may find it very chilly.

The list of candidates for the Conservative leadership continues to grow. Michael Starr is now in the field and Alvin Hamilton is said to be on the way. [Manitoba Premier Duff] Roblin wishes that he had not taken such an active part with his Ministers against me in November's meeting. I have written a summary of the events of that meeting which I forwarded to the President of the Ontario Association, Mr. Elmer Bell, Q.C., and also to Premier [John] Robarts. The summary is a history of events placing the blame on Mr. Bell and various other members of the Ontario Association. They will receive their billet-doux today and I expect a stormy reaction.

I have waited five months and have said nothing and still the attacks continue. Now the Liberal Party have a campaign on against me. Their followers are to write me in the most abusive way. I received such a letter from the Rev. W.G. Onions, a United Church Minister in Winnipeg. It was not the first that I have received from him so I sent him a telegram last Saturday which reads as follows:

"I received your letter of bitterness, abuse and vituperation stop I suggest that starting tomorrow you practise as well as preach the essential principles of faith, hope and love stop If you do you will feel better and so will your congregation"

That holy man would be ready for his Sunday Service after my message – I hope. He sent a worse one to Gordon Churchill who having perused my reply felt that nothing more need be said.

> With all best wishes,
> Your brother
> John...

From John to Elmer   *Office of the Leader of the*
                                        Opposition
                                        June 11, 1967

Dear Elmer,

I am so sorry that you have been deprived of your glasses all week as you helped me out when mine were not available. For some reason none of us recalled whose glasses I had borrowed. It was only today in talking to you on the phone that I learned with regret that it was you....

This week there does not seem to be anything of a troublesome nature in the cards but one never knows what will turn up. Now that [Donald] Fleming is in the field for the leadership, Harkness has thrown Fulton overboard. Jack S. [Sangster] from Regina was in to see me and he claims that Premier [E.C.] Manning is not entirely disinterested. I think his eyes are turned towards Ottawa and he realizes the hopelessness of Social Credit. I have nothing definite in this regard except press references with a certain amount of corroboration by one informant with whom Manning was in conversation. I will know more about this before the week is out but in the meantime nothing must be said about him.

Roblin is angling for support but he is away down at the bottom of the slippery pole. He would have been right at the top had he not listened to Camp's advice in September, 1965, when he was about ready to contest a federal seat in the general election.

I have given no indication one way or another as to whether I will stand but will have to do so shortly. [Eddie] Goodman, who has been anything but straightforward in his dealings, but who is now one of the Co-Chairman of the Leadership Convention, wrote me a day or so ago and I am sending you a copy of his letter [not found]. It has all the appearance of being part of a scheme to find out whether I am going to stand because it refers to a celebration that will take place in my honour and fits in with Fulton's cynical, sarcastic statement which he made about a month ago in Vancouver, that I would receive a warm welcome at the Convention as a prelude to getting out.

Olive and I attended the National Memorial Service on Parliament Hill this afternoon in honour of the 113 thousand Canadians who have been killed in action in wars in which Canada has participated in the last 70 years.

With all good wishes and hoping that your neck condition will improve soon,

                                  I am, yours sincerely,
                                  John

From John to Elmer

Hotel Vancouver
Vancouver
August 14, 1967

DON'T WORRY. In 3 weeks I'll be out of this RAT RACE.

[Unsigned]

From Elmer to John

Box 1728
Saskatoon
August 17, 1967

Dear John,

...The rat race is indeed going at full pace. Fleming was here during the week. I was told there were about 60 present. I heard that it was not too enthusiastic, but they treated him civilly.

I saw a chap yesterday from Brampton who has two brothers here (strong supporters of yours). His name is Wilfred Fitzpatrick & I met him here three years ago. He is related to Pallet, the former member.

In what amounted to almost a prayerful plea he said: "John must let his name stand." He recalls that the Grits called on Ontario farmers just before the last election. He says they know now that they were hoodwinked and they are mad. He tells me that you have terrific support all over Ontario right now. I am a long way from Ontario, but I think that is right from those I spoke to. Fitzpatrick says you could carry the Convention. Others have told me the same.

Fitzpatrick told me that Donald Fleming is not at all popular in Toronto. It would appear so as I heard over the radio this morning that one Toronto constituency pledged its five votes to [Duff] Roblin on the first vote.

This fellow Camp is thoroughly detested and it is generally accepted he ruined the party. In his discussion in Weekend Magazine he admits that he received terrible letters across Canada and with the object in mind of soliciting sympathy, he should have been quiet on that subject. He was a Crown witness against himself.

I don't think I received that Camp issue of Weekend Magazine.

I don't know who is behind the distribution of Weekend Magazine, but apparently everybody is receiving it on arrival back from overseas. I noticed everybody in this block where I am received it. I had a whole load of them when I got back and I find now that others have been receiving it here in Saskatoon.

I am enclosing an editorial from the Victoria Colonist that gives the attendance record of the "rebels" that Camp praises.

After this thing is all over I'll likely go to Expo as you suggested.

I am sure you could carry the Convention but it is up to you to decide. They know now that they are in a mess and the more they talk the deeper they get in to it. Your main thing now is to make the best speech of your career, which you can do as you have always done so, and then they will realize who is top man. You are the only one who can win. You can make no mistake in going after Camp as everyone knows that Camp is an S.O.B., although some do not care to admit it....

It is quite amazing even today, everybody asks: "What is John going to do?" Someone told me yesterday. I must hear that regularly every day and I do. You have them caged on that issue, and you have them even more buffaloed [than] when you withheld your announcement to the last minute when you ran in P.A....

[Letter missing pages]

∽

This is the last letter available from John before the September, 1967 Leadership Convention.

From John to Elmer   *Office of the Leader of the*
                                        Opposition
                                        [Ottawa]
                                        August 29, 1967

Dear Elmer,

The day of miracles is not over.

Regenstreif (whom I designated in 1965 as Ribbentrop, which annoyed him to no end) had an article in last night's paper which indicates that he must be convinced that things are changing. It took him a long time to get around to it but in the last paragraph it shows 101 favourable mentions for me compared with 14 for Camp.

Gordon Churchill was in today to bring me the news from Manitoba.

There is a storm on here concerning delegate stuffing. It is becoming more heated by the hour. Fulton expressed his concern today but he is not going to enter a formal protest but the 88 (whether Liberal, NDP or Conservative) who attended the Montmorency Conference who are automatically delegates seems to be causing some of his concern.

I sent some eight books that were on my library shelves which we used on the homestead to the Provincial Archivist, Regina.

> With warmest regards,
> Yours sincerely,
> John

8

THE OLD LION

OUT OF POWER AT LAST at 72, John Diefenbaker might have been expected to slow down and to enjoy his old age with his devoted wife at his side. It was not to be: politics was his life and his life was politics. The Chief stayed on as a Member of Parliament, harassing the new Trudeau government and often tormenting Robert Stanfield, the Nova Scotia premier selected to lead the Progressive Conservative party in 1967, and his successor, Joe Clark. Curiously, the terrible bitterness that many Canadians had felt to Diefenbaker when he was a power in the land disappeared very quickly once he was no longer party leader. The Chief had become a living icon, a treasured national relic, loved for his perseverance, admired for his House of Commons performances, and his outrageous quips and comments were repeated up and down the land. Diefenbaker's fabled memory was starting to fade, but the public memory of the Chief as the most popular of Canadian prime ministers was already beginning to form.

The last years were hard. Elmer died in 1971, leaving John as the sole surviving member of his immediate family. Olive succumbed five years later. Her arthritis, so painful for so long, had not stopped this warm, charming woman from impressing her personality on countless Canadians. However in December, 1975, she suffered a stroke, recovered with surprising speed, and then returned to hospital with a serious heart condition. She spent most of the last three months of 1976 in hospital, but was released to spend Christmas with her husband. On December 22, John Diefenbaker left for his House of Commons office, leaving her asleep in bed; he called later and found her well, but shortly after noon, Olive Diefenbaker died quietly and peacefully.

John Diefenbaker lived almost three years more, desperately lonely,
yet still a force to be reckoned with. But there is none of the correspondence of his last years in this book – the Family Series of the Diefenbaker
Papers ends with the death of Olive Diefenbaker.

On September 9, 1967, Robert Stanfield was elected as the new leader of the
Progressive Conservative Party.

From Elmer to John   *Armstrong, Ont*
                                              September 18, 1967
                                              2:30 P.M.

Dear John,

We have just left Armstrong on route to Winnipeg and shall be in
Saskatoon in the morning about 8:30.

I trust at the staff party you were happy and the press party tonight
will be as great as the trip down the mall and the reception along the
promenade at Expo.

You were very tired yesterday and so was Olive and this was an anti-
climax to a most strenuous week that very few could have survived. So
many have said that Olive and you were made of steel and that is the sort
of thing that serves as a shining inspiration to the cross-section of people
who call themselves Canadians.

You came through O.K. with Olive and the path ahead is straight and
all you have to do is to heed the order of the Sandhurst sergeant major,
as related by the Indian General – 'at on straight – quick march.

Personally I am most grateful that you are out of this rat race. The
world picture is most gloomy and even the strongest men will break
under the heavy load that is on their shoulders. So many of your most
loyal and staunch friends are most proud of your most distinguished career and they sincerely feel that they would prefer that someone else
other than yourself should crack under the strain of office.

You fought and that is what the general public want. You won – probably not yesterday – but tomorrow.

So take my advice – be happy. This is just a period of transition and
far from being at the end of the road.

I like and admire people who get mad and I know there are thousands
who share that state of mind with myself – that make me anything but a
lonely individual.

I'll meet you and Olive in Saskatoon and I know you and Olive will be happy.

I don't have anything against against Stanfield – I'm just sorry for the man.

I took a good look at the picture today – the one of you and me in your office. I studied it and find it most admirable.

I have been reading the Randolph Churchill book* and indeed it is very worthwhile. The Jews get full marks.

Forget all the trash you've read. Only the feeble-minded take it seriously and in a short time they will forget all about it – the rest of the public will be mad – also foxholes will command a very high price – McCutcheon will have his daily ration of one gallon of liquor mixed with Vodka, beer and wine. There is nothing better for the system. There is nothing that can stupefy stupidity more than the quaffing of bum's mixture.

I met a very interesting little girl on the train. I asked her "Were you ever in the Philippines?" She smiled and said she came from Mindanao. The Filipinos are a distinct type. She is a nurse, was in Montreal for five years and is now on the way back to be with her folks in Mindanao. She knows Manilla well. I told her some of the places I visited. She laughed and was well pleased with these places.

The above is the only advice I can give you and if my picture of the future is not right I'm going to be the most disappointed person in the world. I would be the next to resort to bum's mixture.

[Letter missing pages]

ℐ

This is the first letter from John after the convention.

From John to Elmer   *House of Commons*
                                          [Ottawa]
                                          October 16, 1967

Dear Elmer,
    Herewith cheque to cover the advances you made to me.

* Churchill, Randolph. *Twenty-One Years*. London: Weidenfield & Nicholson, 1965.

I have no Sect'ys now – Miss Pound and Mrs. Wagner have decided to leave.

The new office is a lonesome place.

Everybody is interested in the hunting trips we took.

Olive is in good spirits.

> With best wishes,
> Sincerely,
> John

꙳

From John to Elmer   *House of Commons*
                                        [Ottawa]
                                        October 16, 1967.

Dear Elmer,

The trip back was uneventful except for my seatmate on the plane who was drunk but always gentlemanly. He would go to sleep from time to time and wake up screaming.

I only had an economy ticket but after leaving Winnipeg the stewardess moved me back to First Class. In Winnipeg I met our friends Leonard Claydon, Ted Groves and Bob Steen etc. They told me the story which is a repeat of Saskatchewan – that in Manitoba with the exception of Winnipeg South, there is a strongly aroused public opinion which will show itself at the next election. Indeed, the view was expressed that if Roblin runs in Marquette when a vacancy is created by Nick Mandziuk's resignation, he will have some difficulty.

I have not failed to point out today to the various press people who called on me that the vote in Saskatchewan of 140 thousand in the 1964 Provincial election dropped to 40 thousand in the current election.

The colossal nerve of some people was evidenced today when Ed Nasserden [M.P., Rosthern] called me on the phone and said he wanted to bring someone from Saskatchewan down. I said, "no" after the work you did at the Convention. That ended that! He has followed the course in the last few years of calling on me with some of his constituents to have pictures taken by him – he being a photographer of note according to his own expressed view.

I went in the House this afternoon and stayed for half an hour. This morning some fifteen press men called on me and a nice visit was had by all.

Before I stop I should tell you the visit with you for two weeks was a most happy one. I hope you enjoyed it as much as I did for it is a very long while since I have had so long with you.

> Affectionately,
> John

ᴥ

From John to Elmer   *House of Commons*
                                         Ottawa
                                         October 19, 1967

Dear Elmer,
    Olive must have worked day and night when I was away for everything is in readiness to move. The home to which we are moving was shown in the "Citizen" a couple of days ago and I will send you the item in question.
    We have had two days of continuing rain and while Happy enjoys his morning walk through every puddle hole he can find his way into, his face shows frustration when in his sodden condition he is refused admission to "Stornoway" House.
    I have gone into the Chamber on a couple of occasions but have not stayed very long and do not intend to for the time being.
    I had a long chat yesterday with Dr. [Lewis] Brand who has come to the same conclusion you have regarding the low vote for Conservative candidates in the Provincial election. At the same time in Ontario, while [John] Robarts was returned, the Conservative vote fell from 49% to 42%. What helped the Conservative cause was the large vote for CCF [NDP] candidates which otherwise would have gone to the Liberals. You will have to read of Martin Pederson's outburst. He claims he is on the way to Ottawa where he is going to straighten things out. Yesterday the Member for Rosetown-Biggar, Ron McLelland told me he is very annoyed as he contends he offered to help Martin but was peremptorily turned down by him.

> With all good wishes,
> I am,
> Yours sincerely,
> John

From John to Elmer   *[Ottawa]*
                                        October 20, 1967

Dear Elmer,
    "All quiet" in the H. of C. – Just like a funeral home!
    The G & M attacked Van Horne bitterly today in an editorial.* I am
enclosing it for your edification. I think he will win – but what will happen afterwards is another thing!
    Olive is still working hard but has everything about ready for moving
to our temporary home for the next 6 months.
    I have no Sect'y now – Mrs. Wagner got annoyed yesterday and is
away today. Bunny Pound is in Stanfield's office.
    Today the Speaker advised me of my allotted staff – and hope to have
new personnel next week (1 Asst., 1 Research, 1 Sect'y). That will give
me enough staff to get going.
    Well I must get back to work.

                                        With all good wishes.
                                        John

                            ✍

From Elmer to John   *Flamingo Motel*
                                        Prince Albert, Saskatchewan
                                        October 23, 1967

Dear John,
    Just a line this morning and there isn't very much to report except for
the weather which is very nice.
    You and Olive will at least feel a bit more contented when at least you
will be temporarily in new surroundings. Living in that cold place, as
the both of you have, would ultimately bring very bad results, the polar
bear rug has been a fitting symbol.
    The cold storage plant can now be turned over and I know Olive has
worked very hard under extenuating circumstances.
    I am very glad you have been furnished with a certain amount of staff.
The whole thing has been rotten to the core and the general public have

---

* Charles Van Horne was the Conservative leader in New Brunswick. He was an old-style politician,
renowned for the quantity of his campaign promises. *The Globe & Mail* called him "clownish, wholly irresponsible." In the October 24, 1967 election, the Liberals defeated the Conservatives 32-26,
and Van Horne lost his own seat in Restigouche.

judged the whole thing in a most bitter manner. Leadership assassination has always been the cornerstone of the Conservative Party and the modern streamlined vehicle "Assessment" is the bulldozer, and the means to the end of complete assassination. Nevertheless the wave of protest is strong as it is in the Vietnam war and assessment is now a two way street....

[Letter missing six pages]

I know Olive has had a terrible time with her back condition and everyone asks about it. I get fed up with the "pain in the neck" business, commonly known as Dalton Camp disease, but it is gradually burning itself out. Everybody seems to be getting it.

> I must go,
> Affectionately,
> Elmer

ᴧ

From John to Elmer   *House of Commons*
                                        [Ottawa]
                                        October 26, 1967

Dear Elmer,
    We are about to move – Olive has done the work; I the superintendence.
    I have no secretary except that Miss Pound, while in L/O [Leader of the Opposition] office, helps out a bit. The rest have flown!
    Reg Jones wrote me at length. He claims Mr. [R.W.] Cantelon M.P. [P.C., Kindersley] prevented him from being a delegate because he was supporting me. Mr. C. keeps away from me which lends weight to Reg's views.
    I go into the House for the opening – but don't stay longer than necessary. I put Mr. Nasserden in his place when he phoned me that he had someone with him to call on me. I said "*No.*"
    The PC members of the Camp stamp are full of enthusiasm. The Gallup Poll shows P.C.'s up 14% (!) at the same time it was taken the party vote in Ontario Provincial election fell from 49% to *42%*. In Sask. from 140,000 votes in the provincial election of 1964 to less than *40,000* this year.

New Brunswick stayed Liberal.

This Gallup Poll outfit are close to Camp. Their figures have always been against me. I wonder what the answer is for so tremendous a change in 7 weeks!

> With best wishes,
> John

⌒

From Elmer to John   *Saskatoon*
                                         November 2, 1967

Dear John,

I trust things go reasonably well and I know it has been pretty tough going. Probably you should stay on a bit longer until you can't take any more of it and then tell them to go to hell.

According to the radio last night that crazy fellow Walter Gordon has been talking again. He's harping away on Medicare now.

Camp is Gordon's counterpart in the P.C. Party. The only difference Gordon is not detested – they think he is a bit nuts, but Camp is the most detested man in Canada today. C.D. Howe started off with the reputation of being a man of great ability who wanted to get things done but in the end was almost run out.

However when you start out as a "thug" you are at a handicap. Camp was dramatized on TV a year ago. The public still remember that you flailed him with the accusing finger and Camp looked down. The CBC played that up and the general opinion that you hear: "He can't look you straight in the face." Nobody trusts anybody anymore, but you came out with a clean sheet.

I hope you can get things organized and get your book written – that will tell the story – neither the Grits nor the Tories are home free.

I saw Bill Fair. He is quite a character. He showed me one of the autograph books and he has everybody signed in these books.

I think I got things a bit wrong about Art Pearson. Bill Fair was at Rosetown recently and saw Walter Asseltine. Asseltine told Bill that Pearson was with him constantly throughout the Convention and they were never apart. I would like to get this confirmed. The trouble with me I'm not out with the R.M.A. [Retail Merchant's Association] now. There was a time when I was around the country & I could get the odd bit of information.

This morning it is trying to snow and I wouldn't be surprised if winter will be on the way....

I'm blame lucky being out of the [stock] market as it is going down everyday. Things did not look very optimistic in world affairs so I woke up one morning, phoned Richardson's and told them to sell out everything. I was most fortunate as I would be down $2500 right now and it seems to be more unsettled every day.

If you can believe Walter Gordon, you are most fortunate being out of this mess. With all the responsibility of P.M., you would just worry yourself into the grave. You are just as free now as I am of the present market. I gambled in the market like you did in politics, but the both of us are free now.

You don't know how fortunate you have been. You reached your objective – just one out of 14. I saw Paul Martin on TV last night and the idea occurred to me with all his ability he might have been a great Prime Minister but he will never get there. How would you like to be in his shoes?

Your story will be the same as that of Sir Wilfrid Laurier – everything in common. He was honest and upright but only his conscience dictated what course he was to take. He was surrounded by a gang of bums and scoundrels to whom he himself was completely loyal. Sir Wilfrid finished up alone, but his story is now in the book – get your story in the book. That is more important than anything else.

In your case you are no longer associated with the bums – somebody else is.

I attended the Hozen funeral yesterday at St James Church. The Church was filled and standing in the aisles. It was a most tragic thing. Charles Hozen and his wife were on the way to Calgary to attend a wedding. She was driving, went off into the ditch, and her neck was broken. Charles was in hospital, came out to make the funeral arrangements, and will have to go back to the hospital for surgery.

I phoned the Hays. Beulah is alright now but she was lucky to come out of this mess alive.

I hope you and Olive are settled at least temporarily. Olive has had it tough, and I trust you will have some peace for a change. Fred Hadley is a bit different – he has to live with his wife.

Now I must go,

Affectionately,
Elmer...

From John to Elmer   *House of Commons*
                                        The Rt. Hon. John G.
                                        Diefenbaker M.P.
                                        [Ottawa]
                                        Sunday
                                        December 3, 1967

Dear Elmer,
    You seemed in good spirits on phone this morning.
    I am tired of seeing the "playing around" in H. of C. and a rest at the Coast will do me good. Olive is feeling somewhat more relaxed from pain. The painting of me for Parlt. is far from completed. I am not too satisfied with it – modernistic and unusual.
    I had a card from Dr. Baltzan.
    Dec 10th I have to be in Saskatoon and a day or so in P.A. [Prince Albert].
    Did I tell you Olive got a surprise – a Centennial medal for her contributions.

                            John

P.S. I think Fred Hadley has sold his house. I called today and was advised that he is on the way to White Rock. The Grey Cup Game was a washout. Too bad I prophesized wrongly! I thought Sask. would win. Get your work at your suite cleared up so that you can leave at a moment's notice.
    Keep well! Keep smiling! and worship Camp!!

                            John

                        ∽

From John to Elmer   *House of Commons*
                                        Ottawa
                                        February 5, 1968

Dear Elmer,
    Olive and I were in Winnipeg on Saturday and Sunday and attended the dinner in our honour given by the Gordon Churchill constituency executive. There were about 400 present, there could be no more;

tickets had been sold out a month ago, and under all the circumstances it might have been better to have held the gathering at the Marlborough Hotel rather than in Headingly. It was a most happy occasion. The Reverend Dr. Martin, the former minister of the Ontario and Manitoba governments, and his wife were present. They have been loyal supporters through the years. I had known that he did some painting, but I had no idea that he was as "professional" as he is in this regard. We were presented with a painting done by him of the Assiniboine Park. It is a remarkable piece of work and when Olive told him how sweet it was, all the charm of his 85 years was embodied in his reply, "My dear Olive, there was love and affection in every stroke of my brush."

Today the much advertised and lauded conference of the federal government and the provinces will open. I have stated it cannot succeed and I have no fear that I will be wrong. Much as I would like it to succeed, it is simply an endeavour to have Mr. Pearson leave the national scene in an irradescent burst of oratorical grandiloquence.

Trudeau seems to be the anointed of the press for the leadership. Whether successful or not, he has had the most widely dispersed press of any one of the candidates, and while I am still calling Paul Martin as the choice, it seems obvious that he has slipped in the last ten days because of the Trudeau campaign. I should not call it a campaign as he has not announced his candidature as yet, but it is under way just the same.

I have a large number of appointments in the next 30 days and will have to reduce them. The first of these is the Baptist meeting in Fredericton. I have not been there for a long while and will have to go, although I see no reason why Olive should have to accompany me. She has a tremendous job in furnishing the new home and while she has gone with me everywhere I have told her that it is unfair to have her go to all these gatherings when she has so much to do. There was some slight improvement in her condition during the cruise, but that is all over and she is having the same difficulty getting around that she has experienced in the last three years.

> With all good wishes,
> Your brother,
> John

P.S. I received the enclosed letter [not found] in today's mail from your friend Bob Mackay.

From John to Elmer   *House of Commons*
                                        [Ottawa]
                                        6:30 A.M.
                                        February 9, 1968

Dear Elmer,

   I have stayed home since Tuesday fighting a congestion in my chest –
not serious but it has been hanging on since the Cruise. The stay has en-
abled me to catch up on my correspondence which had fallen two weeks
behind schedule.

   Olive is working on the interior decoration of the house – even
painting!

   The Prime Minister's conference is over – and the provinces agreed to
give the French language equality everywhere in this nation. Robarts
and [New Brunswick Premier Louis] Robichaud will introduce legislation to provide French schools – and to permit the second language in
the legislatures of Ont. and New Brunswick. All of this would have not
taken place if Stanfield hadn't given his support and sanction.

   On Wednesday I shall speak to the Baptist Conference in Fredericton
and on Thursday morning to the University of N.B. student body. I have
too many speaking engagements and must cancel them out. There is no
reason why I should do these "Joe Jobs" any longer.

   Fulton is now Dep. Leader of the Party in the House – which means
that anything or anybody favorable to me is *out* and will receive no
consideration.

   The Liberal leadership race is in full swing. "Who will be chosen?"
you ask. I don't know – but if it is Trudeau (who stands for One Nation,
not two, and no "Special Status" for Quebec), I would be concerned for
PC party hopes in the next general election in spite of his leftist background. He visited Communist China in 1952 and praised its system. In
Moscow he attended a Communist Economic Conference in 1954 (?) and
in 1958 set out for Cuba from Florida in a canoe to visit Castro and was
picked up by a U.S.A. Coastal Patrol when a few miles out to sea! What
a man! But he has greatly reduced Paul Martin's chances to become the
Prime Minister.

                                        With all good wishes,
                                        John

From John to Elmer   *Ottawa*
                                        April 22, 1968

I didn't call you yesterday because I mislaid your telephone number and I was in the midst of helping Olive get the house in shape.

This morning I received a copy of the Saskatoon Star-Phoenix. I am always glad to have them, but wish you would make a mark to indicate what you think I should read.

Today is the big day in Prince Albert as Ed Topping will leave to visit his son's grave in Holland, and then over to Northern Ireland to spend a week. It is sixty years since he left there, and while there have been great changes in Belfast and other urban centres, the rural areas will show very little change.

Our chauffeur is leaving tomorrow. I will have to see who else we can get, otherwise I will have to walk to the House. I don't mind a mile and a half in the morning, but three miles is a little too far, even for me.

Today we learn whether the House is going to be dissolved. "PET" is uncertain. He produced a cabinet that the Montreal and Toronto papers say is one of paste and scissors. If he goes to the country I will have to decide right away whether I will stand in Prince Albert. It is a hard question to decide. If I chose a course for myself, I would not be a candidate. However, I must never lose sight of the fact that not only the people of Prince Albert, but tens of thousands in every part of our country want me to continue. If I stand I will have to make it clear that I want no part of a national campaign so long as Camp, Goodman, Fulton, Harkness, [Marcel] Lambert, and other Camp followers are the makers of policy and direction for the Party.

With regard to the trip abroad, I am just wondering whether I should not also visit the three Baltic countries of Latvia, Lithuania and Estonia.

You might let me know what further plans you have made.

                              [Unsigned]

                                 ✍

From Elmer to John   *Hotel Ambasador*
                                        Bucuresti [Romania]
                                        August 1, 1968

Dear John,
     Since leaving you in Edinburgh I have been cut off from the outside

world. I picked up two English-speaking papers in Moscow, but very little in them. I arrived in Bucharest this afternoon and was amazed to find a letter by yourself from Switzerland. I could not believe it. There are very few who speak English in Russia. Sometimes I can get along with German. I shot the Ukrainian in Kiev, the capital of the Ukraine. I met a woman from Toronto yesterday and we got very friendly. I thought she was a Ukrainian but she was not. She lived in Paris for years, the Argentine and all over. She spoke English but she got on the French – "Parlez-vous français? – Oui un peu, pas trop pire." She liked John Diefenbaker and I received two or three Trudeau kisses from her.

I was deeply grieved to learn from your letter (as you are yourself) that our very dear friend Paul Lafontaine has passed on. Harry Jones always had Paul pinpointed as your very best friend and in this he was so right. I received my last letter from Paul while in Scotland. I shall write his wife tonight before retiring. You have always been completely damned inasmuch as you lost your best friends and the damn fools with sputnik gyrations in the cranium appear to be completely indestructable. I don't know anybody in the world who is as well known as yourself. When I report in, every man and woman calls me by name and just pronounces my name naturally. There were a bunch of Ukrainians in the hotel in Kiev from Toronto, Oshawa and Winnipeg and they simply went wild to meet me in the Ukraine. They tell me your name is proverbial in all these areas. Everyone remembers that speech at the U.N. They say you are a good, honest man – a great man. In Moscow you are well known. I shot the Ukrainian and got a real rise out of them. Ukrainians and Americans have no use for this fellow Trudeau. I had the Ukrainians roaring with laughter when I said "Trudeau – pascudena Subokka" [?] – the local Ukrainians joined the mirth. They knew I was so right, as I knew it myself.

These poor devils come to the Ukraine and meet their loved ones, whom they have not seen over the years, and the most touching thing comes when they have to say "goodbye." One from Toronto told me that he had not seen his mother for 28 years. In parting he said: "My mother cried and I cried too." This fellow is a postal worker in Toronto, ostensibly, as he said, at the moment on vacation resulting from the postal strike being a postal employee and taking advantage of his forced vacation.

I have a ballpoint pen tonight but did not have one yesterday morning. I venture to say I could not find one all over Russia. I signed the autograph for two of the young Ukrainian girls from Oshawa and she insisted I take the pen. I was told by a newspaper man from the Northwest

Territories to take along a supply of 10¢ ballpoint pens and chewing gum and I know now that I should have done so.

Bucharest is a great city of one and a half million inhabitants with smart shops and good-looking people. The stationery on which I write will subscribe to my statements.

I shall be on two tours tomorrow here in Bucharest and the next day to Budapest. The tour ends in Vienna. I shall be at the Hotel Grand Krasnapolsky in Amsterdam August 7th and shall leave Brussels for London on August 12th. I want to see Holland and Brussels on this trip. I've always had a hankering to see Dutch windmills in operation – very much in contrast with Toronto windmills.

I am so glad you and Olive have enjoyed the short visit in the mountains of Switzerland. Olive is so right when she says that is the place to take pictures.

Now that I have been in Russia, I think you would be interested in seeing the country. There is grandeur in Leningrad and Kiev and to an extent in Moscow. You cannot conceive of the luxury in which the nobility were surrounded but the picture is changing so radically all over the world.

I went through the Lavra [Laura], the Community of 1200 monks in Kiev yesterday and through the catacombs. It is eerie – some of the monks remained underground for 11 years – they could not take it any longer and they had to come out – originally there were 12 of them in the 11th century. They were canonized as saints and their mummified bones are there. Sixty of the monks went stark mad and were locked up. It is a self-contained community at Lavra – first printing house was there, bakeries, etc. and a great Cathedral erected that the Germans could not blast during the war. The monks underground were fed by pilgrims. They were almost as the Monk-eys on Bay Street. Well that is about all for now.

Elmer

ᨒ

From John to Elmer   *House of Commons*
                                        Ottawa
                                        October 18, 1968

Dear Elmer,

On Monday I propose to start working on my memoirs. I will be fairly well caught up with my office work and a start must be made without delay.

Olive and I are going to Windsor this evening to attend a dinner in honour of the Hon. Paul Martin. We will go down on the Prime Minister's aircraft and return on another plane chartered for the Members, and should be back around midnight. It is a long trip, but I have to do it because when Cortisone was needed in 1951 [for Edna] Paul heard about it and with the co-operation of the late Brooke Claxton, Minister of Defence, provided a tremendous supply for Dr. Baltzan's use.

A book has just come out written by Peter Dempson*, in which he has you in the Table of Contents as being along on the world trip. He mentions Edna in these words:

"Mrs. Diefenbaker was a pleasant, striking woman with blue eyes and light coloured hair. She was always immaculately dressed and ordinarily was an outgoing person, popular with the M.P.'s and newspapermen alike." He mentioned one occasion when she seemed to be crying because I had an offer as a legal adviser at a salary of $30,000 a year and I asked Dempson what he thought. "Edna says I should take the job and give up politics. What do you think?," to which he replied, "It's an attractive offer, but I'm afraid you wouldn't be happy leaving public life." He says furthermore that when she died in 1951 the Press Gallery took it badly for she had been very popular with the press. He says that I used to take them out for a home-cooked meal. He says that drinks were in plentiful supply, but even when he would wander around with a glass in his hand, "I cannot recall ever seeing him take a sip."

Of Olive he says that she was a widow whom I first met when I was a teenager when I was attending Saskatoon Collegiate Institute. Attractive, matronly, a former school teacher, she had a great understanding of newspapermen's idiosyncrasies and problems. In later years, when Diefenbaker began feuding with with some Gallery members, she was always willing to intervene on their behalf. On only one occasion did Mrs. Diefenbaker speak on her husband's behalf and that was in Guelph where she had once taught school. She was on the platform every night, sending me messages to remind me of something I might have forgotten in my speech. "Perhaps he was rambling; perhaps he was going too fast. She never failed to let him know. Then after the speech-making was over, she would stand for hours to shake hands with the people. It wasn't easy for her. For years she had been having back trouble, caused by a

---

* Dempson, Peter. *Assignment Ottawa: Seventeen Years in the Press Gallery.* Toronto: General Publishing Co., 1968.

slipped disc. She never complained. 'Without her,' Diefenbaker said publicly on one occasion, 'I could never have done it.'"

Mrs. George Swan had a son the day after we left Plenty and is now in the Kindersley General Hospital. A note of congratulations from you and thanks for the hospitality extended to you would be in order.

> With all good wishes,
> I am,
> Yours sincerely,
> John

Happy II was hit by a car on November 22, 1968.

From Elmer to John   *Saskatoon*
                                         Nov 24, 1968

Dear John,

I knew you felt very bad this morning not having Happy along on the route march. Humans have a close attachment for their pets, ostensibly on account of their high degree of loyalty.

I recall the morning that "Mister Budge" (the Budgie Bird I gave mother on her birthday) died. It was a very bad day for me as I was much attached to him.

However, in the case of Happy this thing seemed to be inevitable. He was a very fine dog, but he was not amenable to discipline and I was always afraid this would happen.

It is a horrible thing that these hit and run drivers have no feeling for anything. I am always on the alert when I cross the street.

My suggestion would be to get a dog like an Airedale. He is alert, fast on the trigger, and very loyal. He won't wake up with strangers and he can be tough, if necessary. The golden retreiver is full of the wanderlust and it seems to be in his system.

I sent you the Star-Phoenix and Happy was on the front page and as well your report on Nicholson.[*]

I read about 100 pages. He has a nasty approach and is bound to be attacked by your many friends. The book has not sold at all here and your remarks in print will not help him at all.

---

[*] Nicholson, Patrick. *Vision and Indecision*. Don Mills: Longman Canada, 1968.

I expect Tommy Van Dusen's book* will be here in the next few days. Mrs. Chapman told me if it does not arrive tomorrow, she will phone Toronto.

I have given the book real publicity and everyone is anxiously awaiting it. The advance orders are coming in every day. I tell them to tell their friends and that is exactly what they are doing....

> The Best,
> Elmer

ᔕ

From John to Elmer

> *House of Commons*
> *The Rt. Hon. John G.*
> *Diefenbaker, P.C., Q.C., M.P.*
> *Ottawa*
> *November 29, 1968*

Dear Elmer,

The front page of the Gazette has a picture today in this morning's issue of Cheeko and his master Randy. I have agreed to accept the gift from that wonderful boy and I advised Randy's Mother by telephone this morning that I would do so and she will be shipping Cheeko tomorrow.

There is a very heavy snow storm on at the moment and if it is snowing in Toronto it will mean that tomorrow's Grey Cup game will be played under great handicaps. I was going to go out on a grouse hunt tomorrow morning, but those who were to be with me decided that it is not the kind of weather to be out in so I shall watch the game on TV.

You have worked so hard in gathering up all the odds and ends of letters, papers and things that I hope for your sake you will soon have completed the job. It is tiring and not very interesting. Only your devotion to preserving things for the record has made your task easier than otherwise would have been the case.

With all good wishes,

> I am,
> Yours sincerely,
> John

---

* Van Dusen, Thomas. *The Chief*. Toronto: McGraw Hill Company of Canada, 1968.

[The following letter from Randy Scot Kleckner was attached.]

Dear Mr. Diefenbaker,

I just heard on the CBC news to-night, that your lovely dog "Happy" was run over. I'm so sorry.. you'll miss him so. I was wondering if you would like to have a french poodle pup, 7 weeks old, miniature, and registered. I raise them for pin money, and usually sell them for 125.00$. But because i think your one of the best leaders our country ever had and your a great Canadian (I wish you were still at the controls.) I want you to have him as a gift. His name is Cheeko the 2nd. His mothers name is "Buffy of Sunglow" and the dads name is "Happy" owned by Dr. Chan. Happy has several champions in his family tree. I thot I'd better check with you first, and see if you cottoned to french poodles or not. For one thing, they are very intelligent, and another they don't shed hair all over the place. If you are interested, please let me know, and would you mind paying for the shipping charges? It would come to about 25$ by air. Cheeko is second in a litter of two. The other one was a boy too, and we called him Trudeau, because he had a pink nose and a long neck.. fitting eh?? We sold him last week.

I am 14 yrs old, in grade 6 at the Childrens Rehabilitation centre at the airport. I have cerebral palsey, am in a wheel chair, dont speak, but communicate with people by using my electric typewriter, or a little word board I carry with me, and spell out my wants and thoughts. Its slow and pokey, but at least I can communicate to some extent. There are 3 professors at the University who have nearly completed an "Electronic Word Board", when all the bugs are ironed out, I will be able to push a button, and the word will come out as a spoken word. Isn't that fantastic??? It will surely be a modern day miracle. I can hardly wait. Never underestimate a professor. Sports of all kinds really interest me. Hockey.. (Maple Leafs and Johnny Bower) chess and poodles are my big love. Oh.. and walkothons too. I rolled along in 2 this year, with a good group of pushers. We made the full 22 miles both times: No drop-outs in our bunch.. ha.

It's too bad the kids at the centre missed seeing you and Mr. Stanfield this spring. I was really disapointed. Maybe next time Hey?

I've always wanted a paper route of my own, but realized that I would have some tuff sledding through the Saskatoon snow-drifts with a wheel chair. You know first hand what they are like. Mom and Dad decided, perhaps raising poodles wouldn't require me fighting the elements, so thats what we settled on. My sisters helped me a lot with them. Cheeko is so sweet but spoiled a bit already. He has to sleep with Mom and Dad every night or he isn't happy. Do you think you and Mrs D. would mind sharing your bed with him?? He's as clean as a whistle, nearly trained, and would be a cheap border. He prefers table scraps to dog food. I know he'd have a good home with you. I should also tell you that the upkeep of a poodle is a little more expensive than a Cocker Spaniel. They need a hair cut and nails clipped every 2 months. The price in Saskatoon is 8$ per poodle, but Mrs. Dingwall does both of my females at a cut rate, 2 for 10$.

Please let me know soon, as I have put an ad in the Star Phoenix, this week end, to try and sell him. Snowball, my other female, is expecting just before Christmas, so I really should get a new home for Cheeko.

> Your friend and
> admirer,
> Randy Scot Kleckner

[A copy of John's reply was also enclosed]

> *House of Commons*
> *Ottawa*
> *November 29, 1968*

[Dear Randy,]

Your letter to me offering your French poodle, Cheeko, is one of the most, if not the most, inspiring that I have ever received. I have read and re-read your letter to Members of the House of Commons and without exception each has expressed deep admiration for you. To read of your courage makes each one of us the better for having done so.

My wife and I will be happy and honoured to accept your gift, as I so advised your Mother a short while ago when I talked to her on the telephone. Your instructions as to the care and attention to be given to Cheeko will be carried out.

I cannot tell you at the moment when I will be in Saskatoon, but it may not be before the middle of January, but when I arrive there my first telephone call will be to you so that we can get together.

With much appreciation and with a multitude of good wishes for continuing success, and again thanking you for ensuring that Happy II will have a worthy successor,

[John Diefenbaker]

From John to Olive   *Air Canada en Route*
                                        8 A.M.
                                        October 14, 1969

My darling,

I have just awakened after 5 1/2 hours good sleep.

We are cruising somewhat slower than usual because of heavy headwinds and will be arriving in Copenhagen in a few minutes.

The crew changes and a Russian-speaking Canadian crew takes over.

Everything has been done by Air Canada to make me enjoy my trip. The steward I have known for 20 years – his uncle at one time was bank manager at P.A. The news conference was excellent. I talked to the mayor who is obviously worried over the criticism he is being subjected to.

Joel [Aldred] is fine. [Jack] Cahill of the Star says he will keep "out of my way" and says this is going to be a friendly trip.

You (as always) were so sweet last evening at the airport. You are a wonderful wife – and I do hope that you won't overwork.

Joel is going to take a look at our car when we return for trading value – so it won't be long before we have a car – if we can find a chauffeur.

So long for now,
my dearest,
John

From John to Elmer   *House of Commons*
                                               Ottawa
                                               October 14, 1970

Dear Elmer,

We had a good trip back and an excellent press conference in Winnipeg. On arrival at the airport we were met by a Corporal in full battle dress armed with a machine gun. He accompanied us home and when we arrived there we found four or five soldiers in battle dress and similarly equipped who stayed there all night – one of them inside our home – only relieved by a similar group this morning. I am not allowed to go anywhere without being accompanied by at least one soldier. I think it is the biggest farce that I have ever witnessed and apparently a means whereby the Prime Minister can create kudos for himself and relieve him also of his fear. What is being done with soldiers in full battle dress is giving Canada a bad image and would indicate that Canada must fear a massed attack on Ottawa at any time. I think I will speak in the House tomorrow and if I do I will have something to say about the course being followed and the fact that while the Government was warned a year ago by the Mayor and Executive Council of Montreal and a Royal Commission was asked for, the Government brushed the criticism aside as without justification.

                                               With all good wishes,
                                               Your bro.,
                                               John

From John to Elmer   *House of Commons*
                                               Ottawa
                                               February 5, 1971

Dear Elmer,

I am sorry that you are laid up, and although you gave me your characteristic answer "it is nothing to be concerned about", that in no way allays my concern, for no matter how seriously ill you have been on occasion in the past, I have become accustomed to the same formula.

For me to give you advice to look after yourself would be a needless exercise, but I really think that you should call a doctor without delay, unless there is a marked improvement in the next couple of days.

I made a debating speech a couple of days ago and I think you will find it interesting. I am sending a copy, enclosed herewith, as I know you no longer take Hansard.

I spoke in Regina on Wednesday at a joint dinner of the Canadian Council of Christians and Jews and the Regina Chamber of Commerce. It was the largest Annual Meeting in Regina's history. The mayor conferred on me an honorary citizenship and several gifts were given me, including a very beautiful radio.

> Hoping you are soon
> well again, I am
> Yours sincerely,
> JGD

In early February, 1971, Elmer suffered a heart attack and was hospitalized.

From John to Elmer   *Ottawa*
                                        February 10, 1971

Dear Elmer,

I phoned Dr. Baltzan last night and I was pleased that his observations on your condition was most favourable.

I was up very early this morning trying to finish a small article for the Ottawa National Press Club annual issue. It should have been done weeks ago but I didn't get around to it. You might be interested in the content and I will send you a copy when it is completed.

Somebody from Saskatoon must have given the information to the Ottawa radio, for the fact that you were in hospital was a news item on various radio stations yesterday.

I have a letter from Randy Kleckner and I am sending you a photostat herewith. He is apparently twelve feet tall since being chosen as No.1 Sports Fan in Saskatoon and I am delighted that he was so honoured and I have decided to write the organization which gave him the honour.

Ottawa has had the heaviest snow storms in 24 years, over 100 inches have fallen. The snow in front of our home is 7ft. deep. Cheeko got away from me this morning and the only reason I was able to find him was that I saw his two black eyes and black nose peering out of the snow bank.

On Friday morning we will be arriving in Saskatoon and I hope to see you later that day.

> With all good wishes,
> I am,
> Yours sincerely,
> John

✍

From John to Elmer

> *Hotel Bessborough*
> *Saskatoon*
> *Monday 6 A.M.*
> *March 10, 1971*

Dear Elmer,

Olive and I are being taken to the airport by Dr. Brand and I will ask him to leave this note at the hospital office for you.

It was clear as can be yesterday that you are progressing well – the change for the better from time to time over the last three weeks has been a continuing one. As Olive mentioned last evening any time you would like me to come to see you just have a phone call put in to Ottawa on reverse. During the day to my office number and at any time to my home number. Olive doesn't think you have our home number so I am attaching both hereto.

I will see what books of travel or pioneer days I have and will send them to you at once so that you will have lots of reading.

I will have all the cards and messages acknowledged that I picked up yesterday.

If there is anything that you want done make a note of them and when I phone you (as I will every afternoon) be sure to let me know.

> With affectionate good
> wishes,
> John

Keep on Getting stronger!

From Elmer to John   *St Paul's Hospital*
                                        Saskatoon
                                        March 24, 1971

Dear John,

I have become quite lazy since coming into the hospital but must discipline myself and write a few letters for a change. I keep putting off the job and have come to the conclusion that I should at last get some of this correspondence off my hands.

The little French sister visited me as usual this morning, her face beaming. She laughed and told me every time you came to the hospital you addressed her as "Sunshine." You are very popular around here.

The little French sister told me this morning that I look much better and Dr. Baltzan told me the same this morning.

This is a long drawn out affair but I think I am sailing out of it. I think that I feel stronger.

I have done a great deal of sleeping and that helps. I slept like a log last night. One has to be very patient. My appetite went bad on me but am doing better now.

Beulah told me she will come over this afternoon. She likes Jim Johnston's* book very much.

I have almost finished reading it. It is terrific and I am sure there will be a few raised eyebrows.

I think we might as well get them on the run. I do think that some action can be started to get Arthur Maloney back in the House of Commons after the next election.

Joe McCrea told me that they couldn't defeat the Maloneys in that Irish constituency. The Irishmen were fanatically loyal to the Maloneys. I think we should do something right away about stirring up these fighting Irishmen and get them in there pitching. There is no doubt about it, Arthur Maloney must go back to the House of Commons. It is almost time to get down to business and have some of these bastards out. They are becoming frightened and now is the time to get moving. I am so very sorry that you got the front of your car so banged up. That is terrible – hope you will soon have it out again.

I just received my mail & still get quite a volume.

Looking out the window, the weather seems a bit better. It was very cold for a few nights.

---

* Johnston, James. *The Party's Over*. Don Mills: Longman Canada, 1971.

I must write to Olive. I don't seem to get around to it. I'll try to finish up my correspondence.

> My affectionate good
> wishes,
> Elmer

♋

From Elmer to Olive   *St Paul's Hospital*
                                         March 26, 1971

Dear Olive,

I should have written to you before but have become rather lazy.

I hope you are feeling better and you must not work so hard.

That was so good of you giving me the personal stationery on my birthday and if I have the ambition I shall be able to look after some of my correspondence when I am released from custody. Thank you so much. You are always doing something for somebody and I was pleased that Jim Johnston gave you full marks in his book.

I think the book is great. It is a history covering a certain era in Canadian history that I should rather not talk about.

The Passion Play at Oberammergau is a breathtaking spectacle and finally in the middle of the play I said to myself "Here I am witnessing the annual PC Meeting in the Chateau Laurier."

There is nothing nasty in Jim Johnston's book, but he has recorded as a history of this era in Canadian history.

I have had quite a long session but I am beginning to feel that I am coming to life just like the coming of spring. They have done everything for me and everyone has been most kind.

The little French sister comes in beaming. She grinned, her eyes sparkled and she said every time John Diefenbaker visited the hospital he called me "Sunshine."

The name Diefenbaker is very high around here.

I hope everything goes well and that Cheeko is holding his own.

I am so sorry to learn about the crash of your car and trust it will soon be fixed.

I have to write a few letters now for a change.

> Look after yourself,
> Love,
> Elmer

From Elmer to John   *St Paul's Hospital*
                                         April 3, 1971

Dear John,

I just read a story of Dr. Harry Emerson Fosdick.

An ass and a calf went down to a pool to drink water and they fought among themselves as to which one should drink first.

Suddenly overhead appeared two vultures and then the two started to drink together.

Everything goes well and the nurse this morning told me I look well.

Dr. Baltzan dropped in to see me yesterday. He told me I was fine but he still had a great many tests to make on me and I gathered that I should be out of the hospital after Easter.

I slept a great deal yesterday and last evening took a route march to the end of the hall and back. So one of these days I'll be able to fight my weight in wild cats.

It has been a long drawn-out affair but I'm beginning to work myself out of this mess.

Everybody has been telling me you have been fighting like a tiger in the House. They just eat it up and for the public it is refreshing. They are tired of the performance of dolts and pygmies for so long.

They are trying to discourage the sale of Dr. Johnston's book.

I note that Jim Johnston referred to the great Passion Play sponsored by the Conservative Association of Canada and broadcast live to the nation in color.

Last summer I noticed that the colossal Passion Play at Oberammergau and the big Canadian Passion Play of 1966 was identical point by point. The only point I would say the two great Passion Plays differed, that vicious bellowing mob of lowbrows in Jerusalem, screaming at the top of their voices, did not receive fifty cents for beer.

The Canadian play made a great impression on the Canadian public and they still remember.

I think [Eddie] Goodman should be encouraged to broadcast the play to the nation once a year. It would keep the P.C. Party before the public.

I was glad Jim Johnston referred to the Passion Play....

I trust that Olive is feeling some stronger. She has had it very tough.

I'll be looking forward to seeing you at Easter.

                                         The very best,
                                         Elmer

From John to Elmer   *The Saskatchewan Hotel*
                                        Regina
                                        Sunday 7 a.m.
                                        [April 11?, 1971]

Dear Elmer,

Arrived here at 11 P.M. by the Premier's aircraft and will be leaving at 9 A.M.

It was a happy week we had. You looked exceptionally well and the removal of avoirdupois has made a great difference to you. I wish that I had your secret for not developing double chins!

I am looking forward to your visit on May 14. I shall try at once for reservations, both by air and train, whichever you would like to have. You enjoy train travel but it is your choice. Let me know at once.

The last ten days have been rather hectic – now for two days of preparation for Income Tax!

With all the Best to a wonderful brother,

                        John

                        ✍

From John to Olive   *Hotel Bessborough*
                                        Saskatoon
                                        6 A.M.
                                        April 13, 1971

My darling,

...Elmer may be getting out of Hospital shortly and will go to a rest home. Beulah has visited several and believes that the Sunnyside Nursing Home – 2200 St Henry Ave. (3 blocks south of her home) is the best – the cost is $350 per month. He wants to keep his apt. and could rent it for the time being. I don't want to disabuse his mind of the early hope of returning to his prided place.

The doctor says that Elmer was fortunate that things have turned out as well as they have. Elmer is gaunt and his eyes deeply set but in good spirits – and *like* his brother – never a complaint.

Dr. Brand will be having breakfast with me. He tried to get a dinner convened with Robert Stanfield as speaker. Nobody would come! They wanted me to be asked – but that's out.

I am beginning to fear the NDP in Assiniboia – Lawrence Watson is not well liked!*

> With deep affection and
> Congrats for [your
> birthday] tomorrow,
> John

ᔓ

From John to Elmer   *House of Commons*
                                        Ottawa
                                        April 19, 1971

Dear Elmer,

I got back to Ottawa on Saturday evening, and was met by the CBC TV people, who asked me what I thought of the report that Goodman had been fired. I said I didn't know, but hoped that someone would now be chosen who would have time to look after the Party better than it had been for the past 3 years – in other words, I gave him a swift kick in the posterior! There are a number of reviews out of the Johnston book and I am sending you photo-copies, together with a report of the press conference in Victoria, also a cartoon which appeared in the *Victoria Colonist.*

Olive apparently worked steadily while I was away, in spite of the fact that her arthritis is causing her intense suffering and immobility. She has tried a couple of doctors without apparent benefit, but has been told of one who has brought about considerable improvement in his patients, and she will be seeing him in a few days time. The snow is still piled up outside the house but with the temperatures now up in the 50 mark it will soon bring about the kind of spring you have had in Saskatoon these past few weeks.

I am very pleased with our visit together, it revealed that you are getting along very well; now you have to concentrate on exercise and diet. I'll have to know some days in advance of your discharge from hospital, so that all the necessary arrangements can be made. It may be better to make preparations for Mount Royal rather than Sunset or Sherbrooke, but the decision must be yours. If you would sooner go to

---

* In the 1968 election, Conservative Lawrence Watson was defeated by the Liberal candidate by less than 100 votes, in turn beating the NDP candidate by less than 250 votes.

Mount Royal, call Judge Hughes and make an appointment, and have him arrange a private room. Certainly the cost is much less, but the nursing service will also be much less than at the Sherbrooke.

> With best wishes, I am,
> Yours Sincerely,
> John

From John to Elmer

> House of Commons
> Ottawa
> May 24, 1971

Dear Elmer,

Do you remember that on the 24th May 1907, father and mother went to Borden and you and I went to a slough on Uncle Ed's farm (with trees around it and almost cornered by 10 feet of snow) and jumped into and stayed for three hours in the icy water. It's a wonder that we didn't develop the paralysis that in later years struck down President Roosevelt.

Those were the days! 1907 was the coldest winter ever experienced by us by the Homestead.

I have tried to get in touch with your and my friend Donald Macleod in New Glasgow for three hours this morning but he can't be found. That by-election is not going too well and the PC Executive is pressing to have me speak at a public meeting later this week. I must decide within the next 24 hours as the election will take place one week from today. Frankly I am anxious to participate as it might be that I would speak out on some problems that the Leader is not discussing.

I must phone you now (10 A.M.) and I hope that I can make it possible for you to hear.

Tomorrow I shall see Shuett (your ear authority) and will ask him to make over your earpiece.

Keep up the good spirits of yesterday morning and you will be all right.

> With all good wishes,
> Your brother,
> John

Give my best to that superb nurse – Miss Jones

From John to Elmer   *House of Commons*
                                        Saturday
                                        May 29, 1971

Dear Elmer,

P.M. Trudeau returned yesterday – what his next trip will be isn't known yet! He doesn't like Ottawa because he cannot relax here with so many problems to face – unemployment, inflation and Hellyer.

I received a letter today from the Sec. of the R.M. [Rural Municipality] of Fish Creek concerning the construction and the opening of my old law office at Wakaw on July 1st.

The Committee looking after it is doing a wonderful job and the North American Lumber Co. is giving the lumber at cost to the Committee. You will recall that the same company gave me credit for the lumber to build the office.

As to the farm which you and I have agreed to have deeded to the University of Sask., after we do not need it, it will provide out of the income either scholarships, or other uses will be made.

What do you want it to be, the Elmer C. Diefenbaker Memorial Scholarship Fund, or do you have some other idea?

When I am next in Saskatoon you can let me know.

I have just completed the short census form and sent it to the officials in charge. They were careful not to send me the long form for I intended to answer "Canadian" to question re social origin!

                            With Best wishes,
                            John

∽

From John to Elmer   *House of Commons*
                                        Ottawa
                                        June 2, 1971

Dear Elmer,

I just called you on the telephone but Miss James said you were sleeping.

I am staying at home today as I am very tired after my trip to Saskatoon.

I was pleased to see you and to note progress being made by you – as is Dr. Baltzan.

By the way, two big boxes of papers from your apartment came to the office this morning. They were sent by Tom Lefevre – and I will have them looked into at once. It's a hard job to sort out papers.

You did a tremendous job in sorting out the ton of papers that you had to go through. Indeed if it had not been for you, much valuable material would have been lost.

> With the very best
> wishes of Olive and me,
> Your brother,
> John

P.S. "Cheeko" just barked which would indicate that he joins in wishing you well!

ᗌ

From John to Elmer   *House of Commons*
                                         [Ottawa]
                                         Friday
                                         June 4, 1971

Dear Elmer,

Since returning from Saskatoon on Tues. I have not been in the House as I felt a little under the weather.

Tonight the Kiwanis Club will honor me at a dinner.

Tomorrow Olive and I will attend the Mitzvah for the 14-year-old son of the Israeli Ambassador.

As well George Cloakey will be coming to see us. He has been in Montreal to attend a hospital meeting.

I trust that you are resting. Miss James says that you are. She is a wonderful nurse, isn't she?

> With all good wishes,
> Brother,
> John

In early June, while in St. Paul's Hospital, Elmer contracted pneumonia. He died on June 11, 1971 at the age of 73.

From Olive to John   *[Ottawa]*
                                          December 8, 1971

Darling,
    1971 has been a hard, hard year. Let's hope for an easier, less
troubled 1972.
    But we can handle anything, as long as we are together.

                                          Love,
                                          Ollie

ᔦ

From John to Olive   *House of Commons*
                                          [Ottawa]
                                          January 2, 1972

My darling,
    I just had your phone call and am sorry that you are tied up at the
airport in Toronto although it is better than having the long wait at
Winnipeg.
    You were so sweet and winsome as you left for your flight. Just like
the little darling of 1917-18. Wonderful as always.
    The picture after the funeral service in tonight's Citizen is enclosed.
It's a good likeness of you.
    I will miss you but not for long this time as in 48 hours I will be in
Saskatoon. I will try to visit you after the flight's arrival – that will be
about 11 P.M. – but if you are sleeping will not bother you.
    On Friday morning I will be at the hospital.
    All will be well. God bless and keep you.

                                          With all my love,
                                          John

From John to Olive   *House of Commons*
                         [Ottawa]
                         Wed., 2 P.M.
                         February 24, 1972

My darling,

How I hate to leave you when you need me most – but after the meeting tomorrow night at Thunder Bay I'll come back if you need me.

Do you remember in 1924 it was there that I met you as you came on board the Liner! Mother spied you first – and when she pointed you out I couldn't believe my eyes. So Fort William (now Thunder Bay) has a special place in my heart.

I do hope that you won't be having any surgery before I get back. Arrangements if all goes well will bring me back in the early afternoon of Sunday. If you come to the office... have Betty call me on the phone – to keep me advised – and so that I can talk to you.

Goodbye for now my
dearest,
John

From John to Olive   *House of Commons*
                         [Ottawa?]
                         July 26, 1972

My dear one,

Dates mean a lot to me and I recall the important ones.

On the 26th July 1953 – 19 years ago today – you came to P.A. during the campaign. I had a lot of difficulty finding the meeting at Carlton and with Elmer you went to Duck Lake and got lost – and to the park. It was a great uplift for me to have you and helped me win the "impossible" election. And today I look back on 19 years of happiness with you.

Now all that matters is that you recover your health – and I get out of hospital the 12th August and after a few days rest get working on the campaign with you.

I want to win this my 11th election (including the 1940 one) – but I have no ambition to even think of the 12th! regardless of health or other consideration.

Well I have now covered enough ground regarding the present and future. All that remains is to determine to dry my hands. I'll be phoning you and waiting anxiously for a message from you.

> Goodbye for now, my
> darling,
> John

<p>

From John to Olive

*Air Canada en Route
to Wpg. 11:30 A.M.
January 8, 1973*

My darling,

Even though under unhappy circumstances – with you in hospital – the last two days have been most happy days. You are so wonderful always but especially when things are trying.

Ross R. [?] and I had a good chat both on the way to and at the airport.

He says that he hopes that the Prov. of Sask. Leadership Convention (now set for March) will be postponed until a serious candidate is prepared to contest. Furthermore he advises that the helicopter which Dr. Brand used on the 1968 election lost him many votes. A poll was held in the constituency some weeks before the election was called – and everywhere the same answer was given as the reason for Brand's defeat. They who were asked why felt that the helicopter was the cause. Too high and mighty in using such a means of transportation!

The pilot has just opened his notice that we are approaching Wpg. with "Good Morning Mr. Diefenbaker, Ladies and Gentlemen."

I do hope that you continue to progress well.

> With all my love and
> devotion,
> John

From John to Olive   *Sunday*
                                        January 21, 1973

My darling,

I am so happy as I return to Ottawa. It is quite different from eight days ago when I came here with your operation then ahead.

You looked so beautiful this morning as you moved around the room without the "sceptre" attachment. I hope that this afternoon will show that things have returned to a reasonably normal condition. If not the doctor said you will have to have the attachment on for another four days. I'll be back after either Thurs. or Fri. night.

Thursday may be a rush for me as I will be speaking to the Canadian Club at noon that day. I shall let you know how things are going from day to day.

Now again a determination to go ahead with sections of my memoirs – 1962-3, the 1966 annual meeting, the 1965 when Camp first showed his hand – and I stated to the audience "I know where I stand. I want to know where *you* stand" and turned around to Camp as I said that.

Next the events of the 1967 Convention. I should get the above drafted within two weeks.

I'll be so joyful when you get back to 115 Lansdowne.

You're a dear, dear person.

> With all the affection
> that I can put in words,
> John

From John to Olive   *House of Commons*
                                        [Ottawa]
                                        Monday
                                        February 27, 1973

My darling,

The hours go on slowly for me. If only I could be with you – for I have an "elephantine" touch when it comes to being at a sick bed!

I talked with Dr. R-----. He will get in touch with Dr. L---- so that no saline mixture be given to you.

Mr. Stanfield called – he can't or at least didn't say anything – but sat for a moment and then left to meet some school children.

Trudeau got mad at him today and said he was tired of *Goddamn* questions. If he were around long enough Hansard would be filled with profanity – and worse.

You dear one. I love you so and would feel like taking you to Bermuda for a rest – why? The Beauty Queen of Grenada and her husband, Mr. Craig called on me this morning and will be leaving tomorrow for Bermuda where he's connected with the IBM company.

As well today is election day in Grenada – so the Premier was able to prevent the 18-year-olds from voting – as their right to do so does not come into being until March.

With deep love,
John

I called Carolyn and told her about you. She was calm and collected as "we Freemans" are always.

↜

From John to Olive   *[Toronto?]*
                                        April 16, 1974

My darling,

How I dislike leaving you!

You mean so much to me that I can never express it in words.

Do look after yourself – and if at any time I should come home cable me c/o Can. Embassy at Tel Aviv.

I shall be back soon – and in the meantime will be thinking of you.

As ever,
With all my love,
John

↜

From John to Olive   *Toronto*
                                        April 16, 1974

My dear one,

Here I am at the hotel. Everything put on posh. All that is needed to make everything complete would be you.

I didn't turn back after bidding you "good bye" because I might have shown a tear or two – and that wouldn't do.

What a long trip – leave here at 3 P.M. – in 2 hours in New York – then 5 hours stopover – and then 10 hours direct flight to Israel.

I have made a discovery just at this moment.

The watch has lost 40 minutes since you delivered it to me.

What a mess I'll be in when I try to keep appointments. I'll have to buy a cheap watch – Ingersoll – in Jerusalem!

Have just finished lunch with Dr. S----- and am going to catch a little rest for an hour or so. (I am writing this while lying on my back – hence the poor writing.)

I hope that your medical exams turn out well.

Keep well – rest lots – my darling. 10 days goes by quickly and will I be happy to be home.

> So much love to my
> very dearest,
> John

From Olive to John   *Home*
                                [Ottawa]
                                Monday
                                April 4, 1975

Dear John,

While I'm writing birthday "Thank-you" notes, why shouldn't I write one to you – the one to whom I say "Thank-you" most.

Darling I love my white sweater. How you and Betty find the very thing I need most I can't think. But I do thank you and love you *very much*. Very *very* much.

> Ollie

From John to Olive   *Windsor Castle*
                                            [London, England]
                                            7 P.M.
                                            April 1, 1976

My darling,

   The Queen has just conferred the C.H. [Companion of Honour] on me
and you shall be the first to be informed.

   It was a private and delightful little ceremony and followed by an
audience of some forty minutes.

   She asked me to be sure to give you her best wishes for good health.

   If only you could have been present.

                              With deepest love,
                              John

INDEX OF NAMES

Note: None of the Diefenbaker family and relations have been indexed as their names occur throughout. Page numbers in bold type are in the introductions or footnotes. For the most part official titles have been omitted.